BUDDHA'S FAVOURITE WORDS

Daily Contemplations To Unlock The Essence

BRUNO NUA

Copyright © 2018 by **Bruno Nua**

All rights reserved. No part of this publication may be reproduced, distributed or transmitted in any form or by any means, without prior written permission.

Bruno Nua/Outside In
www.osi.xyz
www.brunonua.com

Proof-Editor: FIONA WHITE [EditCorrectWrite]
Cover Photo: JOSH BULRISS
Cover Layout: JOHN MARSHALL

Buddha's Favourite Words/ Bruno Nua.
ISBN 978-1-9998785-1-1

O S I
U I N
T D
E

www.osi.xyz

Supporting

OUTSIDER INDIE AUTEURS

by BRUNO NUA

FICTION

The Jalu Series:
LONDON CALLING

BUDDHIST PHILOSOPHY

BUDDHA'S FAVOURITE WORDS

Better than a thousand hollow words,

Is one word that brings peace.

BUDDHA

CONTENTS

Dear Reader, ... 17
Foreword 19

Addiction 23
Aggression 27
Amnesia 31
Anaesthetic 35
Anger 38
Anorexia 44
Anxiety 49
Attachment 52
Aversion 54
Awake 58
Awareness 60

Bardo 63
Bodhichitta 67
Bodhisattva 73
Boredom 76
Breathe 80
Buddha 83

buddha 91
Buddha Nature 94

Challenges 101
Change 108
Child 112
Cinema 115
Compassion 118
Consciousness 123
Contentment 128
Contemplation 131
Control 137
Cosmology 141
Creativity 147
Cult 150
Culture 153

Death 157
Delusion 165
Dharma 170
Dream Yoga 175
Drugs 179

Ecology 185
Ego 190

Ego-Buddhism 193
Emotions 198
Emptiness 204
Energy 208
Engaged 212
Enlightenment 216
Environment 219
Equanimity 223
Evolution 226

Family 231
Fear 235
Forgiveness 238
Friends 241
Fun 245

Gentleness 248
Guru 253

Habitual Tendencies 256
Healing 259
Heart 264
Hell 268
Humour 273

Identity 275
Ignorance 279
Illusion 283
Image 286
Imagination 288
Inertia 293
Integration 297
Intention 301
Inter-Being 304
Intoxication 307

Joy 311
Just Be 314

Kaliyuga 316
Karma 320

Let It Be 324
Love 328

Magic 331
Manic-Depression 336
Materialism 339
Meditation 343
Mindlessness 348

Money 351
Mother 354

Natural Mind 357
Neurosis 361
Nirvana 365
Non-Conceptual [Shunyata Lite] 368
Non-Harming 372
Numbness 375

Obesity 378
OCD 382
Ocean 385
Openness 388
Pain 391

Paramita 395
Pilgrimage 397
Pleasure 404
Precepts 407
Primordial Purity 412

Quantum Theory 414
Questions 417

Refuge 420
Remember 423
Respond 425
Retreat 427
Revolution 430

Simplicity 434
Sky 437
Smile 439
Staying In The Practice 443

Teacher 445
Toxins 450

Un-Distracted and Un-Altered 454

Vegan 458
Virtual Reality 463

Warrior 465

X Factor 468
X-Ray Vision 471

Yes 474

Yogi 478

Zeitgeist 482
Zenith 486

Afterword 491

Homage to the Buddhas of the past, present, and future.

May all beings reveal their True Nature,

For the benefit of self and others.

Dear Reader,

May the essential Clear Light of the Buddha's teachings
resonate within you.

May your Natural Mind fully awaken
from its long slumber.

May your Heart Essence flow unhindered
like a vast river of Wisdom and Compassion.

And may YOU, in this very lifetime, bring the
Ultimate Liberation to all beings!

Foreword

The words spoken by the Buddha around 500BCE are contained in the Sutras. Nothing can compare to actually studying them. Together with commentaries and other works composed by subsequent generations of meditators who attained full awakening by following the Way of the Buddha, the Dharma has become a vast area of study and contemplation, which ignites in us a wealth of blessing, wisdom and compassion.

But for many people there is not enough time or energy left in our busy, fragmented lives to devote ourselves completely to making a thorough study of the Dharma – to say nothing of putting it all into practice. These days, many awakened and highly skilled Masters encourage their students to unlock the very essence of the Buddha's teachings and to practise that, as a matter of priority and great urgency. This is the path I myself am following with the guidance of my own spiritual masters, whose teachings I have remembered and reflected upon in this book.

It is with tears of deep gratitude and devotion for my Masters, therefore, that I offer this volume of essential yet profound teachings remembered, as a homage. Without the immeasurable love and patience of Sogyal Rinpoche, Ringu Tulku Rinpoche and Thich Nhat Hanh, I might never have heard even the faintest whisper of the truth that liberates all.

To the reader, the entire lineage of the Enlightened Ones sings a primordial prayer, from the heart to the heart: May you fully awaken to perfect buddhahood in this very lifetime!

In order to present the core teachings of the Buddha in an interesting and managable way, I have laid them out in a series of short readings that could be used as daily contemplations. They are not at all suitable for devouring one after the other.

Using a single word or phrase to unlock an entire spiritual teaching is a rare but highly effective method of offering the Dharma. With this in mind, I have imagined a list of words that might have inspired the Buddha if he were alive today.

If there are parts of this book that are of benefit, it is because the essence of the Buddha's words is so pure and utterly transformative. It works! As such, whatever benefit may come is because of the tremendous blessings of my teachers. Anything that isn't so helpful, well... let's put that down to me being such a lazy student and practitioner. Profound truths half-remembered, half-digested, and unskillfully scrawled by someone with a huge ego is not ideal, to say the least.

But one thing is clear, though. The Heart Essence of the Buddhadharma is on every page: You are already a buddha. You are already perfect to the very core.

My only motivation is that this profound truth is fully realized and that you allow the natural state of openness and contentment to blossom within you.

May each one of us fully awaken to our True Nature,

And may we bring ultimate benefit to all beings.

Samet, 2017.

Addiction

This human life of ours is so precious and rare. We hardly know just how special an opportunity it is.

We are born with the capacity to become self-aware. But somehow we have misunderstood reality almost completely. We have turned that self-awareness into self-obsession.

When I live in the realm of the Ego, I am ignoring my True Nature.

I quickly become preoccupied with my ego-self. Even subconsciously, I become obsessed with my own personal happiness. That is not an entirely bad thing, however. Of course, I must look after myself. But, when I do it to the exclusion of others I am missing the meaning of life entirely. I am truly wasting this precious opportunity.

In my pursuit of happiness, I misguidedly waste a lot of time and energy running after and grasping onto whatever I imagine will bring me lasting contentment: people, experiences, intoxication, food, wealth... The list is endless, and will occupy us our whole life – maybe even lifetime after lifetime.

The quest for happiness becomes deeply ingrained in my psyche. So much so that I devote myself to it tirelessly. The quest first becomes an obsessive pattern, then a compulsive

Habitual Tendency. The search for happiness becomes such an integral part of what we do, eventually we identify with it so strongly and so naturally it simply becomes who we are.

Like a drowning man clutching at a leaf on the surface of the lake, our grasping knows no reason. We soon discover that the endless wish-list of distraction and desire cannot fulfill us. However, our grasping is so strong we dare not let go, perhaps for fear of the abyss. We have become addicted, and that brings tremendous suffering. Even if we have released our grasping, our body still hurts and suffers tremendously. Withdrawal symptoms set in and we feel miserable and hopeless. Yet another of our schemes has backfired.

This is not to say I would be much happier without loved ones or food, for instance. On the contrary. Life may offer us many healthy options if only we didn't become addicted to them.

I must acknowledge how addictive I am. My distracted small-mindedness, and even my physical body, is prone to craving. Then, if the object of my desire actually delivers a little happiness and pleasure, I am hooked!

In the case of drug and alcohol addiction this is very clear. But the same principle applies to a host of supposedly less extreme situations too – relationships, food, work…

Looking deeply into my own preoccupations and addictions, I must learn to shine the pure light of awareness on what I see within.

Soon I may come to a clear insight about my own addictive nature.

Every being wishes to have lasting happiness. So we all share that in common. But human beings, while having tremendous potential and strengths, are also very fragile indeed.

Our ego-mind longs for contentment for a variety of unhealthy reasons. Perhaps I feel empty inside and look externally for something to fill that void. Maybe someone else is feeling profoundly incomplete and desperately wants a relationship – an 'other half' – to make them whole again. For some people the problem is boredom; we seek insatiably for newness, freshness, anything to relieve the post-modern jaded malaise – travel, shopping, sexual partners, hobbies, even spirituality.

Drug addicts are just like me. Whether an addict becomes hooked on drugs to relieve suffering or just for entertainment, I must recognize that we are all like that.

Some day, hopefully soon, I will recognize my own addictions and slowly begin to find a solution that works for me.

It could be I have to cut through the whole sorry mess in an instant – quit, go cold turkey, temporarily suffer the withdrawal, avoid all future contact with that substance or person. Or, in other cases, simply seeing the problem clearly, perhaps from a different angle entirely, might prove extremely helpful. Or maybe I could have a much healthier relationship with that person or thing – not cut them out of my life entirely, but learn to be with them in a different way; more moderate, less grasping, more mindful of the consequences of completely losing myself in the same old way again.

Who knows... I may even find myself in the process.

The teachings of the Buddha help us to do precisely that. They point the way towards lasting happiness. If we are ready, willing and able to walk that path ourselves we will discover that the happiness we have sought externally for aeons was already inside each one of us all along. We only had to realize that truth by turning our mind inwards and revealing our inner happiness, which is inexhaustible and limitless. That internal source of happiness has many names. It is known as our Buddha Nature, our True Nature, The Natural Mind.

Once we connect with it permanently, we unleash its vast qualities of Love, Compassion and Wisdom. When these energies start to flow, there is no stopping them. Because of Wisdom, we come to see ourselves and all phenomena as they truly are. There is no more grasping. We are completely open and content. Our focus has switched from ourselves to others. Love and Compassion drive us to work tirelessly for the benefit of all beings.

Nolonger self-obsessed, the ego is first diminished, then eradicated entirely.

When that occurs, we are completely and vibrantly awake.

This is the day we have become enlightened.

We have become a Buddha!

Aggression

When we are not running after certain desirable things, the Buddha discovered, we are prone to running away from the things we do not want [but which come our way nonetheless].

This also leads to a profound state of unhappiness.

We become exhausted and worn down by seemingly always meeting the very circumstances we wish to avoid. A new negative pattern, a strong habitual tendency, is born within our fragile ego-mind. As usual, we blow it out of all proportion and fixate onto it.

Now we dwell in a paranoid state, dreading that which may never even come our way. We become worriers, ever-watchful, guarding our ego-selves against the unwanted dreaded bogey-man.

I expend precious energy avoiding like the plague anything and everything I feel may possibly bring me suffering. And, if my repulsive scowls and growls don't ward off life's unwanted visitors, woe betide all the uninvited undesirables that dare to cross my path.

Aggression, according to the Buddha, is one of humankind's most profound obstacles to uncovering our True Nature. It is never helpful. It can only lead to a negative outcome. Reacting aggressively always makes things worse and is a hard habit to break.

For this reason, the Buddha's core teachings were dedicated to cutting through aggression. Each one of us can and must eventually achieve this by disarming, pacifying and stabilizing ourselves. Ultimately, the teaching goes, I personally must make a solemn vow to bring about world peace and harmony – starting with me.

The Way of the Buddha is perhaps the most challenging assault on the ego. It goes against all that we believe in.

In our current way of seeing things we have a primary duty of self-preservation and self-defense. We practise fight or flight, just like our animal cousins. But we are not merely animals. Fear should not dominate our lives like that.

We must learn the crucial difference between my ego and my true self.

Leading by example, I must learn to observe my body, speech and mind.

I must learn to perfect these methods of mindfulness, and from moment to moment I will consciously work towards total non-violence.

The good news is this sacred goal is actually achievable. Many saints, and masters, and ordinary people like you and me have done it.

It is not even a question of becoming a Buddhist.

As human beings, we must all learn to go way beneath the apparently crazy, chaotic, and almost unnatural surface energy of the mind. We must learn to go deep into the heart of the enlightened mind, the Natural Mind. Once we connect with the stability of our Core Being, we tap into the limitless [and largely unused] resources there.

Then everything is possible! Happiness. Peace of mind. Non-violence. Unconditional love.

Revealing our True Nature, according to the deepest teachings of the Buddha, is not about turning our being into something new – something it was not beforehand. Neither is it a kind of spiritual evolution... becoming enlightened. The most profound, ultimate truth is that we have always been enlightened. Just like the Buddha, there has never been a single nano-second when we were not already awake.

However, the Natural Mind, our Buddha Nature, is temporarily obscured. At the moment, we are unable to perceive its luminous primordial purity. It's as if our Core Being is covered up, like a dust-sheet over a priceless antique, or a precious wish-fulfilling jewel that has become dull, smeared with the darkest slime - the filth of countless lifetimes of neglect and disuse.

In our case, the two obscurations that prevent our Natural Mind from spontaneously radiating benefit for all beings are Addiction and Aggression, also known as Attachment and Aversion.

Whatever we call this pair, they are ruining our lives! Although we claim not to want suffering, we run headlong towards it. We experience suffering acutely, yet we do nothing about its causes.

Our state of mind is the key to lasting happiness.

When I react to the world with aggression, I reduce myself to the level of a trapped animal or some kind of caveman. If only I could remember my true nature - how it could never ultimately be harmed, in any way whatsoever. My view of life would be so different.

Maybe I could finally realize a few much-needed home truths:

There's more to me than meets the eye.
Aggression makes things worse.
The more stable I am, the happier I become.
Ultimately, there is nothing to fear.

Amnesia

The difference between a Buddha and an ordinary person, like us, is that an enlightened being knows who they are and we do not. A Buddha realizes their true nature because they have reconnected with their innate Wisdom Mind. Buddhas work for the ultimate benefit of others because of their Infinite Heart of Compassion.

We, on the other hand, have no clue what or who the hell we are. You might say we are suffering from the most profound kind of amnesia. It's like we are wandering about aimlessly and have forgotten who we truly are. We have lost our memory completely and instead of looking inwards to discover the truth about ourselves, and our incredible potential, we create a surface personality to present to the world, to protect ourselves somehow, to show that we do actually know what's going on, and that we are in control.

Whatever we don't remember, we simply invent – personality, role, hopes, fears, aspirations...

Look about you and you may notice an intriguing paradox about others: they are busy reinventing themselves on the surface, and yet they have a deep thirst for spiritual self-realisation.

No one, not even a Buddha, knows exactly why this veil of amnesia has descended upon beings. But it appears to be all-pervasive and universally disturbing. It's as if there has been a cosmic train-wreck and the people have just drifted off into the world, stunned, blank, and desperately trying to put the pieces back together.

We are suffering.

Because we are ignorant of the truth of who we really are, we appear to waste much of our time searching externally for hints and any shred of evidence that may help us solve the eternal mystery: *Who am I? What's going on? How did I get here? What is the purpose of my existence?*

We turn to psychotherapists, spiritual gurus, mediums... anyone... in our search for help with our identity crisis. We even allow our peers and loved ones to define who they think we should be – we would try almost anything rather than take personal responsibility, turn our minds inward, and do the work ourselves.

Of course we all need help to guide us through what will be the most profound and exciting exploration of our lives. But who can we trust? The teachings suggest that we find someone who has already realized their own True Nature, a Living Buddha. Even in this dark, turbulent age there are many. They shine like diamonds on a rubbish heap. We only have to choose one we can connect with and who will accept us as their disciple.

The buddhas see our suffering and our longing to reveal the truth about who we really are. They recognize it for exactly what it is – the Universal Buddha Nature in each being stretching and yawning, beginning to wake up from its deep sleep, just starting out along the path to full enlightenment. The buddhas know the way and understand their job is to guide us.

However, we must also trust our *Inner Teacher* to guide us. No matter how powerful the Outer Teacher is – even if the Buddha himself were alive and guiding us – they could not do the work for us, they couldn't make us enlightened.

Ultimately, enlightenment comes from within. We just need a skillful helping hand. Our True Nature is longing to awaken. It *will* happen. That's exactly what the Buddha Nature does... it wakes up! It's the most natural thing in the world!

However, many many human beings are not yet sufficiently aware of their Natural Mind or interested in its potential. But when they are ready, help will be at hand, in abundance.

Chances are, if *you* are reading this, you're already on the path to awakening.

Authentic mainstream Buddhist teachers, therefore, do not look for new students or converts to their new 'ism'. Ultimately, there is even nothing called Buddh-ism. It is a universal, living lineage, a Wisdom Tradition that holds: when individual beings are ripe for these teachings, they will find them.

Then, and only then, can the mists of ignorance and amnesia begin to lift and eventually be dispelled for once and for all.

May all beings take a little break from the exhausting busyness of addiction and aggression.
May we all discover there's so much more to life than attachment and aversion.

May I dispel the darkness of ignorance, and may we all remember our True Name.

Anaesthetic

While we continue to be disconnected from the Natural Mind, we drift on the unaware, unconscious, surface of mind.

On the surface level of mind, we are prone to our moods and are tossed about like a tiny boat on a rough sea. Without the anchor of being connected to our True Nature, we are indeed lost – but worse than that, our mind is tortured, always looking for somewhere to call home, somewhere reliable and stable.

This suffering mind wanders endlessly astray on the perilous surface of the infinite ocean the Buddha called *Samsara*. If only we knew the peace and stability we crave was right here inside us all along, our very essence, waiting to be awakened.

According to the Buddha's teachings, our deluded mind searches in vain high and low for the Natural Great Peace we already possess but don't realize.

In our 'post-modern' era of jaded Western mindlessness, we are exhausted by the continual search for contentment. Many of us have already begun to recognize experientially, and instinctively, the universal truths we now find in these precious teachings.

However, more of us are not yet ready.

We are suffering greatly and reach out for something – almost anything – to ease the pain.

Anaesthetics dull the senses and disengage the brain temporarily. They take the edge off life with all its raw, incessant assault.

For some people it is intoxicants they turn to. For others, it's new experiences – lovers, travel, general distraction.

Or it might be the familiar we cling to – family, role-play, routine – in the vague hope of finding profound peace there.

Many people, especially in the West, don't even anaesthetize themselves with substances or experiences. We simply switch off.

A true sign of our jaded, worn-out times is that people become *numb*.

Maybe our senses have become numb from over-indulgence and burnout. Or maybe we have deliberately numbed ourselves, just for a break, to put some distance between ourselves and the daily bombardment we must endure.

Dropping out of life or withdrawing into our shell might offer some protection, who knows. However, it's still a kind of anaesthetic – a barrier between us and reality.

But, one thing is sure –

Prolonged use of anaesthetics leads to lasting mental health problems. The chemical wiring of the brain, it is being discovered, actually changes [sometimes irreparably] according to whatever substances or habitual experiences we submit it to.

Worse still is the sad truth that all anaesthetics wear off.

Either we will overdose eventually in a tragic attempt to remain numb or we will inevitably return to our full senses and have to face reality anyway.

Buddhist meditation techniques achieve precisely this. We train, re-habituate, and re-wire the mind to remain in the present moment. Unperturbed by reality, we learn to neither indulge nor suppress what we experience. Acknowledging the temporary nature of all phenomena [good and bad], we come to accept whatever arises then let it go completely.

The truth of the Buddha's essential teaching has been arrived at experientially. Life itself, and our own innate Wisdom, has revealed to us there is no barrier between us and the world – nor is there any need for one – no separation whatsoever.

There is nothing to fear.
Lasting happiness comes from within.

Anger

We inherit many qualities and traits, good and bad. They come to us both genetically and socially.

All human beings have the seed of anger to some degree or other within them – just under the surface. Once the right circumstances arise, it will manifest with all the suddenness and ferocity of a forest fire.

Instead of *responding* to life, we are quickly drawn into *reacting*.

Anger is just like all other emotions. Though strong and seemingly beyond our control it is nonetheless a habitual tendency, a pattern that is reinforced every time we indulge it. It is therefore possible to eliminate entirely by never indulging it. As one living master Sogyal Rinpoche says, *Don't go there!*

In my own recent family history, anger played a hugely damaging role. My grandfather was a monstrous brutal force in my father's life. And, though less so, my father was a very angry man and had a deeply negative effect on his children. Even when we learned to avoid him and tip-toe around him, for fear of setting him off, there always seemed to be something to annoy him. Anger enveloped our home like a fog – blinding us to reality, pervading our every move.

But, perhaps worst of all, anger nearly destroyed my father's own life. It was like a progressive mental illness. We all remember occasions when – even though we were completely silent, and had said nothing to provoke him – Daddy would shout things like 'I heard that' or 'I know what you said just now under your breath'. He would even say 'I can see what you are doing behind me!'

These little illustrations from life encapsulate what is at the root of anger.

My father had inherited the predisposition for anger and compounded it habitually. The purpose of anger is *self-protection*.

We all watch and wait for a moment when we feel we are under attack. Then we strike out like a cobra to defend ourselves.

This is not our *true* self we are defending, but our *ego*.

The ego cherishes itself above all else. It deludes us and obscures our True Nature. Ego preoccupies us with an exhausting cycle of negative activity: attachment and aversion, addiction and aggression. Its mantra is 'I want' and 'I don't want'. What a waste of time and energy! How ignorant to believe that would ever bring lasting happiness to ourselves and those we love.

One of the ego's many ridiculous ploys is to keep the guns of anger fully loaded and ready for use against intruders. To prevent the unwanted from harming or annoying us we create an imaginary force field around us, supposedly to set up a barrier between ourselves and the world – an early warning system against enemy missiles.

We even go so far as to employ a policy of pre-emptive strikes, very common in modern warfare. Our anger is unleashed even on those who have not yet provoked us. We imagine the whole world will fall at our feet when they hear of our wrath. Our might will be the stuff of legend and our superior reputation will be a deterrent to anyone thinking of messing with *us*.

Funny as it seems, this is real. I saw it in my father. I see it in myself too. Look around you. You will recognize it everywhere for yourself. The TV news follows war like a soap opera – we can observe and analyze every strategy from a safe distance. Recalling our own school days is also helpful. Remember how children treated each other in the playground. Bring to mind the bullies who, to protect themselves and their fragile egos, wreaked so much havoc and misery.

Now, returning to our own anger we recognize that we too can be just like that, given the right circumstances.

The Buddha and all the *living* Buddhas of our age are clear on this point. In order for the world to change, I must change *myself* first.

I am part of the problem, so the solution must begin with *me*.

The whole Buddhist path is about disarming the ego – dissolving it completely. Literally, by *seeing through* the ego we glimpse the Buddha Nature within. And gradually, glimpse after glimpse, revelation after revelation, direct personal experience of the Natural Mind after direct personal experience, we come to have a steadfast unshakable conviction of its existence. We also come to know how *un-natural* the ego is and that its superficial layer of negative patterns does not really exist at all. They never really did.

We do not have to go to war with the ego or destroy it. It is said that enlightenment is like switching on a light in a dark room. We did not have to get rid of the darkness. There was no need to work on the darkness, slowly chipping away at it until every last bit was removed.

Light is simply the absence of dark.

Enlightenment is the absence of delusion.

We may come to see things as they really are by many means. We can enter the enlightened realm through many gates. In fact every passing moment is offering us a blessed opportunity to do just that.

Anger may be just the ticket!

One precious Master, Ringu Tulku Rinpoche, once gave me some private time to ask him about anger.

He said this –

Anger is like a fire. When it arises, it comes up very quickly. It burns strongly – almost out of control – and can do a lot of damage to oneself, and to others.

But always remember, though strong, fire is short-lived. It will burn out.

Don't let your anger do any damage when it arises. Just watch it and wait for it to burn out.

Experience the emotion rising. Look directly at it, don't run away from it. Shine the light of awareness on it – observe your mind, how it is, how the emotion feels, but don't indulge the anger either – just let it be, let it go, observe...

You will see that, like everything else, the anger changes from moment to moment – sometimes stronger, sometimes weaker, always changing, soon dispersing.

I never forgot this priceless teaching and remain so grateful to this very day that I write his words with a lump in my throat.

When you find a method like this that really helps, really works for you, *remember* it. Hold it close to your heart. Make it your main practice. Treasure it like a precious jewel, a cherished loved-one. It will become your best friend.

Use the method in every situation, at every given opportunity. It will work with all phenomena that arise, not just anger. It is not just *a* method, it is *the* supreme method – the whole teaching of the Buddha is contained within it.

You see, when we observe phenomena like this we are actually observing from the viewpoint of our own Buddha Nature. That primordially pure, spontaneously present, spacious openness is our very essence. It is literally larger than life.

Whatever may arise, will simply pass through – if we allow it to.

So we can come to identify more and more with this Natural Mind as it manifests and reveals itself through mindful experiences like this, and less and less with the risings that occur.

Instead of thinkng 'I *am* angry', there will be a realization that *'there is* anger'. I am not the emotion I perceive momentarily, it's just passing through. No need to block its passage, let it come. No need to invite it to move in with you, just say hello. No need to grieve its passing on, just blow it a kiss goodbye like an old friend – who may return, but is gradually becoming more of a passing acquaintance really.

When we view phenomena this way, we become increasingly aware that the one who is observing is the Buddha within.

The trick is not to just read these lines and say: *Yes, that makes sense to me* - but do nothing about it. Or to try it once or twice and think: *Um, that was an 'interesting' experience. I might find that method very useful sometime in the future.*

We must practise it with exertion, become experts in it just as we dedicated our whole lives to becoming experts in the ways of the ego up until now. It must become our life's work, the project of a lifetime – as if our life, our sanity, depended on it. It really does!

The cessation of our ego life will be the greatest gift we could give to ourselves, and to the world. This inner disarmament will bring peace and love to everyone. It will change everything, entirely, forever.

May all beings, beginning with me, recognize their enlightened nature.

May we manifest for the world as beacons of wisdom and compassion.

May my anger be replaced with patience and stability.

And may the love and light we embody nourish both ourselves and others completely.

Recognizing patience and love as the antidotes to anger, may my own gradual blossoming inspire others to turn their minds inward and do the same.

Anorexia

Anorexics look at their bodies and do not see what is truly there. Their perception of reality is completely wrong.

According to the Buddha, this is true of all humans; we do not perceive reality *as it is*.

I've always been fascinated by anorexia myself as it encapsulates so many of our common problems as deluded human beings. Therefore, contemplating anorexia can help unlock the very *essence* of the Buddha's highest teachings.

The usual public understanding of anorexia is very superficial. We imagine these unfortunate people have an exaggerated aversion to eating, or that they have an unhealthy attachment to becoming a size zero like so many models they see in magazines. But we fail to look beneath the surface of what is really going on. The anorexic is suffering, just like you and me, from delusion. Their misperception and self-obsession plays out in a very overt and often tragic way. Ours is much more subtle.

Most people have something about their bodies they don't like. This leads to self-consciousness [usually at an early age], which invariably becomes a kind of self-obsession as we grow older. Our ego-tendency grasps onto it and, if we are not careful, can turn it into low self-esteem and even self-hatred. Essentially, we become extremely unhappy and over-protective.

We look at ourselves and all we see is our particularly hideous deformity. We don't see the whole person and we rarely see the Buddha that lies within. If only we could transform that self-consciousness into *self-awareness* of our true nature.

In the extreme case of an anorexic, however, all this is amplified. They look at emaciated flesh in the mirror and the folds of skin hanging off them literally appear like rolls of fat. Once they make the connection between that misperception and a possible solution in dieting, exercise, even laxatives, a tragic pattern is set and their downward spiral follows. This pattern is often established in early childhood nowadays, long before anyone else has begun to suspect there might be a problem. The individual's self-absorption can quickly lead them to a place of debilitation, where they are of little benefit to themselves or others.

The essence of the Buddha's teaching speaks precisely about this issue of perception. We do not perceive things as they truly are – ourselves, others, the world, all phenomena. And once we do experience them directly, without any delusion whatsoever, free from all sense of being separate, then we are enlightened – literally *awake*.

Anorexia offers us some insight into the human condition and proof, if we needed it, that not only the eyes but our whole perception is playing a cosmic trick on us.

We need to regain a universal perspective. Our view should be vast as the sky. Seeing the bigger picture can only be achieved through spiritual practice like meditation.

When we turn our mind inwards we glimpse our true nature and eventually come to perceive reality as it really is all around us. Tapping into our own innate inner peace releases bliss and clarity. An enlightened being, and there are many of them around us even today, has purified their perception to the point where all ego-clinging has ceased and they fully experience the innate goodness of everyone and everything around them.

By dwelling in the present moment like this, they have changed the world. As Jesus put it, they have established heaven on earth.

We make so many mistakes and self-limitations by reducing our perception of ourselves to this physical body when we are so much more.

Teilhard de Chardin, a Christian mystic, once wrote:
We are not physical beings having a spiritual experience,
We are spiritual beings having a physical experience.

When we come to see phenomena in this way, we are not being mystical or Buddhist or esoterical or anything. We are being True. If we believe the truth will set us free, why wait tilll some time in the future or when we die? We can experience that truth right here, right now, in the present moment.

The Buddhist path offers various tried and tested methods of learning to live in the here and now.

It's not secret, magical, mysterious, or even holy. Neither is it reserved for those special beings living in monasteries or in a cave in the Himalayas. It is for ordinary folk like you and me.

We all possess the keys to our own salvation within us. With some practice and hard work, focus and commitment, and the guidance of a genuine spiritual master, our inner bliss can be unblocked, unlocked, revealed for the benefit of self and others.

Once we take our focus off the ego the rest, we are lovingly assured, will follow.

Most people look at themselves in the mirror. If you like, from now on, we can also turn that superficial task into a spiritual practice.

Looking deeply and lovingly into our own eyes we can connect with our inner beauty for a while.

Seeing clearly what lies just below the surface, we can begin to experience our true potential, the Natural Mind with all its store of limitless wisdom, love and compassion.

Touching our Buddha Nature deeply is *the* practice.

It will reassure us, and ground us in the Absolute Truth. Gradually, with regular repetition, we undo old habitual patterns and become refreshed, healed, content and open like a blossoming lotus flower.

After we become comfortable with this practice, we might add some mantra phrases to deepen its effect. Each pair of phrases offered below is a separate practice and can be chosen according to our needs. They are said calmly and quietly in the mind.

Breathing in – I am in the *present* moment
Breathing out – Everything is *ok*

Breathing in - I am already completely *perfect*
Breathing out – I send *love* to the person in the mirror.

Breathing in - I *rejoice* in this openness and contentment
Breathing out – I *radiate love and light* to all beings.

Anxiety

The whole universe and its inhabitants are essentially ill-at-ease. We all just want to have lasting happiness and be free from suffering.

We would even settle for having some more control over our lives, but we don't and that produces anxiety. You might even say it is the background soundtrack of our lives.

Instead of turning the mind inwards and finding that which we so desperately long for, our mind is turned outwards – lost in its own projections. We could have *Nirvana,* perfect peace in the here and now, but we create for ourselves a living nightmare. A kind of hell on earth.

Sometimes this nightmare is vivid. But, more usually, there is a dull, all-pervasive sense of dis-ease. We are rarely content. As the French say, we do not feel well in our own skin.

However, like a drowning man, all our struggling just makes matters worse. We must first learn to accept how we are, and then grow through the experience.

But we do not look for the cause of our malaise. Our insatiable appetite for distraction just leads us astray, temporarily diverting us into a seemingly endless cul-desac. It postpones the day when we'll inevitably have to work with the root of our problems – the mind itself.

Why delay, always putting everything off? We could be *so* happy today.

Perhaps the most common mental illness of our time, our mind's dis-ease with its environment, is *anxiety*.

It's not that we are anxious *about* anything in particular, necessarily. Or even that we're simply worried about the future. The anxiety we feel is much deeper than that. The creators of Western psychology described it as *angst* – perhaps that's a better term. These days we even talk about post-modern angst as if our generation had discovered some new form of neurosis, thus making us even more special and privileged somehow. The ego is like that ...

'I went to my analyst today, Darling',

'Oh really, Sweetheart?'

'Yes, he says I've got post-modern angst now. Apparently all the best people are getting it'.

A contemporary interpretation of the Buddha's teachings might understand angst to be much more primal, more endemic to the human condition regardless of the era or country we live in. Because we are temporarily 'un-enlightened', we are deeply uneasy and restless. We do not realize our true nature and we are all adrift. The teachings remind us that all our homes, wealth and even our family cannot completely fulfill us.

Through the practice we will come to an un-distracted state of comfort and ease. A great serenity will emerge from within and this sense of stability and well-being alone has the power to completely transform our minds. As the

Buddha Nature becomes more and more manifest, all negative feelings and perceptions are cut right through. Their power is completely and irreversibly done and over with. We still think and feel, of course. But whatever may arise in the mind is seen as just passing through. It is met with non-grasping and, as such, is allowed to subside again.

We choose instead to operate at the most profound, core level of our being. Our wisdom and compassion are pure and inexhaustible.

In place of old anxieties, we're now driven by a fresh energy and new aspirations.

Whatever homes, wealth, or family we may have are seen as a precious opportunity to benefit others.

We transcend our previous small-mindedness and wish the very best for all beings. We work for *their* enlightenment because only that will bring them lasting happiness and freedom from suffering of every kind.

Attachment

From beginningless time, the Buddha says, for countless lifetimes we have refused or been unable to recognize our true nature. We live in a murky, misty state, which is called Ignorance [or Delusion].

Because of Ignorance there is an undercurrent of Suffering in our minds – we struggle to find happiness and to avoid the very suffering which appears to saturate our existence.

The mental struggle we endure manifests as *Attachment* and *Aversion*.

In its most raw state, Attachment is all about grasping. Ego mistakenly latches onto various experiences, people, things that we find pleasurable or comforting. Forgetting they are by nature impermanent, like all phenomena, the ego grasps onto them in the foolish hope they will make us truly happy and in the fear that somehow they will be taken away from us. It's as if the ego stockpiles, like a squirrel continually on the look out for nuts to store just in case whatever it already collected will not be enough to satisfy our needs.

What our old friend, the ego, is most attached to is actually itself. Ego's self-cherishing knows no bounds. Poor thing. You can't really blame it though. Life can be tough. One might almost think the ego knows that sooner or later it will be destroyed and the Natural Mind will triumph over it.

In the Buddha's time, he and many of his followers chose to live a monastic life free from possessions – a hugely simplified existence. Today, however, most of us would never dream of doing such a thing.

Afterall, it is attachment that is the main problem here, not *having*.

A simple monk or nun could remain attached to their garments or to their uncomplicated way of life.

Billionaires, homeless people, the mother of a new-born baby, you and me – we all cherish *something* or someone. We hope it will make us happy and fear losing it.

The very essence of this teaching is that we must learn to *have without attachment*. Overcoming attachment means that we become liberated fundamentally. Beyond hope and fear lies a blessed way of life where we *can* have it all – or nothing – and rejoice in that. However much or little we have in our lives, we can all find positives. When we nolonger fear losing them, our liberation is vibrant and blissful. Every moment, lived mindfully like this, brings with it a shower of blessings and halleluias.

Aversion

The flip side of Attachment is the scourge of Aversion.

Sometimes we get precisely that which we do not want. It makes us miserable and we fear it may never go away.

Big or small, life has a way of bringing to our door experiences we do not want. Because of our ego's inflated sense of self-importance, we actually believe that we should not encounter anything negative.

Like a rich person who feels protected by their wealth, or a king who can command this and that, the ego is astonished when the universe has the gall to serve up flat champagne!

Fundamentally, none of us can avoid unpleasant things entirely and cause ourselves to suffer more when even the most trivial of unwanted negative experiences comes our way.

Our suffering is all the more exaggerated when we get something we have always dreaded.

No, no, no... this is the very thing I didn't want, the ego cries. And a desperate struggle ensues. In so doing, we actually worsen the experience instead of allowing the misery to eventually subside, as indeed it will. All phenomena do.

Reflecting on our own minds in this light, recall situations when we experienced tremendous physical pain. It washed over us in waves, building up to an unbearable crescendo then releasing its grip momentarily only to come again. Contemplate awhile to see how your mental attitude may have contributed to the force of the attack.

We can all recall arguments we made worse by completely losing our minds. Or how a certain mindset when receiving bad news made all the difference between being quite naturally shocked or sad and being so devastated it led to a total nervous breakdown.

It's not pessimistic to acknowledge that life brings difficult situations sometimes. It is only being realistic. The more stable we are the less likely we are to be completely blown away by tragedy.

The ultimate test of our attachment and aversion will be the process of our own death. Since the Natural Mind does not die, we can safely say it is the ego who finds it so difficult to accept death and let go. Even the physical body itself has been so well trained by the ego it can take a long time for it to allow death to occur.

Next to our strong aversion to death, it can be quite fun to observe the carry on of our inner drama-queen when faced with the small stuff life throws up. Go on... I dare you. Don't be embarrassed! By sending yourself up you have only your ego to lose!

Oh, alright then. I'll go first...

Remember the children's story of The Princess and The Pea, I observe with a broad smile how long it takes me to get to sleep some nights. Everything must be just so or I'll never drop off – the mattress, the pillows, the temperature... the list is endless!

Or Buddha-forbid I should ever go for dinner to a friend's house and they serve cabbage! I can feel the vomitous aversion rise up in me this instant as I type!

The other day in a Thai restaurant I methodically searched through an entire plate of veggie fried rice – trying to be a good vegetarian – to make absolutely sure they hadn't inadvertently allowed a shrimp fragment to get in there.

Even as I write on a balcony in Thailand, watching the sun set gold and crimson over the bay, I am also aware of a morbid phobia I have of being swept over the wall somehow and plunging headlong down the eleven storeys to the carpark below – where, eventually, some local will find my shattered dead body dressed in a cheap imitation of last season's beachwear and a pair of plastic flip-flops!

On a more serious note I recall how my mother died in my early twenties from cancer, which she'd fought for many years before. She was my best friend and I adored her. Despite her terminal illness being part of all our lives for so long, the night she actually died I was so shocked and disturbed I unleashed upon myself a breakdown of sorts that lasted most of the year.

You know the old saying 'Be careful what you pray for....', well I'm positive the opposite must also be true –

Be careful what you dread, because life has a funny little habit of giving it to you anyway.

A life without aversion must be such bliss. A blessed release from all that worry, to say the least of it.

No fear, is one key aspect of what defines a Buddha.

We simply must come to appreciate that it's through life experiences, and not by avoiding them, that we grow and come to realize the cosmic truth of what lies within.

Awake

In the *Sutras,* the Buddhist scriptures, there is a very charming but very strange story.

One day, a Hindu priest called Dona was walking through the countryside. Noticing the splendid footprints of the Buddha, and the extraordinary effect he was having on all around, Dona decided to follow the footprints that he might see with his own eyes this holy being.

By the time he caught up with the Buddha, he was sitting in perfect meditation posture under the shade of a large tree. Even from a distance, he could see his shining presence. Pure peace and love. Enchanted, and deeply curious, Dona approached the Buddha to investigate more closely.

As a holyman himself, it was Dona's sincere desire to enter into a spiritual dialogue with this strange being he'd encountered on the road but the Buddha appeared beyond the need to chat or debate.

Dona was a man of great insight and clearly saw the Buddha's transcendent qualities illuminating the space he inhabited, like a Blue Lotus untouched by the mud or even the water from which it has arisen..

Convinced the Buddha couldn't possibly be an ordinary human being, he asked:

"Are you a god?"

"No," came the simple reply.

"So, are you an angel?" he ventured further.

"No," Buddha replied.

"Well, you must be a Nature Guardian spirit then?"

"No."

"But surely you're not a human being, are you?" said Dona, persistent to the end.

"No," the Buddha answered enigmatically.

Shocked and exasperated he couldn't categorize the Buddha at all, Dona gave up.

"Then what on Earth *are* you?" he asked.

"I am *Awake*," said the Buddha.

Awareness

The Tibetan master, Dudjom Rinpoche, famously wrote 'Pure awareness of nowness is the real Buddha'.

Dwelling mindfully in the present moment, therefore, is the path to enlightenment.

To be a Buddhist means that we undertake to train the mind to rest in its true nature. Then we remain open and content there, aware of our innate goodness, which we radiate for the ultimate benefit of all beings.

This awareness has within it the realisation that there is no separation between self and others. This is the Wisdom of all the Buddhas of past, present and future. That is why the Compassion of the enlightened ones is all-pervasive, awake, and effortlessly directed for the welfare of others.

Ultimately, Buddhism is not about sitting on meditation cushions – that is only a training ground. Enlightened activity is the raison d'etre of one who is awakened.

We train in the various levels of mindfulness and awareness so that we may be of more and more benefit to others. In the process, our own welfare is more than adequately taken care of. His Holiness the Dalai Lama reassures us that when we have compassion for others, the first beneficiary is ourselves.

Put another way, we become happy, healthy, whole human beings by loving. We don't have to wait for enlightenment to do that.

Broadening our awareness to include all beings, is precisely the means by which we skillfully radiate our innate compassion towards others.

Now we face the question, 'In what ways exactly should I benefit beings?'.

I could focus in a small way on those around me. Or I might wish to change the whole world!

But, according to the teachings, the greatest benefit I could bring to beings is to do whatever I can to inspire them to realize their own Buddha Nature and to manifest their true potential.

For some people this may be rather shocking. Shouldn't we try to eradicate poverty and disease first? Of course we should. That would be incredible! But the bigger picture offered by this Wisdom Tradition is that we view all beings as Buddhas-to-be. As such, our ultimate focus has to be making that a reality.

As we may already have observed, the rich and the healthy are not necessarily enjoying the lasting happiness free from suffering which, according to the Buddha, is what we all really want.

If I truly wanted to bring about the ultimate happiness of others, I would not merely strive to offer them states of being which are intrinsically impermanent.

A universe filled only with enlightened beings would, of course, bring about physical well-being and peace as a consequence. But their lasting happiness would not depend on the presence of those things.

In the meantime, of course we must attempt to bring about world peace and wellness. That much is clear and necessary - perhaps now more than ever as we stand on the brink of destroying our precious planet and all the miraculous species who have manifested on it.

The hidden miracle, however, is the Buddha Nature within all beings.

When we become aware of this, both internally and externally, it colours everything about how we perceive self and others. All our actions and aspirations take on a fundamental sense of urgency. The greatest tragedy of all would be for this Ultimate Truth not to be realized.

> Dwelling in the present moment,
> May Awareness shine like a torch,
> Dispelling the darkness and misery of the world,
> So that all beings may fully realize their True Nature.

Bardo

This contemplation is all about the famous French movie actress, *Brigitte Bardot*... No – only kidding – it's about death again! LOL! Oh those crazy Buddhists and their twisted sense of humour!

Bardo is a Tibetan word meaning *transition*.
Every moment, it must be said, is actually a transition. Each moment bridges that gap between past and future. In fact, the present moment is really all we have. The past is gone, and the future has not yet come. The bardo of the present moment is a vibrant precious thing, pregnant with endless possibility. Moment to moment, both we and the entire Cosmos manifest from it.
The most important aspect of this moment is the golden opportunity it offers. If we open up to the present moment we can actually encounter our Buddha Nature. This present moment is truly a wonderful moment. When we live it with mindfulness, awareness and a sense of spaciousness, we have the chance to become enlightened.

The Natural Mind only manifests in the present moment. So, if we want to experience it, that's where we have to look.

If it doesn't happen in this particular moment – not to worry – there'll be another one coming our way ... well, in just a moment.

According to the teachings, some moments actually offer a stronger possibility of success than others. There are certain times in a human life when one is more ripe than others – usually when we surrender all need for control and the mask of Ego has slipped temporarily. These moments range in duration and importance from a sneeze to an orgasm, from the dream state to the bardo of death.

When we sneeze, nature takes control momentarily and we can do nothing except let go of everything – all our baggage and neuroses – and just allow the moment to be *as it is*, pure, naked and aware. But a sneeze passes by so quickly.

During an orgasm we experience unbridled rapture and ecstacy, but it's still a very ordinary joy we are feeling none-the-less. It belongs more to the realm of superficial emotions. However, at this time we also have the possibility of connecting to something much more profound. It could be a portal to the *Great Bliss* that characterizes the inner radiance of the Buddha Nature itself. These days, unfortunately, this particular avenue has been hi-jacked by 'new age' self-styled gurus and there are practically no remaining authentic practitioners, even in the East.

When we sleep we dream. Sometimes it's like going to the cinema. We usually think the dream is real, and get carried away by it. We don't recognize the delusional nature of it – just like the so-called daytime *reality* we think of as real. Though still quite secret, there are *dream yoga* practices we can learn. These could be very helpful as they offer us tools to experience the dream state as unreal and within our control. Because we don't have a physical body in the dream and are less inhibited emotionally, we are more likely to make a spiritual breakthrough.

But the Bardo of Death, especially according to Tibetan Buddhism, is a very special opportunity indeed.

For most people, the actual moment of death flies by in an instant. We don't even notice the various phases that are contained within it. We are propelled by the winds of karma, and our own mindlessness in life, towards our next rebirth. But for people who were adept at dwelling in the present moment during their lives, and who may have reconnected with their true nature, the moment of death appears a slow, gradual psycho-spiritual event with various stages – each presenting us with an opportunity to realize our Buddha Nature and become enlightened.

Many great beings have attained liberation this way. In their next manifestation as a spiritual teacher, they described every step of the process by which they did it.

These precious Bardo Teachings are very detailed. They describe all the stages of the physical body's consciousness dissolving and the spiritual body's gradual journey as it dissolves into Pure Awareness. If our consciousness manages to merge with the Buddha Nature at this point, it means we have merged with the nature of everything. This glorious reunification is likened to a child running towards its mother and jumping into her lap – all safe and snug – the most natural thing in the world.

More adept practitioners usually train in the methods of the Bardo, just in case.

For less experienced practitioners, like you and me, this chance may not arise. It could be no sooner have we left our death-bed, and all the cherished associations of this person we think of as *I*, and we're in our next mother's womb preparing to be born.

The Bardo of the Present Moment, therefore, should be our preferred gateway to realizing our True Nature. That's why the most common teachings of the Buddha found all around the world are those instructions on meditation and the way of compassion.

Only by training the mind and opening the heart in this way can we truly aspire to living fully in the present and so bring ultimate benefit to beings.

Bodhichitta

If I were a Buddha this very instant, what would it feel like?

This is not a mere fantasy or wishful thinking. It is a fundamental consideration on the spiritual path. By contemplating the very essence of buddhahood, and with determined effort, we can begin to manifest as a buddha ourselves right now.

If we knew what a buddha was supposed to be and do, we could measure ourselves against that, recognize the positive qualities we already possess, rejoice in them, and become more and more like that.

The teachings guide us to touch the core of buddhahood deeply and – starting where we are right now – move gradually in that direction.

Bodhichitta is a Sanskrit word meaning *The Heart of the Enlightened Mind*. It is all the many glorious good qualities found in the heart of a buddha – peace, loving compassion, wisdom, and the power to benefit beings. But, not only that. Arising out of our love and compassion, for Bodhichitta to be present a deep longing to bring others to full enlightenment – even before ourselves – must emerge.

We should remember that we already possess such beautiful qualities in *our* core being. They are the very seeds of our own eventual enlightenment. But not just seeds – these qualities are already active in our lives. When we operate from the space of innate goodness towards others, in our ordinary daily lives, we personally experience the truth that we can and do show love, compassion, wisdom, and the power to benefit beings. No matter how small, these seeds and activities are already vibrant within us, longing to become fully manifest. What we must do now is expand them beyond all limitations and stabilize them until we are of maximum universal benefit. The catalyst we need to ignite that unquenchable fire is Bodhichitta – the profound desire to bring all beings to enlightenment.

When we begin to train in Bodhichitta, we may find it a little difficult to make it feel *real* somehow. Suddenly it may be hard to relate to others as the teachings instruct - *longing to bring all beings to complete enlightenment.* Pretty daunting, huh? Maybe we actually feel indifferent towards all these unknown beings. Maybe we find it difficult to connect with them in this way. What we need is a key that will unlock the whole situation and propel us forward.

At present we are more interested in ourselves than others, largely speaking. So the Buddha used that very tendency as the starting point. We re-train the mind to have a more altruistic tendency by first considering any given being as *just another you.* They are exactly like you in every way. This being just wants to be happy and not suffer. No matter who or what they are, we are essentially the same.

Seeing others in this way makes it much easier to feel *engaged* and to actually connect with them. Now we feel we have a personal insight into all beings and just what makes them tick – they're just like me. So whether I am sending love through my practice, in private, on a meditation cushion, or I am volunteering in a hospice cleaning an elderly lady's ass, the attitude is the same – oh it's just another me... no drama... I wipe my own ass everyday without a second thought!

Once I've begun to break through my personal barriers and come to *Equalize Self and Others*, as above, the next step is to *Exchange Self and Others*.

This is a crucial step for developing Bodhichitta. As before, we use specific meditation practices and real life situations. We begin to train the mind to give all our happiness to others and to take on their suffering.

At first this seems quite a shocking proposal. It's the one thing the ego doesn't want to hear! Love and Compassion, however, herald the death of the ego. These two practices, Giving Love and Taking On Suffering, are only uncomfortable for the ego – not our true selves. There are many twists and turns in the Dharma, and here come two more. When we give all our happiness away, it generates infinitely more for us. When we take on the suffering and delusion of all beings – even if we actually *could* remove it – we ourselves would not suffer in the slightest. Only our ego would become diminished and eventually destroyed.

These practical meditations can be learned at most mainstream Buddhist centres. In such places, you should also be offered study-courses on Bodhichitta. It is very important not only to become a practitioner but a scholar too. Dharma study helps us to see the path ahead in great detail and our present position within that context. We see our own progress.

The Bodhichitta at the heart of the enlightened mind can be understood in two ways. There is an Absolute and a Relative dimension.

Absolute Bodhichitta is to do with the Natural Mind, our Buddha Nature, and the Wisdom of its vast view; all phenomena are changing and therefore impermanent. Flowing. Because all things are *open* in this way, everything is interconnected. The Buddha Nature pervades and connects every being, every thing. Thus the buddhas rest in their true nature and so have a connected, blissful, liberated spaciousness about them which manifests as a compassionate courage and perseverance by which they intend to lead all beings to Liberation.

Relative Bodhichitta, on the other hand, embodies the concrete, specific ways a buddha *achieves* this – what they actually *do*. In the Relative dimension there are two distinct aspects to be adopted: the Bodhichitta of Aspiration and Action.

The Aspiration of a buddha is realized by heartfelt *prayers* and *vows*. The prayer is 'May all beings attain buddhahood'. And the vow is 'May *I* personally be responsible for bringing that about'. This is known as the *Boddhisattva* Vow. It is a saintly but eminently practical aspiration. A Bodhisattva is a being who puts others before themselves and, therefore, works tirelessly for the enlightenment of others instead of themselves.

The Action of a buddha is all-embracing and skillfully inventive. It is broadly understood to manifest in the following ways, known as The Six *Paramitas* or Transcendent Perfections -

1. Generosity (Skt. dāna): to cultivate the attitude of giving of oneself to others.
2. Discipline (Skt. śīla): refraining from all harm.
3. Patience (Skt. kṣānti): the ability not to be perturbed by anything, to become expert in peacefully remaining.
4. Enthusiastic Diligence (Skt. vīrya): to find deep joy in what is virtuous, positive and wholesome.
5. Meditative concentration (Skt. dhyāna): not to be distracted – at the highest level, to rest in our Buddha Nature.
6. Wisdom (Skt. prajñā): the perfect discrimination of all phenomena – to perceive everything purely, *as it truly is*.

Whether we're already enlightened, or baby buddhas-to-be, these six are what we can and must do in the here and now. Living mindfully, we should actively look out for opportunities to put them into practice.

The beauty and strength of the Bodhichitta teachings must be taken to heart and understood courageously not as something we might embody at some point in the future but *as we are* right now. Bodhichitta is enlightened activity. The spiritual path – training the mind and opening the heart – is none other than this. Embarking upon it right now, no matter how modest our progress, will be the direct cause of our own liberation too. By acting like a buddha, we become one.

The great Indian Buddhist saint, Shantideva [700 CE], wrote the following on Bodhichitta, The Compassionate Heart of the Enlightened Mind:

> It is the supreme elixir
> That overcomes the sovereignty of death.
> It is the inexhaustible treasure
> That eliminates poverty in the world.
> It is the supreme medicine
> That quells the world's disease.
> It is the tree that shelters all beings
> Wandering and tired on the path of conditioned existence.
> It is the universal bridge
> That leads to freedom from unhappy states of birth.
> It is the dawning moon of the mind
> That dispels the torment of disturbing conceptions.
> It is the great sun that finally removes the misty ignorance of the world.

Bodhisattva

Bodhi-Sattva literally means *Enlightened Warrior*.
The Theravada schools limit the word to mean anyone who is well on their way to being enlightened but has not yet reached that point. For example, the famous Jataka Tales are a collection of stories about the Buddha's heroic good deeds in previous lives.

The Mahayana schools have a different view. A Bodhisattva is a courageous, saintly person who may already be enlightened or just on the verge of it. Either way, they have the focus and demeanor of a warrior and will not give up until all beings are enlightened. They nolonger think of their own welfare and are continually reborn for the ultimate benefit of others.

In the Buddhist tradition, as a whole, there are different categories of Bodhisattva:

Like a king, who himself becomes enlightened and then leads others towards it by example and whatever means he has at his disposal.

A boatman, who ferries all sentient beings across to the far shore of liberation and in so doing, as a consequence, inadvertently becomes enlightened at the same time himself.

A shepherd, who walks behind his cherished flock steering them in the right direction, with no thought for himself. Until every last being is liberated the shepherd will not accept enlightenment.

The last example is the one I have heard most about from my own teachers and I also recall His Holiness the Dalai Lama remarking that this *good shepherd* must secretly already be enlightened to have such vast Bodhichitta.

His Holiness is himself a fine example of this gentle warrior shepherd - although he would never admit it.

There can be no Bodhisattva without Bodhichitta – the desire to bring all beings to enlightenment – and there can be no Bodhichitta without a surging realisation of egolessness. The emergence of the Enlightened Warrior heralds the death of the Ego altogether.

I myself have no Bodhichitta. I just embody a huge ego that loves to hear itself explain things. So, without having to elaborate further, perhaps the best examples of Bodhisattva Aspiration and Action are to be found in the vows and prayers used regularly by HH Dalai Lama.

In explaining his greatest sources of inspiration he often cites a favorite verse, found in the writings of the renowned eighth century Buddhist saint Shantideva:

> As long as space exists
> And beings endure,
> May I too remain
> To dispel the misery of the world.

If you have seen the movie *Kundun*, you may well recall the young Dalai Lama as a child trying to memorize another prayer of Shantideva's.

May I be a protector to those without protection,
A leader for those who journey,
And a boat, a bridge, a passage
For those desiring the other shore.

May the pain of every living creature
Be completely cleared away.
May I be the doctor and the medicine
And may I be the nurse
For all sick beings in the world
Until everyone is healed.

Just like space
And the great elements such as earth,
May I always support the life
Of all the boundless creatures.

And until they pass away from pain
May I also be the source of life
For all the realms of varied beings
That reach unto the ends of space.

Boredom

We have many spiritual teachers in life. Our inner teacher, the Buddha nature itself, also manifests externally in order to wake us up to the true nature of reality. If we are extremely fortunate, this will happen in the form of an enlightened being who has dedicated their life to waking beings up. But that is not the only form the inner teacher takes on.

Spiritual teachings may occur in the form of other people, situations or seemingly random events. The universe itself functions as an outer teacher. Our life experiences would be a force for gradual awakening if only we could look deeply into them.

Many of us are prone to such a sense of *boredom* it pervades much of what we experience. We may feel so numb and essentially unmoved by life that a boundless stream of wake-up calls appears to pass us by. We are learning practically nothing from life.

We can even experience boredom on the spiritual path. Instead of being refreshed or profoundly transformed by our meditation, the practice itself may actually become an obstacle for us. In this case, we must remind ourselves that obstacles *are* the path. Obstacles are not preventing us *from* becoming enlightened, they are the opportunities *through which* we attain liberation. Seen in this way, working with boredom *becomes* the practice itself. Learning to accept things as they are specifically includes being bored while meditating.

Boredom, it must be said, goes far deeper than a subset of practitioners who find meditation boring.

The feeling that reality, as it is, is not enough pervades the perception of all beings. On the deepest level, it's almost as if we misinterpret our own *Empty* essence [*Shunyata*] as a hole that needs to be filled somehow. We seem to panic and throw ourselves into a chaotic cycle of filling that perceived void. We fill the mind with an avalanche of thoughts and emotions, and fill our already hectic lives with more and more unnecessary stuff. And so, we embark on a quest for interesting experiences.

Boredom, then, not only makes us fidgety and dissatisfied with our meditation, it preoccupies us our entire lives. A strong desire not to be bored usually gets us into a lot of trouble!

We don't feel complete in ourselves so we turn our minds outwards and get lost in a sea of unrealistic expectations. We run the risk of drowning in a mess of our own making. We need too much from others. We want too much from travel. We may well end up with a string of disastrous friendships and relationships behind us, and a pile of mounting credit card bills in front of us – and precious little to show for our trouble.

Having spent some time many years ago contemplating the nature of boredom, instead of doing my meditation practice of course, I accepted an invitation to tea and a chat with an old friend one afternoon. The experience turned out to be a huge teaching for me. It was almost as if the Universal Buddha Nature was confirming what I was coming to suspect.

We met in the café of the Irish Museum of Modern Art. I arrived a bit early and, bored, wandered aimlessly through some of the exhibition there. It struck me that a lot of the art had been created by minds trying to express – or fill – the void within themselves. They seemed to think too much, their cleverness exploding onto the canvasses to relieve their boredom.

Then I went to have tea with my friend. He suffers a lot with his mind and just couldn't stop talking. He chattered without pausing for breath or a sip of his tea for over an hour. It hadn't always been like that. Years before, he had been physically ill. He had to quit his job, stay home, and allow the healing to take its slow course. Instead of that being the end of his problems, he became mentally ill he says from having nothing to do. He was a meditator, but had become so scared of the emptiness of his own mind he could nolonger meditate. He felt the endless babbling of his stream-of-consciousness was helpful because it appeared to give his mind something to *do*. I felt my heart breaking for his suffering and a deep, compassionate longing emerged in me. I wished I could remove his suffering altogether. But the best I could muster in the situation was to remain open, listen, and send him all my own peace and love through our eye contact.

Then, out of the blue, he announced the real reason for our meeting and reached deep into his backpack. As unopened post, used tissues and crumpled banknotes spilled out of his bag onto the table, my friend produced a present for me. It was an old Dharma book containing rare Tibetan Buddhist teachings. He'd inscribed it for me and pressed exquisite rose petals between the pages ... he was literally giving the teachings of the Buddha to me. The whole encounter taught me so much.

By the end of our meeting, I felt quite drained. However, something in *me* was still unfulfilled. I left my friend with a kind of empty feeling inside. Still looking for something *else* to do, almost bored, I drifted into the museum bookshop, perhaps to see if an impromptu purchase would fill the gap. I was still wondering if we think too much because we can't bear the natural perfection of the empty silence inside. I remembered, yet again, the Buddha's words... *With our thoughts, we make the world.*

There were no books apart from the usual over-priced mighty tomes on the fabulousness of modern art. Determined not to leave empty-handed, I glanced at the postcards and there it was... the perfect summation, a cosmic punchline to the whole day. Honestly, I laughed all the way home and I'm looking at the card right now. It reads:

Boredom is the Cause of Everything

Breathe

Vietnamese Zen master Thich Nhat Hanh inspiringly sums up the teaching of the Buddha in a single phrase – *'Breathe. You are alive'*.

The essence of this teaching encapsulates all of meditation itself. When we become mindful and aware of our breathing, we have given ourselves the greatest gift there is. Returning to the present moment like this arouses in us a joyful consciousness of the fullness of life. Without too much fuss, or preparation, we are actually meditating already and have the opportunity to experience directly our own true nature and reality as it is.

Observing the breath in this way can be a formal practice in itself or it can be a trigger for mindful living in daily life. The key is not to fixate on the breath or manipulate it in any way. We do not need to have a running commentary in our heads: *'Now, I'm breathing in. Now, I'm breathing out'*. Rather, we simply rest the mind and loosely settle our focus on the natural flow of the breath. *Natural* is perhaps the most important word here. There is no need to force anything at all. The Buddha Nature, the Natural Mind, will reveal itself with comfort and ease the more uncontrived we become.

This is the very essence of the Buddha's words. Since the breath is always with us we have a constant, portable, and free method of connecting with our true nature. For this reason, the whole Buddhist path begins with learning to meditate and culminates in the awakening of the natural, inexhaustible Wisdom and Compassion that our Buddha Nature contains.

We must not become fixated on the breath to the exclusion of everything else around or within us. It is better to devote maybe a quarter of our attention to *watching* the breath, and another quarter to over-seeing that we are not becoming too distracted – when our mind wanders, we gently bring it back to the breath. The rest of our consciousness – the larger part – in time will be empowered to remain naturally spacious, free to engage with phenomena. Thus we learn to accept and let go of whatever arises. We do not *block* reality. All the senses remain open and accepting. All our thoughts and emotions, and stimuli from the external world, are greeted spaciously and allowed to settle again quite naturally.

The breath is the gateway to the Natural Mind and, as such, is our best friend – our constant companion in life. It offers us direct access to our true nature at any time and in all circumstances. With practice, mindfulness becomes our *new habit*. Eventually, it allows us to settle the mind on whatever we choose. Our mind becomes so flexible and pliable that we can apply it, one-pointedly and without distraction, however we want whilst still being spacious enough to multi-task and remain relaxed, alert and refreshed.

In a formal meditation session, more experienced practitioners may skillfully use the breath to inhale and remove the suffering of all beings while exhaling love, peace and joy to them. Or they may use the breath to turn the mind inwards and rest in the Buddha Nature. Practitioners who are new to all this learn to *observe* the breath spaciously and without too many concepts. They learn the skill of simultaneously being alert and relaxed.

The gift of meditation teaches us to allow ourselves to be naturally present – to just *be*, right here, right now. We are naturally open, content, aware and refreshed by the practice.

Breathe in... Breathe out... What bliss!

Buddha

The Buddha's life story reveals the awakening of an ordinary human being, like you and me, to the state of full enlightenment. It is told in such a way that it's meant to parallel our own potential spiritual evolution. To best enjoy the details and for the beautifully poetic flow of the language, I strongly recommend reading *Old Path, White Clouds* by Thich Nhat Hanh.

There is a single theme running right through the life of the Buddha – Bodhichitta – the strongest possible desire to liberate others from suffering and bring them to the state of lasting happiness, enlightenment. It was his Bodhichitta that created the right causes and conditions for his own enlightenment and which provided his life with a clear purpose thereafter.

His given name was Siddhartha Gautama and he was the son and heir of the king of the Sakya clan. It was a small kingdom in the foothills of the Himalayas in northern India over 2500 years ago.

When Siddhartha was born [somewhere between BCE 563 – 483] his parents were thrilled and the whole Kingdom rejoiced and celebrated the birth of their future king. But a court holyman predicted Siddhartha would either be a great king or a great spiritual teacher. So the king proceeded to do everything in his power to ensure his son would never be distracted from his royal duty. His father's biggest fear was Siddhartha might be so moved by the plight of ordinary people that he would abandon his crown in favour of seeking spiritual answers to life's questions.

Despite the king's best efforts, this is exactly what happened.

Even though the king protected Siddhartha from the harsh realities of life, he could not shut them out entirely. The story goes that when he was a young married man with an infant son of his own, Siddhartha escaped the confines of the palace compound in which he'd spent his whole life. He knew he had been kept in the dark – totally ignorant of how life truly is.

Once out in the world, he experienced everything first-hand for himself. What he witnessed moved him so deeply it aroused his Bodhichitta to benefit beings. Traditionally we speak of life's sufferings being represented by the all-inclusive phrase 'Birth, Old Age, Sickness and Death', but I'm certain Prince Siddhartha also saw the suffering of teenagers, the lonely and marginalized, the poor, the mentally ill and so much more. Instinctively he knew the world could never provide true happiness – he had seen it for himself from both sides now. The young prince decided to dedicate his life to discovering the universal answer to the suffering of the mind. This quest would lead him far from home. Even if he lost his wife and child, his entire kingdom, the transformation had to be made for the benefit of beings. It was his father's worst nightmare come true.

In some versions, we are told Siddhartha then glimpsed a wandering Hindu monk and his heart leapt. Maybe that could lead him in the right direction and provide some answers.

So motivated was Siddhartha that he quietly returned to the palace to say his goodbyes and began his spiritual quest.

The next section of Siddhatha's story is taken up with his spiritual journey from teacher to teacher perfecting the highest meditation techniques available at the time. He progressed quickly and was ripe for the ultimate breakthrough, enlightenment itself. But this he had to do alone.

His journey had also taken him into several dead-ends. At one point he joined a small group of master-meditators in the forest. These hermits practised a path which involved extreme self-denial. Eventually it occurred to Siddhartha that he had simply gone from one extreme to the other – from total luxury with no spiritual practice to total æsceticism. Since neither would produce lasting happiness for himself or others, this blossoming bodhisattva decided to courageously strike out on his own and explore the *Middle Way*.

His experience of the India of his day – and not much has changed since then – led him to deduce also that secular and religious life needed great reform. The removal of the caste system, and creating a non-ritualized spiritual path for all, were two major themes he would return to again in later life.

Back on his own wandering path, Siddhartha eventually settled under a tree near a small remote town, in what is still one of the poorest regions of India. He vowed not to get up from his meditation until he had cracked the ego wide open and attained absolute liberation.

You or I could be just as determined and maybe nothing much would happen. But Siddhartha was ripe for enlightenment. The full force of all his past positive karma and, in a way, the Wisdom energy of the whole universe, and the inevitable spiritual evolution of all beings was propelling him towards it.

The Buddha became enlightened under what is now known as the Bodhi Tree, just outside the bustling dusty little town of Bodhgaya.

His transformation was evident to all who encountered him. Similarly, if *you* find and meet an enlightened being, you will undoubtedly experience their incredible transcendent qualities yourself.

At first, the Buddha didn't know where to begin explaining the true Nature of Mind or how others might discover it for themselves. But his enlightenment radiated to others and they wanted to learn from him. His Bodhichitta flowered into a tireless effort to help beings liberate themselves. He knew he could not do it *for* them, only show the way.

The Buddha went back to the forest and found his hermit friends. At first they were uninterested, so immersed were they in their own views. Buddha did not try to convince them, so they became curious. These filthy, emaciated practitioners were, however, also ripe for *their* final breakthrough. They became Buddha's first students and, with his guidance, quickly realized the Natural Mind.

Soon a growing community of student meditators, both monastic and lay, was emerging. In fact, the Buddha's aunt, his wife Yashodara, and son Rahula were amongst the first wave of monastics.

The community benefitted from the charity and patronage of kings and simple local people alike. They moved about en masse according to the weather, establishing residential retreats for each season.

The Buddha had realized the primordially pure, undistracted, compassionate nature of his own mind. And now, gradually, so did others. The Buddha's Bodhichitta was bringing about results. His teachings and guidance is known as *The Path* [Skt. Dharma]. Most of it came to be memorized by the first generation of his followers, and was later written down in Sutra form. He taught beings according to their ripeness and ability to understand. Therefore some of the Buddha's teachings were not written down since they were not intended for general consumption. These teachings were passed on orally as appropriate and are available to anyone, even today, provided the master is qualified and the student is ready. Otherwise they make no sense and will have no spiritual benefit, however mentally stimulating or mind-numbing they may be.

Far from being a personality cult, the community of practitioners [Skt. Sangha] were meditators on their own path to enlightenment and the Buddha was their guide. The Buddha often said to them, 'Look, if I could enlighten you myself of course I would have done it for you, long ago. But I can't do that. I can only point the way. You must be the one to liberate yourself through practice. There's no other option'.

Buddha was determined his Sangha become a community of practitioners not fans. Interestingly, he forbade them from making images of him. However, within a few generations there were geometric shapes created to represent the Mind of the Buddha rather than his outer form. And within another few generations, there were paintings and statues everywhere.

For a long time at first, the Sangha was a place where the caste system and all other forms of discrimination were abandoned. Similarly, there was no ritual – no bells or smells – only meditation.

In a later era, the whole of India was Buddhist under the saintly King Ashoka [BCE 304 – 232]. Important sites connected with the Buddha's life were marked and famous monasteries and universities were established.

But India being India, there came an even later period with a deeply entrenched need for a societal class structure and the caste system slowly returned with gusto. The monastics – now mostly men – had simply become yet another stratum, though highly elevated above ordinary people. They were privileged for the most part and revered, but rarely taught the Dharma. India's love affair with ritual [Skt. Puja] also returned and Buddhism soon expressed itself through the mystery of sound, sight and scent. What had emerged was a two-tiered spiritual contract. The people supported the monastics in return for their pujas and prayers. How the lineage of enlightened beings wasn't actually broken at this juncture is a real mystery.

Although not yet mainstream, there is an academic school of thought nowadays which holds that the eventual decline of Buddhism in this period was largely due to the ordinary people and many practitioners simply walking away from it in droves. They felt Buddhism had become no different to the old Hinduism, which was still around. After Emperor Ashoka died, a succession of new kings ruled and Buddhism never benefitted from the same degree of royal support again. Some monarchs even persecuted it. The ancient cults and religions enjoyed a renaissance and Buddhism declined. Travelling Chinese scholars attested to this having already begun in the 5th to the 8th centuries CE. There was a further marked decline with the fall of the Pala Dynasty in the 12th century.

Either way, the Muslim invasion was just around the corner and Islam would soon replace both. Beginning slowly in the north of India in the 7th century, the conquest was complete by the 11th. The Buddhist priestly class was disbanded and banished altogether. And most of the temples, universities and now forbidden images were completely destroyed.

Whatever various forms of the Buddha's teachings had taken root previously in other parts of Asia was pretty much all that remained. But Buddhism grew strong in those foreign lands and its authenticity shone bright there for many centuries. Now it has come from those treasured second-flourishings, where it is tragically currently in decline too, to the West where it will surely enjoy another revival. The big question on everyone's mind is 'Will Westerners practise meditation? To the point of enlightenment? Do we actually care enough about others to arouse Bodhichitta? Where do we even start all this?'

Some time before he passed away, the Buddha was asked by a very simple student, 'I still don't get it. Please, explain in the simplest way possible the main point of the Dharma'.

The Buddha replied:

> Don't do anything negative.
> Only do positive things.
> Achieve all this by training your mind.

buddha

The Buddha is not the only buddha.

There have been many buddhas already, even before Prince Siddhartha, the buddha for *our* time. Many traditions speak of Samanthabhadra, the Primordial Buddha, who is said to be the origin of all buddhas wherever and whenever they may manifest to benefit beings.

Therefore we speak about the source of all buddhas being outside and beyond time and space. That is also the origin of the Buddha Nature that pervades everything within time and space, including ourselves. The teachings often speak of '*The deathless, unending Nature of Mind*' for this very reason. It is '*unborn and unceasing*'. So we could say the spiritual has manifested physical form in order to create innumerable opportunities to further express its boundless love and compassion. *That* is the meaning of life. The *Changeless* compassionately embracing the Ever-Changing in order to liberate it.

So we can differentiate between buddhas, who are said to *emanate* from the source, and beings who *reincarnate* within the multi-dimensional layers of space-time.

A bodhisattva defers attaining complete enlightenment so they can continue to reincarnate for the benefit of beings. But once a bodhisattva is fully enlightened, by definition, technically they have become a buddha and are nolonger reborn. Therefore we understand why Bodhisattva Siddhartha, after having attained enlightenment, did not reincarnate.

There are still beings today who continue to destroy their ego through practising Bodhichitta. They will either blossom into reincarnating bodhisattvas or become fully enlightened buddhas and cease to be bound by this realm.

The teachings say the particular epoque we live in now is on the slippery downward slope of just one of many peaks and troughs that comprise an expanded view of time on earth. Eventually, they maintain, the Wisdom Teachings that lead to enlightenment will be completely lost and forgotten, yet again. Then it will be necessary, in some future era, for the next emanating buddha to manifest and reveal them.

When *we* see time in this expanded way, and our own tiny role within it, we have a choice. We can either become overwhelmed, or we can be all the more determined to help. We must come to see ourselves as significant players in something huge!

We have had the good fortune to encounter the teachings and practices that end all suffering. We know in our hearts that we and everyone around us is suffering terribly. Therefore it is our duty to do something about it. Without any trace of ego, we must realize that *this* is why we were born!

May we have the courage to train our minds.
May our hearts open and go out to all beings.
May we allow our true nature,
which we share with all the buddhas,
To awaken from its long slumber.
And may we be the cause of all beings finding
perfect peace.

Buddha Nature

We share the same essence as all the buddhas. Our Buddha Nature [Skt. *Tatha-gatha-garbha*] therefore is also the source of everything that is. To illustrate this truth the Buddha himself said the most amazing and enigmatic thing:

> We are what we think.
> With our thoughts, we make the world.

I never cease to be shocked and inspired by this teaching. It summarizes everything the Buddha discovered when he became enlightened.

Because our *perception* of reality can often be so wrong, fundamentally it must be said we are negatively colouring that which we perceive. Depending on our state of mind, we literally create a different reality.

If our minds are occupied with neurotic ego-centricities, that is the world we create for ourselves to inhabit.

On the other hand, if our mind's focus is the purity of its own true nature we create inner strength and peace, and we dwell in Heaven on Earth – the Great Perfection. A world of endless possibilities to benefit others opens up.

Through our meditation practice and all the activities of Bodhichitta, we must develop an unshakable confidence in the powerful presence of our own true nature.

Sogyal Rinpoche often tells his students, 'Remember, *our* Buddha Nature is as good as *any* buddha's Buddha Nature'.

Just look at what the buddhas achieve. We must never forget that we can do the same if only we have faith in ourselves. The entire purpose of our True Nature – the Natural Mind – is precisely that ... to do what comes *naturally*.

When we dwell in the narrow-minded realm of the ego our lives are hijacked. We are not free. Everything about us is temporarily *un-natural*. It's like we have no say in what we're doing. We seem to be driven along by every fear and whim. We have no self-control. We have no clue whatsoever who or what our *real self* is.

We become fragmented and shattered. Every scattered impulse is followed.

Spiritual practice will help the mind become peaceful. When we become whole again – reassembled – we develop a new perspective. Nolonger prey to every conceivable distraction, we experience first-hand the limitless power of our own nature. The Natural Mind brings with it a much broader view of phenomena. We experience the big picture.

If the Buddha Nature could talk it would probably not have so much to say about itself or its nature. Because the Natural Mind *knows* it is completely perfect, open and content already its focus would be entirely on *others*. The agonies and the ecstasies of beings would prompt our true nature to a*ction*. It would not necessarily get sucked into the minute detail of all the drama of other's lives, however compelling. The primary objective of the Buddha Energy, if we can call it that, is to help beings cut at the very root of their suffering – the ego – and to rest in their true nature.

The Natural Mind is not an indifferent, vacant *void*. It has a strong heart at its core and it beats for the welfare of others. It has been compared to the sun. The sun isn't particularly wondering to itself 'Ooh... what shall I do today then? Shall I shine or not? Should I shine here, or there?' The sun's nature *is* to shine, constantly and impartially. The Buddha Nature, like the sun, offers light and warmth to beings. Its light is Wisdom – it sees phenomena clearly as they are – and its warmth is Compassion. This means our true nature has the wisdom to see the Buddha Nature of others and to see through their suffering to its fundamental cause, the surface mind. The compassionate aspect of our Buddha Nature displays the tireless determination to remove those causes forever.

It is nice, but fundamentally misguided, to think we'll only be able to re-connect with our Natural Mind by creating the *perfect meditation space*. This is not true and might lead us on a magical mystery tour, with the ego as our guide.

Believe me... many of us have distracted ourselves for years like this to little or no avail. We have re-modelled our homes to make them more zen-like living spaces, creating the perfect corner in which to meditate with exquisite buddhas sitting on elaborate shrines. We have even travelled far and wide in search of the holiest spiritual places on earth so we can *meditate well* there.

This is like a person who, wishing to find their elephant, follows his footprints endlessly throughout the entire forest, while the elephant was at home all along!

The *perfect* place to meditate is *right here*, wherever we are. And the *perfect* time is *right now*.

Granted, as total beginners, it is vital to find a spot that is conducive to meditation – somewhere peaceful and inspiring, without distraction. But to be able to *transform* ourselves – especially to glimpse the Natural Mind – we need to become very skillful and, as Ringu Tulku Rinpoche reminds us, we must learn that *we ourselves* are the practice.

By this is meant that *our mind* is the environment in which we practise perfectly. The mind is the root of our suffering and it is also the root of our own Liberation. We could follow our master around day and night, practising by her side or at his feet. However, most people may only be lucky enough to *glimpse* the Buddha Nature. To become *liberated*, we must do the work ourselves. Starting where we are now, we must become experts in observing the way *our* particular deluded mind works.

The most valuable lesson is to realize that *we* are the practice. Comfy meditation cushions, inspiring shrine-rooms and elaborate formal ritual practices, in themselves, are not.

The ego mind is already adept at attempting to turn every life situation to our advantage. We also have highly skilled imaginations. Now we must learn to put both these human traits to a higher, more noble task.

When we view life itself as a wake up call, we begin to *use* every situation that comes our way. We can gradually awaken our Bodhichitta for the benefit of all beings and, in so doing, *realize* our own Buddha Nature – not only discover it, but actually make it *real*.

Let us return to the idea of the sun. As we discussed earlier, the sun's light and warmth provide us with a very inspiring teaching on the wisdom and compassion of the Buddha Nature.

So wherever we are, whatever the weather or time of day or night, we can imagine the sun this very instant and meditate in the following way...

Imagine the sun as the embodiment of the Universal Buddha nature.

Its rays bring light and warmth deep into our very being. The blessing and healing grace of all the buddhas and bodhisattvas of the past, present and future gently stream towards us.

Imagine the sun's rays vividly. They cross all of space and time, and touch our hearts bringing profound peace and well-being.

Breathing in – receive everything that is positive and wholesome...

Breathing out – let go completely, for once and for all, of everything that is negative... low self-esteem, ill-health, doubts, fear...

Continue like this for some time...

Imagine your very soul is gloriously opening up like a lotus blossom... and your hard-hearted ego is melting and dripping away like a block of ice left out in the sun, until it is gone...

When you feel open and refreshed, take some time to really acknowledge how happy, well and safe you feel from your very core... already perfect... primordially pure.

Now, imagine yourself... in every detail... Your physical body is light and luminous.

Recognize that *your* Buddha Nature shares the same qualities as all the buddhas... the wisdom that knows things as they truly are... the compassion that cares ... and the power to benefit all beings.

Arouse a very strong desire to share your love with others...

Allow yourself, through compassion, to dare to be the one who is going to take away their suffering...

This time, breathing out first – Send beings all your love, from the depths of your true nature. Imagine it flowing towards their hearts like a stream of pure, white, healing light.

Breathing in – Fearlessly, remove the suffering of all beings, without exception. Imagine their minds being liberated.

... The teachings urge us to practise continually like this – in meditation sessions and in daily life – until what we imagine becomes reality.

We practise in this way without distraction and without getting caught up in the story that surrounds the suffering of others.

We must remain in the moment with a vast spacious attitude that is egoless.

When the session has finished, simply drop the method completely – all thinking, all imagining. Let the mind itself drop, pure and simple.

Rest like this for some time before any new activity.

Challenges

The Buddha did not set out a canon of beliefs for his followers to adhere to. He did not start a religion, or an ideology, or an *ism* of any kind.

Rather, he described the truth of reality and challenged us to measure those descriptions against our own experience. Therefore it cannot be said that Buddhism is an *ism* at all. Nor can we think of ourselves as becoming a Buddh-*ist*. There is no club to join and no set of ideas we must accept. The Buddha himself warned his students not to accept what he taught out of respect or love for him, but to examine the teachings and put them through rigorous experiential tests.

Believing *in* something could never help us attain enlightenment. Liberation is a transformative personal experience not a concept.

Transformation, of course, is a process. Therefore the challenges of the Buddha's teachings may take some time to sink in, become absorbed, to be verified by experience. It is important not to lose heart during these challenging, testing times, but to persevere as if our lives, our very sanity, depended on it.

The principal challenges laid down by the Buddha himself are sometimes known as The Four Seals. If you are just encountering these for the first time – *Courage, mon ami!* Fasten your seatbelt, Darlings. We're in for a bumpy ride!

All compounded things are *impermanent*.
All emotions ultimately bring *pain*.
All phenomena are *Shunyata* [empty, open].
Nirvana is peace *beyond all concepts*.

I can just hear readers around the world flinging this book on the floor and running away screaming -

'Oh My God! I am SO not a Buddhist! *All emotions bring pain* ?! Are you freaking kidding me!? Why can't we all just get along? ... And dance naked in the park at full moon with crystals around our necks?!'

All compounded things are impermanent.
EVERYTHING that exists, or at least *appears* to exist, in fact does not exist. They have no intrinsic lasting qualities. All is in a perpetual state of flux, ever-changing, ever dependent on the various components that brought it together in the first place. It is said that things *appear*, like a mirage or a rainbow, but once the causes and conditions shift – even slightly – it disappears again. Every compound that comes together falls apart eventually. Look deeply into your own body, or a passing emotional state, or any phenomenon whatsoever – they are all made from various

other phenomena that *co-emerge* temporarily, change constantly, then move apart again.

Vietnamese Zen master Thich Nhat Hanh famously encourages us to look deeply into this page, for example. When we shine the light of mindfulness on the components of paper we see it is not simply *one* thing alone. We realize that paper contains within it the forest, the earth that nourished it, the people who toiled and harvested the tree, the sun and all the vast array of weather systems that cared for it throughout its life, the entire universe that shapes our planet and its life-giving conditions. We also know it will biodegrade, so it is changing even as we look at it.

He goes even deeper, concluding: Paper is made *only* of non-paper elements. Pause for thought. Pause again, considering *everything* to be like this.

Now for an age-old conundrum... A profound paradox...

Even the Buddha Nature does not *exist*, so to speak. It is not bound by space and time. Its origins are beyond. Therefore, since the Natural Mind is *un-compounded* it is, in fact, the only *changeless* thing. However, we must be careful not to fall into the trap of thinking it is an entity like a spirit or, furthermore, a *single* un-connected entity, perhaps like a soul. The opposite is the case.

We are not like a physical shell containing a spiritual ball of energy we can identify as our *self*. When we die it will not transmigrate like a soul with wings. It may not even remain intact. It may disperse into many incarnations. We *embody* the Buddha Nature. Our particular manifestation gives it expression. Moreover, it is always interconnected with all other manifestations. It is never separate or independent.

All emotions ultimately bring pain.

This is a huge stumbling block for many people perhaps because we identify so strongly with our emotions. Even the very language we use – I *am* happy, I *am* angry. Why not *'there is* happiness', or *'there is* anger'?

Eventually, though, even that viewpoint changes. We come to see our thoughts and emotions as the surface activity of the mind, not the mind itself. Emotions just arise within the mind and pass through [if we allow them]. We could think of them as bubbles fizzing to the surface in a glass of champagne, but they're not the champagne.

Enlightened beings continue, of course, to have emotions. But they experience them passing through their mindstream in a very different way to us. They don't block their passage, they allow them to come. They don't grasp onto the nice ones or struggle with the nasty ones, they simply allow them to pass through. Letting go is the answer.

The Buddha taught that emotions bring pain not so we might shun emotions altogether – they come anyway – but so we could learn to see them *in perspective*. They are the fizzing energy of the mind's natural radiance. More often they are released by hormones and chemical reactions in the physical organ of the brain.

The reason why all emotions can be seen as *ultimately painful* is actually simple enough.

When we have a positive emotion, we cling onto it as it passes. Because of our ego and its habits, we grasp onto nice feelings and the object we assume has caused it. Then the problems begin. We fear losing it. And we add to our suffering when it changes and passes on, as it inevitably must. Positive emotions sometimes actually spoil an otherwise wonderful experience, both for ourselves and for those around us; think of romance, we are so clingy and fearful of loss. They water the seeds of Attachment within our consciousness.

When negative emotion arises, instead of allowing it to pass, we grab hold of it and a struggle ensues. We want to push it, and whatever we think has caused it, far away from us as soon as possible. It is the very thing we don't want and now it is here, in our face. Clearly, negative emotions bring suffering, both to ourselves and those around us. They water the seeds of Aversion.

All phenomena are Shunyata [empty, open].

Viewing phenomena as ever-changing and impermanent brings a totally *fresh* perspective to how we relate to ourselves and everything else we perceive. When we truly take on board the inter-connected nature of all phenomena, we understand the web-like pattern of all that appears. There is *no separation*, no duality at all. Whatever happens in one part of the web affects everything. Even a modest amount of good or bad done by an individual fundamentally changes everything.

To paraphrase Thich Nhat Hanh, '*Thanks to* Shunyata *everything is therefore possible*'. Each moment we practise meditation and live mindfully, the whole universe benefits. Imagine then the cosmic shift when a single being is enlightened!

The Buddha teaches that every being and every atom is by definition *open* and connected to the whole. If they weren't, nothing could change or grow. Everything would be frozen solid instead of flowing spontaneously through time and space.

That is one good reason to never give up on our true nature. No matter what past negative *karma* has brought us at any point in our lives, we must not become fatalistic about our lot. We should never forget that everything changes and *can be changed*.

The possibilities are limitless.

Nirvana is peace beyond all concepts.

Since *Samsara* is the mind turned outwards, lost in its own projections, *Nirvana* then is the mind turned inwards, resting in its true nature. So we equate Nirvana with perfect peace and harmony. It is also said to be beyond *extremes*. That is, resting in our Buddha Nature does not merely hurtle us from one end of the spectrum to the other – from a chaotic realm of unbearable suffering to a blissed-out, spacey mindlessness. The peace that Nirvana represents is said to be so perfectly peaceful, open and content, that it's beyond all description. Therefore, the phrase 'beyond all concepts' is used. Even when the Buddha himself became enlightened, at first he couldn't find the words to describe it to others. After much contemplation he found appropriate similes and metaphors to teach others what it was like, how it would be most beneficial for self and others, and what methods to use if you wanted to attain that state yourself.

Furthermore, we must remember that enlightenment is an *experience*, albeit beyond the phenomenal, conceptual realm. This is why we can be offered a glimpse of *Nirvana* when we are in the presence of a realized master. We can literally experience the Natural Mind for ourselves. The glimpse may be quite brief at first but, thanks to the blessing of the master, it is usually enough for us to gain confidence in the existence of the Buddha Nature and inspire us to switch on that connection permanently.

Once the self-cherishing ego and its grand illusion is shattered for once and for all, we have revealed our true nature and realized Nirvana.

Change

Things change.
If they didn't, everything would be frozen, incapable of movement or progress.
Thanks to change, *everything* is possible.

When we observe the world around us – and the *internal* landscape as well – we quickly learn that change *is* the nature of everything. Looking deeply into something ... a plant, a wall, an atom, our opinion, an emotion ... we reveal the truth of change in all phenomena. Every particular thing depends on several other things for its very existence. There is a delicate balance going on. Phenomena appear and exist not as individually solid entities, but as living, changing occurrences.

Sometimes the rate of change can be observed, sometimes it's not so easy. But, because of the universal principle of change, we can deduce that all phenomena are in a perpetual state of flux.

This is also true of the human mind. Our thoughts and emotions come and go. Look deeply into any one of them – even for an instant – and we can observe how it is not at all fixed. Nothing lasts forever. Things change.

Because of this state of affairs, we do not become over-attached to pleasant phenomena. They will change. Similarly, we do not become overly troubled by unpleasant things. They too will change, eventually.

Furthermore, we acknowledge it is the nature of the deluded, ego-mind to be ever-changing. For this reason we have hope. Every cloud has a silver lining. The ego and whatever obstacles currently obscure our Buddha Nature from shining are all temporary events. Just as they have arisen, they will subside. It is the most natural thing in the world that our true nature will eventually be fully revealed.

Through spiritual practice we can participate in this process of change. We can actually speed up our progression towards enlightenment. Re-training the mind will help undo the tangled mess that has led to all our delusion.

When we realize just how flexible and malleable our minds actually are, we can *use* those same qualities of mind to manipulate it from within and drive change in the direction we want to go.

Most people can observe and accept change in the external, natural world. Many can even accept change when it affects them personally in an extremely painful way. Now we must learn to observe the mind on a far more profound level, and make use of the mind's innately flexible quality.

Instead of fighting *against* the ocean of change, we must first learn to float then develop a talent for *surfing* on the ever-changing waves. In this way, we skillfully use the energy of change itself to arrive at our ultimate destination.

The practice and the teachings provide us with the know-how necessary to embrace change.

The Wisdom of the Buddhist path is so life-affirming, and reassuring. It helps us to accept change and impermanence. Ultimately, however, it also speaks of a much deeper reality.

If *all* phenomena are changing and changeable, including the mind, is there anything that is **unchanging**?

The Buddha taught that all phenomena have their origins *within* space and time and, therefore, are subject to change and suffering. However, there *is* one exception – our Buddha Nature.

The *Tathagatagarbha*, our true nature, is described as *unborn, unceasing, with nature like the sky*.

Therefore, since it was never born, it can never die. It is not governed by any of the laws of the changing universe. Its open, spacious, sky-like nature is unperturbably content and wishes to help all beings become like that too.

The Buddha Mind is so vast and the deluded aspect of our mind so tiny, complete enlightenment is not only possible but inevitable. The *Unchanging Natural Mind* is drawing the changing, deluded aspect of mind towards itself. If we dwell in the realm of ego, that gravitational pull towards awakening may create fear ... fear of the unknown, fear of annihilation, fear of letting go, fear of change itself. It is all part of our grand delusion that we do not see change as a natural, potentially positive force in life.

> May all beings learn to embrace change.
> May we also learn to surf fearlessly whatever comes our way in life.
> Realising our vast True Nature is completely beyond suffering,
> May all beings swiftly transform small-mindedness and delusion into full awakening!

Child

Consider for a moment that beings actually *do* reincarnate.

Science confirms that matter can neither be created nor destroyed. It is simply transformed, endlessly, from one manifestation to another. So too with our *true nature*. In the future, modern science will also confirm the existence of the spiritual energy – let's call it the Buddha Nature – how it underpins and connects everything that manifests, and how our minds are in fact producing the appearance of everything ... lifetime after lifetime, aeon after aeon.

In this context – the big picture – it goes without saying we've all been around the block a few times before, to say the least of it. We have all known eachother intimately in many lifetimes before. We have manifested in a myriad of forms. We have hated, loved, murdered and given birth to eachother.

I have been your *only* child and you have been mine. It is said we've had this close bond of mother and child countless times already – and it was a beautiful, healthy relationship.

We have had this precious connection with *every* being that now appears – in every form and circumstance, in every realm and dimension – we have personally loved and cherished each one of them. So why not now?

When we wish to arouse and deepen our Bodhichitta – the Compassionate Heart of the Enlightened Mind – we retrieve our parental instinct towards all beings.

No mother could bear to see her child suffer even a scraped knee and do nothing to help. This is all the more true when we develop some wisdom and clear insight. The deluded ignorance and consequent suffering in the minds of beings will arouse in us an instinct to rush to their side and do *whatever* we can to take away their suffering. This instinct over-rides any ego tendencies we may have. We'd do anything to save our child! And when we recognize that our children are also baby-buddhas, the job of raising them to realize their full potential becomes paramount.

That is the vast attitude we must arouse when embarking on the spiritual path. We undertake to thoroughly heal and strengthen *ourselves* through the practice first. Then we are fully prepared for the Bodhisattva task ahead. We are also less likely to *burn out*. Reflecting on this, it becomes clear we must be like an olympic athlete who dedicates her life to training first – maybe for decades. Then and only then is she truly ready to achieve her ultimate goal.

We don't have to wait till we are actually enlightened to best benefit beings. Our mind training practice and our bodhisattva activity must go hand in hand.

The practice will help stabilize our minds. This is essential for genuine compassion. We must benefit *all* beings, not just the ones we find easy to love. The difficult people in the world and in our lives pose the greatest challenge to our Bodhichitta. If we don't have equanimity, stability and openness towards *all* beings, we do not have compassion. Our emotions impede the scope of our effectiveness.

Every being who does not yet realize their true nature, who does not yet live to benefit others, is *equally* deserving of our compassion; the sick, the starving, the marginalized ... serial killers, genocidal dictators, *all* of them. Just like ourselves, they all need to find inner peace.

Recognizing this, may my mind turn towards the spiritual path.

May I view all beings as my children who are suffering the most horrendous nightmare.

May I be the one to awaken them and bring them to lasting happiness.

May this Natural Great Peace erupt in the hearts and minds of all who are languishing in their own private prisons.

And may liberation, love and light flow across the cosmos like a torrential river removing all obstacles for beings, returning them to a state of unending bliss!

Cinema

The superficial ego-mind is confused. It doesn't see things as they truly are.

In order to make sense of the world, our small-mindedness *projects* its opinion onto whatever it perceives. Everything is judged in relation to the false sense of self the ego cherishes so dearly; is it something I like, or something I don't? Based on previous experience and deep habitual patterns of old, we continue to operate – at least temporarily – in the dark.

Imagine we see an object and deduce it must be a flower. Immediately we are drawn into a self-centred, analytical *story*; it looks like it might be a beautiful flower... not like those rather ordinary flowers that grow between the cracks in the pavement... I wonder how it smells... I would like to possess such a flower... I suppose I could cut it and take it home... but then it would surely die and I'd end up with no flower at all... how about I go online tonight and research all about this flower and maybe find out where I can buy the whole plant... oh yes, that would be fantastic ... oh, I *am* clever...

On and on the story goes. Not content with simply *experiencing* phenomena, we launch into a cycle of superficial, subjective judgement. I like, I don't like. I want, I don't want... me, me, me.

We're sadly unaware of the true nature of reality and, worse still, we do not realize the true nature of the *I* who is observing that reality.

The Tibetan master Sogyal Rinpoche compares this process to the cinema. We sit in the darkness watching the movie and get sucked into wherever the story takes us. We literally lose ourselves in the experience and get completely wrapped up in the make-believe, taking it for reality. We are swept along by the emotion of it all.

In the cinema we are prepared to suspend our disbelief; we know it's not real but we're willing to be won over by the magic of the silver screen in the hope of entertainment. Even if the story is potentially harmful to our psyche, we allow the toxins to permeate our mindstream, planting who-knows-what negative seeds for the future ... all in the name of a *harmless* cheap thrill.

Rinpoche encourages us to step back from the screen and what is on it so we can contemplate the projector itself awhile. The film, complete with all its technicolor surround-sound melodrama, is merely passing through the projector. And behind the whole process is a light bulb. The bulb is not involved in the story, or swept away by it however gruesome the bloodbath or arousing the love-scene. But one crucial thing is clear: without a bulb there is no projection and no drama.

The source of the light is like our Buddha Nature. It's said to be the source of the vast display of *all* phenomena. But it is not swayed in the slightest by it.

When the mind is turned outwards, lost in its own projections, there is no peace. Chaotic superficiality reigns over a mind trapped by self-made suffering. This is called *Samsara*.

If we turn our minds inwards, and rest in our own true nature, there is a natural great peace surpassing all concepts. The mind is self-liberated, for the benefit of others. This is *Nirvana*.

Compassion

Language has many strengths, especially in the creative arts such as poetry and literature. But it often falls down when it comes to expressing spiritual truths.

Despite Buddhism being in the West for many decades already, it has to be said the translation of some central concepts is still in its infancy. Already we can see how beautiful Sanskrit words such as *Shunyata* [*Openness*] are commonly mis-translated into English as *Emptiness* thus giving it a negative, defeatist, almost nihilistic meaning.

This is unfortunately true of *Karuna*. The English word *Compassion* seems to limit the whole concept from the very beginning.

Com-passion suggests that we *feel with* another person – their pain, their suffering – that somehow we share in their suffering as a sign of our love. While *compassion* connotes *empathy* it must never be allowed to include *pity* or any element of *helplessness*. We do not aspire to *suffer with* others.

When we look elsewhere in the English language, and in Christian theology, of course the real meaning of *Karuna* is there.

I remember my mother always used the expression *My heart goes out to them*. Watching horrific suffering on the evening news, or on hearing about someone's tragedy, *My heart goes out to them* continues to be a common response in Ireland.

I also remember gazing at Jesus on the Cross in our local church, blood dripping from his wounds and his dead face. Or at the picture of The Sacred Heart in our house, Jesus's beautiful eyes staring directly into mine as his hand opens his shirt to reveal his tortured beating heart. Nobody I asked could adequately explain the meaning of these images. Ironically, I had to become a theologian myself before any of it made sense.

The true meaning of Compassion is present, though hidden, in those horrific images. Literally, The Sacred Heart is *going out to you* from the picture and Christ Crucified shows a Bodhisattva who, according to St. Paul, *Emptied himself* and *Took away the sins of the world*.

The Buddha taught Compassion [Karuna] in this way.

We recognize the suffering of beings. Though some are more obviously in pain, we are *all* suffering ultimately because we do not realize or rest in our true nature. Seeing this, the first response is that our heart goes out to them.

We are not content with feeling their suffering, sharing in it. Neither do we pity them.

We must acknowledge that each and every one of those beings was our mother in a previous lifetime. Finding their suffering unbearable, we resolve to actually take it away from them. This is the ultimate act of self-emptying. Compassion is *egolessness in action*.

Since the ultimate, most profound suffering of all is *Delusion*, we can go one step further and pray that all beings experience enlightenment.

If we are inspired to become *enlightened warriors*, bodhisattvas, then we vow that we ourselves are going to take away the suffering of all beings by leading them to enlightenment.

How wonderful for a simple being like you or I to have the depth of compassion that gives rise to such Bodhichitta!

One thinks not only of Jesus but the many saints and prophets of all religions. One also brings to mind the more *secret* saints who remain largely hidden – sometimes in plain sight – and whose tireless work for the benefit of beings does not seek praise but goes unsung.

Some bodhisattvas work in small ways. They prefer to act locally whilst thinking globally. Others have a cosmic energy about them that's larger than life and work to benefit beings in the most enormous ways imaginable. Perhaps poverty is one saint's main focus, whilst universal enlightenment is another's. Either way, the compassionate motivation is the same.

As well as our meditation practice, which trains the mind and opens the heart, we must also enter into contemplation about our personal strengths and how they might be further developed to benefit the world around us.

Ever-watchful for our dear friend the ego, we undertake to express our compassion in a buddha-like fashion. We don't have to consider it as doing something *holy* or *serious* or whatever. In fact, we don't have to consider it at all. Once we identify how we can help, we just *get on with it!*

If ego gets involved, there is no buddha.

If *I* am part of the equation, then *I* am part of the problem not the solution, and there is *no* true compassion whatsoever.

Our compassionate focus is on others and their *ultimate* needs.

Recognizing that internal mental suffering often has external causes can lead us in either of two directions.

Either we try to eliminate *all* the external causes of suffering, for example *poverty* or *war*. Or we can cut at the root of *all* suffering – the mind itself – by eliminating *delusion* and *ignorance*. One path is the work of global politicians and ordinary good-hearted people. It could be achieved in an instant with the stroke of a pen or sadly it might never be *entirely* achieved. However, the other path is the work of spiritually awakened people, at every stratum of society, and in every country. This universal awakening has already begun. It is so focused and determined, it *will* eventually succeed. The key to its success will be selflessness. And its method will be Bodhichitta.

Just like St Francis of Assisi who prayed '*Make me a channel of Your peace*', our greatest prayer should be a song of compassion.

May we become more and more useful to others.

May we manifest in order to bring about the enlightenment of all beings.

May our hearts go out to all those who suffer in darkest ignorance.

And may we begin this instant, just as we are, right here, right now.

Consciousness

Humans have used a multitude of models for investigating and speaking about the mind. It is said the Tibetans have 100 words that English can only translate as *mind*.

Whereas Buddhism has been investigating and *directly experiencing* through meditation the various levels of consciousness for over 2500 years, Western Psychology is the new kid on the block. Just look at the difference between them! One brings about lasting happiness and an end to the suffering of the mind. People from all walks of life manifest as buddhas. The other relentlessly stirs up the *surface* thoughts and emotions of the mind in the name of healing, and medically anaesthetizes those it cannot help – often against their will – making them numb or blank. It's the difference between one person actually *going* to the very heart of Paris, and when they return inspire others to go themselves with descriptions of the beauty of it and clear directions for how to get there – or another person who just goes as far as the outer suburbs and returns only to discuss it *ad nauseam*. No prizes for guessing which camp I favour. Although there is a fashion for dialogue between the two these days, I suspect the psychologists and psychiatrists will be the main beneficiaries.

The Buddha insists we must go deep into the mind – and indeed the nature of all phenomena – if we truly wish to understand the *causes* of mental health symptoms manifesting on the surface.

Buddhism draws very skillfully on several models for speaking about the make up of the mind and the various levels of consciousness. There is a tried and tested experiential know-how behind it all. The proof is the enlightenment of beings, and our own experience, so we can follow with confidence what we are taught.

Whatever model we use to explain the mind's inner workings, it all boils down to the same thing. There is gross attachment and aversion because we don't realize our true nature.

The following is a very insightful and clear model:

The Eight Consciousnesses

This model presents a multi-tiered picture of how our perceptions of phenomena filter through the various layers of consciousness. It takes us all the way from the exterior physical sense organs, through the brain and down through the mind itself. At that point there are two possible routes with two very different outcomes, depending on how we process our perceptions.

The first 5 consciousnesses are the sense organs themselves: sight, sound, taste, smell and touch. Through those gateways, the world around us is filtered and encountered.

The 6th consciousness is enigmatically labelled in English as the <u>m</u>ind [with a small 'm' to distinguish it from the Natural Mind which lies at the core of all being]. At this level there are two possible outcomes. If we do not *react* to the stimuli with attachment and aversion, it has been processed in a *healthy* way. It's been perceived purely and leaves no further trace [*karma*] in our stream of consciousness. In that case there are no further layers of consciousness. There is *Pure Perception*. If, however, the incoming stimuli are met with attachment and aversion, which arises from ignorance of our true nature, we become caught up in it. This event creates a deeper level of processing.

The 7th consciousness is brought about *because of* attachment, aversion and ignorance. It is the level of *opinion* and *judgement*. We label the experience as good or bad or whatever, perhaps for all time. We create a habitual tendency, a knee-jerk reaction strategy for future reference, and file the whole episode away in the next layer.

The 8th consciousness is only necessary in sofar as we didn't process phenomena in a healthy, sane way at the sixth and seventh. Now it has gone through the layer of being judged and categorized, and has left a deep trace in the *Storehouse Consciousness* [the eighth layer]. These traces take the form of Karmic Seeds that lie there until they inevitably ripen and become circumstances in our lives. Negative actions, such as reacting with attachment, aversion and ignorance, plant negative seeds [*karma*], which produce negative circumstances. Positive actions – such as the *first five* of The Six Paramitas [generosity, discipline, patience, enthusiastic diligence, meditative concentration] – create *merit* which produces positive circumstances. The nature of the cause creates the nature of the effect. The outcome, after this stage, cannot be avoided. Every time we repeat the pattern we water that particular seed so the habit becomes harder and harder to break.

One opportunity to break the negative karmic cycle presents itself when the karma ripens. This manifests as a particular circumstance in our life. If we react with attachment, aversion and ignorance, we are back into the same old habit. In fact we have just made the tendency deeper. However, when we do not *react*, but wisely *respond* by accepting and letting go, and by resting in our true nature, the result is completely the opposite. Thanks to *Shunyata* – the *open* essence of our true nature – the cycle of suffering is broken and no new karma is created.

This 8th layer is often called the *Alaya*. It is the final barrier that prevents us from experiencing enlightenment. The masters compare it to a layer of dark oily scum that has accumulated on the surface of the Natural Mind over aeons of deluded reactions. It's all that obscures our Buddha Nature. This layer of filth is quite thin compared to the vastness of our true nature. However, it is very difficult to purify entirely, especially since we don't yet realize it is there and we continue to add to it by creating new karma.

The *Eight Consciousnesses* is a very skillful and practical mind-map. It comes from the Wisdom Mind of the Buddha himself. You can read further about it quite easily. The version presented here comes from two separate traditions – both Mahayana – the Zen lineage of Vietnam, which came from India via China, and the Tibetan Dzogchen lineage, which came directly from India. Their wisdom traditions compassionately provide us with a step-by-step analysis of the cause of suffering and its solution.

Contentment

When we say we are *content* in ordinary speech it might mean a spectrum of things. We might feel simply OK, not bored, relaxed. Or we might want to express our satisfaction with life. We spend so much of our lives chasing the more extreme emotions such as ordinary happiness, excitement, or ecstacy, that admitting we are simply content rings of having given up somehow on life, the passive 'waiting for God' of the elderly, or that we've ceased to take life by the scruff of the neck. We have settled for a lesser reward.

But there is another meaning. Someone who is said to have found profound contentment in life is a person we often have great respect for. They have discovered a way to simply be in life that brings *them* the kind of happiness and joy that springs from the ordinary, the everyday – the simple things. They are like a kettle that has already boiled and is now on a low heat, simmering away in the background, always ready for tea and a cosy chat.

Contentment in a Buddhist context, though, is on a much deeper level. It is a quality that is experienced with enlightenment. Since Buddhists follow a *Middle Path* – free from extremes – the essence of the result is also characteristically beyond extremes.

When a great being rediscovers their enlightened nature one of the many concepts used to point to what they experience is profound contentment. Obviously this does not refer to an emotional state. This kind of contentment is not superficial in any way. It comes right from the core of our being.

For some people, enlightenment is said to be instant. One second they were deluded, then the next they were not. However, for most of us it will be a long process of gradual revelation culminating in that final breakthrough. Therefore we could say that our enlightened qualities are actually manifesting right now. They are already there, active in our daily lives. These small beginnings are growing all the time, as we become more realized as spiritual beings.

It seems we mis-read these budding enlightened qualities, perhaps mistaking them for ordinary emotions. It's said that all thoughts are actually the Wisdom aspect of our true nature manifesting in an as yet gross, un-purified form. So too, all emotions are our Compassionate nature beginning to blossom.

We should look for the positive side of our emotional life and rejoice greatly in it, in the knowledge that what we're experiencing is our own gradual awakening for the benefit of others.

When we establish *some* amount of contentment in our lives, we should rest assured this is a sign of greater things to come. An even keel is the very seed of our inevitable enlightenment. So we should nurture it and focus on further stabilizing and deepening it.

Our contentment will become incrementally more nourishing and refreshing. In time it will even grow into the kind of enlightened quality that is unshakeable, *In situations good or bad, in circumstances high or low* – as one famous Tibetan prayer goes. Because of the innate contentment of our true nature, we can *completely rely* on it remaining stable through thick and thin. It does not depend on external factors.

The more we practise like this, the stronger the contentment will become. Old negative habits dissolve and an infinite, new habit takes over.

Contentment is never smug or self-satisfied. Therefore we should be on the lookout for telltale signs of ego. True contentment is seen as the highest blessing, the fruition of the practice. It comes both from within and from the buddhas and masters who work towards our enlightenment. If we have true contentment, we accept it joyfully. It's an opportunity to let go completely of all concerns and fears for ourselves. Contentment, seen in this way, frees us up. It liberates us from our *selves*. Now we have a carefree dignity, which allows us to work for the benefit of other beings.

Contentment does not merely guarantee us a good night's sleep, or a quiet life – although for some that would be heaven on earth.

The contentment that emerges through gradual awakening will actually bring *us* benefits beyond our wildest dreams. But, more importantly, contentment ultimately empowers us to liberate *others*.

Contemplation

A vital component of daily spiritual life should be contemplation. It can be seen as combining the twin aspects of Buddhism – Practice and Study.

When we contemplate a dharma teaching, or some essential crucial point from our master, we don't just devote time to mindlessly sitting there *thinking* about it. Thoughts alone will never awaken the Natural Mind. In fact, it could be said, that too much neurotic thinking is precisely what got us into such a fine mess in the first place.

Rather, it is recommended we set aside time – daily if possible – for contemplation as it offers us a rare opportunity to get to the very heart of the Buddha's teaching and *measure it against our own life experience*. This will give us a much-needed chance to reveal the truth of the dharma *for ourselves*. When we test the dharma like this, we are doing exactly what the Buddha requested of his students. Only by unravelling life's mysteries for ourselves can we develop an unshakable, confident faith in the antidotes that lead to awakening. In time, even the process of awakening itself must be contemplated and tested. Otherwise we'll find it very hard to perceive that positive change is actually occurring, however gradual and modest it may be.

In the Tibetan tradition, it is suggested that beginner-to-intermediate level practitioners, such as ourselves, benefit greatly by adopting the following sequence of contemplations before any other formal practice:

Begin with a short period of sitting meditation to settle the mind and create the best environment for the contemplation.

After a while, allow the meditation method itself to drop altogether and simply rest the mind.

Then we use the following four essential teachings [in *italics* below] as a catalyst. We do not obsess or over-think about them... mindfulness and spaciousness are the key. Be loving and gentle with the mind and all will be well. At first we may choose to focus on only one of the four. Maybe we find that particular one very inspiring, or challenging. But, eventually, we will get used to the whole process and contemplate all four in one session.

The Preciousness of Human Life.
How joyful to have this human birth! – Difficult to find, free, and well-favoured.

This human manifestation we have right now is so precious because it is such a rare occurrence. In fact, the odds of being reborn as a human being are extremely slim – very *difficult to find* indeed. We must have benefitted others tremendously in our previous lives to get to this point. Therefore, we rejoice wholeheartedly and resolve not to waste this golden opportunity. For now – in this very lifetime – we have the chance to awaken both ourselves and all beings.

It's also a precious time in our spiritual evolution because we have encountered the very Wisdom Tradition that leads to enlightenment, and we are *free* to follow it. So, if we put our hearts and minds fully into it, our chances of awakening are *well-favoured*.

Death and Impermanence

But death is real. It comes without warning. This body will be a corpse!

We know this from personal experience. Sooner or later, death touches all our lives. But we never quite take on board that *this body* we cherish and pamper, and drag around with us all day, will soon be a corpse.

It has been said the only constant is *change*. And we are dying from the moment we are born. But we only accept these notions intellectually. We do not live our lives fully in the light of this truth.

We ignore the gloriously liberating power of the present moment. Instead we bungle forward through life as if we were going to live forever and nothing we do now has any negative consequences whatsoever.

Deeply touching the possibility that we could even die unexpectedly puts a new perspective on life. Better not waste a single moment. But *how* should this precious life be lived? The next contemplation has some challenging suggestions.

The Law of Karma: Cause and Effect

Unalterable are the laws of karma. Cause and Effect cannot be escaped!

To live mindfully, and for the benefit of beings, means that we embrace the consequences of our actions. *Everything* we do with our body, our speech, and our mind has far-reaching consequences. We are creating karma right now that must find fruition somehow. We not only affect our own future greatly. The principle of the universal web, the *inter-connectedness* that links all phenomena, means our actions affect *everything*.

Therefore, when we sit the whole universe meditates with us and becomes slightly calmer and more harmonious. When we practise Love and Compassion, all beings really do benefit.

We recall the challenge the Buddha set down for his disciples –

"Don't do anything negative.
Only do positive things.
You will achieve this by training the mind."

The detail of this moral code is largely left up to us to work out for ourselves.

Moreover, in this particular contemplation, we must check to see if our experience backs it up at all. What consequences have occurred from our past actions? Could we really be linked in this way to every other person and thing? If not, there's no need to bother about it at all, right? But, if the law of karma is true? ... Better get our act together quick, huh?!

Samsara: The Suffering Mind
Samsara is an ocean of suffering – unendurable and unbearably intense!

Samsara is the word we use to describe the bitter dissatisfaction, emotional turmoil, and profound suffering of this un-enlightened, deluded *ego-mind* we now call home.

We are clueless – completely lost at sea. And we don't realize we contain within us the very remedy that will end *all* our suffering.

For some reason, many miss the whole point about Samsara. Maybe we think of Samsara as a place – the world perhaps – the place that is not heaven. That is a *grave* mistake; we may eventually come to think of it as not such a bad place afterall. We may look at our loved-ones, and all our worldly goods, as fine compensation indeed.

Samsara is actually our current, *deluded state of mind* rather than some place we live in. Our mind is what enables suffering to hit us so hard. It is *unendurable and unbearably intense* precisely because we are blind to the whole truth of our Buddha Nature. When we create a profound spiritual shift in our mind, *everything* changes. It is said to be like bringing the mind home to its rightful dwelling place. Our consciousness rests in its true nature and even external circumstances are perceived completely differently. The ego has been dissolved and there is an end to suffering.

We must look deeply at how our mind suffers. If we do not think we are suffering, then we are in denial. If we think the suffering is not so bad actually, then we'll likely do nothing about it. We will waste this particular human life and the opportunity to be free. Who knows when, if ever, another chance will come along?

So why waste precious time playing about and wallowing in the Samsaric mud? We could begin to cut through the whole sorry mess right now!

Traditionally, an extra line is said quietly to oneself after all four contemplations have finished –

Recognizing all this, may my mind turn towards the practice.

When practitioners contemplate these 'four thoughts', they acknowledge the whole purpose is to utterly *renounce samsaric mind* – for once and for all.

However, the contemplation session itself should be organized so it's not too heavy-going. It must bring much-needed insight and illumination. In order for it to be enlightening, we must infuse the whole session with an air of spaciousness.

One should drop the contemplation method completely after each one and simply rest the mind. Take a short mindful pause before starting the next one.

Similarly, the entire session should begin and end with a dignified, refreshing meditation.

Control

Delusion manifests in so many ways. It drives us to manipulate phenomena. We imagine it will make us feel more stable and secure. Because of delusion, we don't know who we are or what's going on. We perceive ourselves and all phenomena as spinning wildly out of control. It make us feel all at sea, drifting powerlessly, unable to depend on the outcome of daily life.

Some of us prefer to have others create a safe environment for us. We turn to lovers, family, the state, to provide us with a sense of security and direction.

However, most of us also attempt to take control of our lives ourselves. From the time we are babies we learn how to manipulate the outcome of events in our favour. Apart from sowing the seeds of self-centredness, this manipulating, controlling streak builds up a strong pattern – one that is very dangerous to both ourselves and all around us. Far from bringing the happiness we desired, it destroys lives and entire planets.

But, on occasion, our strategy actually pays off a little and we become even more convinced that control, pre-emptive strikes and damage limitation is the best way forward in life.

It could be, even from the time we are developing in the womb, we mistakenly perceive the *Shunyata* nature of everything within and without as a kind of chaotic empty maelstrom. This brings *fear* and anxiety that can only be quelled by us at least trying to take some control. A lifelong crusade begins. It's us against the world and we can't afford to fail. Falling into the abyss of nothingness, we think, would be the end of all that keeps us sane – all that we think we are.

With misperception and fear comes the exponential growth of the *ego*. The rest is history!

Abusive, controlling relationships of every kind are just a bunch of people genuinely trying their best to achieve stability and happiness. You could even argue that Hitler, Pol Pot, all mass-murderers and serial killers, are essentially trying to do the same. You see, the Great Lie of our age is that we *can* bring order to chaos – either real or imaginary – that we *can* achieve inner peace that way.

We all need urgently to stop – create some distance – examine our own personal lives, and see to what extent this scenario is true of us.

Some tortured people go to extremes in an attempt to exert a small amount of control over their lives. Anorexia, bulimia, self-harming, suicide are all considered nowadays to be not so much a cry for help but a private, last-ditch attempt to regain and express at least *some* control in a life that seems to be spiralling away from them.

Buddhism is about letting go – not that we should become a doormat, not at all! What we are letting go of is the ego and all its self-cherishing and grasping at a false sense of *I*. That does not mean we do not exist. On the contrary, we must take care of ourselves and protect this precious human life. When we embrace *Shunyata*, instead of trying to eliminate it, we will discover hidden layers of fearlessness and endless possibilities to achieve lasting happiness, free from suffering – not just for ourselves, but for all.

As Thich Nhat Hanh says, *Thanks to Emptiness, EVERYTHING is possible!*

Properly understood, *Shunyata* loses all its misperceived negative connotations. Emptiness is revealed as *Fullness* ... *Openness*.

Somewhere far beyond hope for control and fear of annihilation lies a distant shore. This paradise brings lasting openness and contentment. But the journey does not involve a boat *per se*. The skillful means of getting there surprisingly involves practising the goal itself. If I want to be open and content, then *that* is what I must put into practise right here, right now. If I want to be a fully awakened buddha, then the *present moment* is the only opportunity for it to happen.

The present moment has been hijacked by the ego for aeons to create a hideously false comic-book realm governed by the evil Dr Fear and his manipulative side-kick Control Freak. We can begin to reclaim the simple beauty of the present moment with just a single breath. Wow! The answer was there all along, right under our nose!

Mindful breathing is the key. It opens up the present moment. We enter a wonderful realm, a possibility that was always there although we didn't realize it – buddhahood at our fingertips! Nolonger governed by the drive for self-preservation, this kingdom is concerned only with the welfare of others. The reign of Ego has evaporated in the morning sunlight. All fear and insecurity is done and over with. No need to control anymore. Because we experience the Natural Mind directly, and abide by that, we *know* that everything is ultimately OK just as it is. This realization is our birthright, our inheritance from the buddhas.

The teachings say: *Realizing Shunyata, have compassion.* Now we must work hard so all beings may realize their own true nature and end their suffering forever.

Cosmology

The Buddha was Hindu, just as Jesus was Jewish. The culture and ancient history of India offered the Buddha a framework and vocabulary with which to speak about the world.

Essentially, the cosmology he used was an Indian one. It has always been the great strength of Buddhism to take on, recycle, and illuminate local beliefs as it spread and transplanted into new societies. Many Buddhists in the West remark how easily they understand the teachings especially when they are skillfully related to Christianity by a Buddhist master. In my own case, as a lapsed theologian and recovery catholic, I still find nothing more inspiring and uplifting than to receive Christian teachings from my Buddhist masters and to receive Buddhist teachings that further illuminate the Western mindset.

The Indian mindset however is the stuff of legend and mystery. For over 5,000 years a strong vibrant culture has been flourishing and evolving there. It is a huge landmass and its inhabitants continue to think of themselves as Indian first, Asian second. They have defined themselves as a nation, united by a common language and culture, for far longer than history can record.

India was entirely Buddhist at one period. Later came the ravages of the Muslim invasion, and the more recent catastrophe of the British Empire's inhumane occupation and botched withdrawal. Nowadays India is the world's largest democracy. It's set to soon become the most populous country on earth. Her people are largely English-speaking and computer literate. By embracing change and learning to adapt, once again India is poised to re-emerge as perhaps the greatest force on the planet. However, despite all this, India still understands the universe and the sufferings of its myriad classes of beings in the ancient ways.

Naturally, the Buddha in his day also used the Hindu cosmology to speak about the sufferings of beings. It is a useful paradigm. But what is really and truly striking is how the various categories of beings it describes, and their primary concerns in life, relate directly to the *emotional* states of mind of each one of us, from moment to moment. The Buddha had this insight whereas others continue to take the ancient cosmology literally. Fundamentalism has invariably stunted the spiritual growth of humankind.

India has always been concerned with everyone having a place in society and, more importantly, everyone being kept in their place – enter cosmology, the caste system, arranged marriages...

Speaking specifically about the various categories of beings in existence, and the many ways in which they suffer, the Buddha adopted the following six-tiered cosmology – look out for parallels from each level to your own life at one time or another :

On top of the pile are the *gods*. They have every thing and every pleasure imaginable. However, they dwell in a kind of intoxicated high. They are only concerned with themselves. Blissed-out, and somewhat jaded from pleasure, their suffering is that of someone who fears losing what they already have. They know, in the grand cosmic scheme of things, their next rebirth can only take them down the ladder.

Below them are the *demi-gods*. Although they are delighted not to have a lower incarnation, they're jealous of the gods above them. They suffer the anxiety and struggle that goes with plotting and wishing, and with all self-obsessed upward mobility.

Then come *human beings*. Our sufferings are manifold. Traditionally these are encapsulated in the phrase 'birth, old age, sickness, and death'. We are trapped in the endless cycle of reincarnation – and, unlike all the others, we *know* it. We are intelligent in the ways of the world, and have some insight. But we are deluded to a high degree in terms of the ultimate reality. We endure a variety of emotional and mental sufferings and preoccupations. But, perhaps our greatest problem is we don't realize our true nature and how that holds the key to liberation. It is taught that we humans are the only category of beings who – if we only knew how – could liberate ourselves and all others from suffering.

Animals are traditionally considered dull-witted and stupid. Of course, this is not strictly true. Animals are extremely sensitive to suffering. Although they don't share our pathological neurosis, they are, however, single-mindedly obsessed with their own drama. They suffer because they fear attack and are concerned with getting their next meal. Their survival instinct is very strong and this leads to territorialism and the need to procreate. Then we have the added dimension of animals being killed or enslaved by humans. Whether you are a wild or trapped animal, nothing could cause suffering more than having to face being slaughtered for food.

Even worse off than animals, though, are the *hungry ghosts*. They roam about largely undetected, invisible, and uncared for. Their suffering is tremendous and is represented by the image of a being with an enormous stomach and a tiny mouth. They feel so empty all of the time. They can never get enough in to fill their bellies. However they are obsessed with trying. What else can they do? The main characteristics of this level of suffering are unbearable craving and a sense of destitution and utter misery way down deep inside, like a terrifying void that nothing could ever fill.

Finally, at the very bottom of the pile are the *beings in hell*. Their entire perception is that of intense, unbearable suffering. Every kind of sensation is instantly perceived as utter torment. Traditionally, they speak of extreme heat or cold, or being tortured and devoured only to be reborn straight back into the same nightmare, or worse. Beings who endure the hell realm have no other thought or emotion except the all-consuming, endless suffering of their all-pervasive pain.

These six realms provide a very insightful paradigm for us. We can even see how a single human being could conceivably go through all of it in one human lifetime, or even in one day! But most of all, contemplating the sufferings of beings arouses profound compassion deep within us and the longing to remove their suffering and its causes, the six main negative emotions: pride, jealousy, desire, ignorance, greed, and anger. In fact, the Buddha taught that each of these emotions has actually *created* each of the six realms in turn. Our emotional state is constantly creating the *reality* we perceive around and within us. It is as though the emotion itself crystalizes and takes external form to create the realm we appear to inhabit.

The Six Realm Cosmology shows that all beings suffer wherever they are. There are no other forms of suffering other than those it describes. The model encapsulates it all. No matter how many sub-divisions of beings we make, or how many realms, dimensions or parallel universes may co-exist, one thing is clear – however or wherever beings exist, *this* is how they suffer. It has to be understood, though we languish terribly and unbearably, we languish unnecessarily.

The ancient cosmology clearly shows that, ultimately, all suffering [regardless of its cause] is experienced in the mind. Maybe we couldn't totally eradicate *every* conceivable source of suffering, but we *can* utterly transform the mind that experiences it.

This is the unique experience of the Buddha.

The ancient Hindus knew that suffering pervades life. The Buddha showed *how* to turn that around.

The greatest tragedy of all would be if beings didn't realize their true nature and its incredible power to end suffering.

Creativity

Our creative streak is very important for human beings. Whether we are creative artists or simply making dinner, each one of us is driven in one way or another to express ourselves. But who, we may ask, are we expressing ourselves to?

Partly, we long to assert our individuality. That must surely stem from the ego and is directed mainly for the benefit of oneself. It usually manifests as showy, borderline-incomprehensible displays, meant to impress others and boost our ego even further.

Seen another way, much of what we create remains on the level of entertainment – dull soul-less dance music, bottled sparkling water, a soufflé ... all harmless fun with not much substance to it. However, at least entertainment is largely created primarily for the enjoyment of others and must therefore be given kudos for being semi-altruistic.

But there are some creators whose effort is solely directed for the benefit of others. One thinks of J S Bach who could have spent his entire career – such as it was – composing mediocre music for his local church. Who would've been able to tell the difference there? But he didn't. Bach's music uplifts the soul and celebrates the meeting of God and humankind. Similarly, one might recall a dark, depressing, wintery day when our mother prepared the family's favourite meal, just to cheer us all up – a simple act of love and human kindness.

Creativity, the Dharma teaches, comes from the same sacred part of us as love and compassion. *Anything* mindfully prepared for the benefit of others, in the spirit of elevating their consciousness, and introducing them to the true nature of their mind constitutes the apogé of human creativity.

The creative arts, particularly when done in conjunction with the spiritual path, give the creator a wonderful opportunity. We can gain access to the Natural Mind through the process of genuine creativity. Then we can allow the mind's true nature to express *itself*. Our Buddha Nature is *always* expressing itself creatively anyway. The Buddha taught, *With our mind we create the world!* Therefore, the Arts offer our true nature yet another positive avenue to awaken ourselves and others.

Think about it. Whatever is prepared mindfully, with a love that intends to uplift, and a compassion that eases the suffering mind, is truly a work of art; a painting that clearly rejoices in the ultimate potential of humanity, a haiku poem that encapsulates a single instant of pure illumination, a freshly arranged Insalata Caprese one glimpse of which delights the senses and draws them into the joy of the present moment, a perfectly made hotel bed turned down with care and attention, a toilet bowl that has been cleaned and polished till it gleams by some invisible chamber maid just so we can sit our weary asses on it and poo.

Whatever does not ultimately *benefit* beings is not truly creative. Emanating from the ego-maniacal, lowest-common-denominator, dregs of the blah-blah-blah mind, it just adds to the mindlessness and the relentless round of distraction and denial that already infuses our jaded, post-modern mindstream. At worst, they serve to further obscure our view of our true nature. At best, they only help us pass the time till death comes.

Whatever we do for others in perfect concentration, with a good heart, and with the sole aim of bringing them into the wonder of the present moment – thus potentially liberating them from suffering – *is* Art of the highest order.

We should aspire to become so uplifting in whatever *we* create. Our whole lives – our every move – could become a creative revelation and a perfect embodiment of ultimate truth.

If we were enlightened this instant, even the very breath we exhale would shower all beings with a multitude of blessings and a host of gentle encouragements towards enlightenment.

Cult

Most of us were born into one religious *cult* or another.

Looking back on it, that may seem clear now. But at the time? Not so easy to recognize at all, really. This begs the question: *What IS a cult?*

There are many definitions, of course. And, although they are not difficult to find, they can differ quite substantially depending on the bias of the one making the definition. There are extreme cases such as those religious groups where the leader persuaded the followers to follow his every command, including mass suicide. And there are more subtle psychological definitions of *cult* where a central figure – or even peer pressure – controls the behavior and attitudes of the group. Seen in this light, even a family or any group of friends could be considered to have crossed the fine line between relative sanity and blind madness.

My spiritual and social interests continued to steer me along a path that seemed to lead from one cult to another. From the time I first began to observe it in my own life, I still immersed myself whole-heartedly nonetheless then gradually withdrew from one controlling environment after another: the Roman Catholic Church, my father and some of my family members, certain toxic friends and social groups [an on-going pitfall], the Capuchin contemplative religious order, the Anglican Church, even my first encounter with Tibetan Buddhism involved turning a blind eye to cultic 'group mind' and the teacher's very harmful behavior [about which we all knew but ignored in order to receive the Buddha's teachings].

However, the plain truth of the matter is you simply do not recognize it when you are actually in a cult. You just don't believe it.

Personality Cults especially are everywhere. And they use the *gravitas* of one thing or another – anything they can summon up – to legitimize their authority, add weight to their outlandish claims, and above all to control and manipulate their followers lest they awaken to the truth of the farcical soap opera and walk away.

Speaking Truth to Power can be a perilous path. Being threatened with *Hellfire and Damnation* can be overwhelming, particularly if you believe it exists. It's not for everyone, the path of righteous indignation. Unless you're that rare breed such as Jesus or Ghandi, perhaps quietly slipping away and leaving them to their own devices is the more dignified approach.

That said, we must remember the Buddha himself adopted both ways. He walked away from everything *and* spoke truth to power. He was a true visionary and actively critiqued and attempted to reform the long-established Hindu cult of the day.

In his own emerging spiritual community too, he demanded his disciples live with *equanimity* and *openness*. But more than that, even to his dying day, the Buddha instructed each individual practitioner to take personal responsibility for their own path to awakening.

We shouldn't believe *in* what the Buddha said simply because it was the Buddha who said. We must put it to the test and above all *experience* the truth of it directly for ourselves. The path to Awakening is clearly laid out for us. And it is there to be tried and tested by the individual.

Good advice, ultimately, since the Buddha eventually passed away and left the community to follow the path without him.

Although they loved the Buddha deeply, he went to great lengths to avoid any culture of dependency on him. He even forbade his followers from allowing images or representations of his physical form to be created, as continues to be the Hindu custom.

The Buddha considered himself and his most experienced students to be *guides* not saviours. Ultimately, he taught the path to *Self-Realisation*.

True Buddhism, therefore, never descends to the level of a personality cult or 'group mind'.

Culture

Everyone comes to The Teachings with a personal perspective. The most pervasive problem we bring to the process is our ego. But there are other things that create a kind of barrier between us and the Buddha's teachings. We all have our own cultural differences and, when we receive the teachings, our cultural baggage sometimes gets in the way. Being mindful of this dimension is very important. We ought to be aware how we may misunderstand or misinterpret the Dharma because of our particular cultural background. Like a pair of tinted glasses, our culture creates a coloured filter through which we interpret everything. Seen in this way, *Culture is not your friend.*

The Buddha himself had his own culture too. A small kingdom in the foothills of the North Indian Himalaya was not without its 'issues' either. However, once he attained enlightenment, the Buddha had a wide open view of reality that transcended his own personal and cultural background.

For this reason, we infer that the Dharma taught by the Buddha is pure. The way we hear and interpret it may not be so pure.

Similarly, as Buddhism spread and took root in other countries, it must be remembered that it merged with the local culture there. This often involved taking on the appearance and concepts of the local ancient religions. Buddhism also became infused with local customs and prejudices.

This is true of all the cultures where Buddhism flourished – and it will be true of Western culture too. So, we must be mindful of precisely *what* we are encountering when we go along to a Dharma centre. We must understand we are meeting the pure Dharma through many layers of culture. Tibetan Buddhism is very Tibetan; it is full of the earlier *Bön* religion, and the images and chants used are uniquely Tibetan in their aesthetic. A Zen centre is very Japanese; rooted in *Shinto*, and so on.

But we must rest assured that, at the core, *all* mainstream Buddhist traditions have preserved the pure teachings of the Buddha. Because of their lineage of enlightened masters, they have a chain of fully realized teachers that stretches back through the generations to the Buddha himself. Therefore, these lineages also have the oral teachings, practice advice, and essential *know-how* instructions that help us awaken.

Some newcomers are overwhelmed by just how *foreign* Buddhism can appear, on the surface. Therefore, it is important to include this contemplation here. Other students, take to the new cultural layers like a duck to water – perhaps a little too much. We have to be aware, either way, of the role ego is playing in our initial encounter with Buddhism. Maybe ego will encourage us to run away because it's all too foreign and difficult, or to become completely distracted and enamoured *by* the foreign-ness itself ... Some people get so caught up in the cultural surface layers that they get stuck there and don't get to the core teachings.

This is yet another good reason for having a personal connection with a realized master in one tradition or another. They can observe just how we are interacting with the cultural elements, and steer us accordingly. They are also supremely qualified to answer whatever questions we may have. A truly realized teacher will always bring our questions down to the core teachings of the Buddha and not what the Tibetan or Japanese culture, for example, has to say on the matter.

All Asian countries – just like the rest of the world – are patriarchal and have strong opinions on all the usual issues. Scratch the smiling surface of the East and you find sexism, homophobia, etcetera. Depending on their age and how 'westernised' they are, speaking to a selection of masters from Asia about these topics may illicit a wide variety of responses. Some pass on the prejudiced views of their upbringing, others give you the enlightened truth.

Many years ago, I was disturbed by reports that a highly respected teacher had given an interview to the American press saying it is wrong to be homosexual. Eventually, when one of my masters was in Ireland, I had the opportunity to speak with him privately and plucked up the courage to *come out* to him and raise my concerns at the same time. His response was astonishing on so many levels. The interview was brief and clear, and full of love.

I told him I was gay. He said, *That's no problem.*

I told him about the statement I had read in the newspaper. He said, *He's wrong. That's just his personal opinion. The Buddha said nothing whatsoever about gays.*

I decided to go a step further and ask if homosexuals and heterosexuals were equal in Buddhist terms. He said, *Oh yes, absolutely... both totally equal... both the same... Heterosexual, homosexual, it's all attachment!'*

As I walked out into the sun away from his cottage, that afternoon I realized something. I had previously identified so strongly with my sexual orientation, I needed Rinpoche to tell me I was OK as a human being. Instead, he reminded me that sexuality is such a superficial matter ... *I want... I don't want...*

I turned a corner and, seeing the breath-taking view of the ocean, I understood. We are *all* perfectly OK. We are already equal, not because of our sexuality or our gender, but because we all have the Buddha Nature as the core of our being.

From then on, I resolved never to become distracted or confused again about the vital difference between culture and Dharma. Hopefully, in the future, so many beings will become enlightened that the global culture will change immeasurably. If humans must have a culture at all, an *Enlightened Culture* is surely the way forward. Using Wisdom and Compassion as our guiding forces, equality, world peace, and harmony would only be the beginning. The culture of *me, myself, and I* – with all its misperceptions and prejudices – will have become extinct.

Death

In the West especially, we have sanitized death to the extent we are almost in denial of its very existence. Of course, if we die a natural death we ourselves will have to face the inevitable and hopefully come to terms with it somewhat as the great transition actually occurs.

But, for many many people, we still prefer not to think about it at all during our healthy years. Death doesn't really fit in with any of our plans so we just ignore the possibility.

When loved ones die, we hide their bodies as soon as possible – under a white bedsheet, beneath heaps of makeup and some nice clothes, in a grand coffin, underground in a cemetery outside of town. Or we make it disappear behind acres of white lace curtains as they slowly close, layer upon layer, at the crematorium until the body is conveyed to the funeral pyre somewhere out back.

Statistics reveal that, despite their express wishes to die at home with a loved one or dear friend as their witness, a shamefully great many elderly people die alone in a hospital bed with a curtain pulled around them for 'privacy', a bunch of grapes and maybe an old magazine on a nearby side-table.

Why do we continue to do this to eachother? Why do it to ourselves? Where on earth is the Wisdom, the Compassion?!

At least in the past, there was a real old-fashioned wake. The person died at home in their own bed, their body was lovingly washed by those closest to them, and laid out to be seen one last time by their loved ones – including small children – and all those who visited for the party. Psychologically, it can be very important to *see* with your own eyes that our loved one is dead. We see the truth. A dead body doesn't look like it's sleeping. It is a shell.

Hopefully we can return some dignity and enlightened courage to the whole process soon, before it's too late. We must learn to write *living wills* too, telling doctors and family how we would prefer to die and be treated afterwards. We must make modern science and medicine work for *us* and be made freely available to all to respect their dying wishes wherever possible.

The Buddha showed through his teachings, and at the time of his own death, that the circumstances surrounding the moment of passing are crucial. The state of mind of a dying person is so important. Just as our state of mind in life colours our perception of phenomena, so too with death.

If our illness, with the help of the right balance of medicines, allows us to die with a degree of consciousness, then we can practise what we've learned and rehearsed while we were well. We can die mindfully.

As death occurs, for most people all awareness of space and time slips away quickly. For an experienced spiritual practitioner, however, their familiarity with their true nature and with dwelling in the present moment actually gives them the opportunity to turn the experience of death into a powerfully transformative event – maybe even enlightenment itself.

Because the present moment is technically without beginning or end, by dwelling in it time appears to slow right down. What usually flashes by in an instant mostly unnoticed, opens up to a dying practitioner. The vast expanse of their Natural Mind is revealed to them as the physical and mental body dissolves. Before them, a panoramic display opens up.

The dying practitioner's karma surrounds them, propelling them this way and that. However, they can *see* ahead of them the warmth and the *pure light* that embodies the *Universal Buddha Nature* – the underlying essence that connects all.

It is said there are many irresistible or frightening distractions lying in our way. These are experienced as very strong images and sounds that threaten to turn the mind away from its intended target. The *Pure Light* essence, however, is drawing us into it if we could only remain in our true nature, undistracted and unaltered. This is where a lifetime of practice may just pay off.

We're not talking here, necessarily, about the commonly reported Near Death Experiences of *life review* and *going towards the light*. What we are discussing is much deeper into the process of death and *after* brain death has actually occurred. An advanced practitioner's death happens so mindfully and subtly. Meanwhile the average person is already well on their way to their next mother's womb.

If the dead practitioner merges their Buddha Nature with the Pure Light, it is said to be like the water in a river reuniting with the vast ocean, or like a small child running into her mother's arms. There is complete and perfect Liberation. Full *enlightenment* has occurred. A new buddha has emerged for the benefit of beings. Then there is a choice to be made. Either the enlightened being chooses to take a physical manifestation and return once more, or they pass into formlessness – this is called *parinirvana* and actually affords a buddha the freedom to benefit beings from beyond *all* the limitations of having a physical body. The teachings remind us, 'Just think of a buddha, and they are there!'

Some great practitioners may not attain full enlightenment, but still they can choose their own reincarnation – who they will be, where and when.

When a great being passes away, there is nothing special to be done with their body. They are beyond any of that having an effect. However, every Buddhist lineage around the world will have its protocols and traditions about how to treat the body after death. Some great practitioners arrange it so they die sitting up doing their practice. They are often left alone like that, after physical death has already occurred, for seven days while they complete their *samadhi* meditation processes. In such now-rare cases, there is no decay or bad odour and often when the samadhi is complete, only then will the body go cold and dissolve. This is frequently accompanied by displays of multi-coloured light as the elements disperse and a marked shrinking of the physical form.

But, perhaps even more important for *us* right now is the issue of how to approach our *own* death and the treatment of our corpse afterwards.

Nothing is totally clear and different masters give different advice to their students depending on their tradition and the student's potential.

That said, here are some thought-provokers. They are offered in the spirit of making the passing of an ordinary person or fair-to-middling meditator as natural and beneficial as possible. This is not a list of rules. It's an *ideal*. Inevitably there will be compromises or just plain *no-can-do's* at every stage.

Contemplate, plan, and write a Living Will. In the event you do not die suddenly or in an accident, your wishes may actually be very important.

Especially consider balancing pain medication [that usually knocks you out], with the possibility of having a degree of lucidity and awareness so you can practise while you are passing. Practice brings mindfulness and the possibility of spiritual transformation, and that is the healthiest, most sane way to live and to die.

Discuss your wishes long beforehand with anyone who may be there with you.

Tell them of your love and gratitude and that you will be OK no matter how dying *appears* on the outside.

Ideally your life previous to passing should be infused with practice. It is not a good idea to postpone practice and then panic, as your passing begins, thinking: *Oh no. I haven't been practising. I must prop myself up somehow and start doing some now!*

If you can't sit, lying down is also good. The Buddha is depicted as dying on his right side doing a meditation technique that is widely taught.

At all times, remember your Buddha Nature and your connection to your master if you have a personal relationship with one. They embody the Universal Buddha essence we spoke of earlier and while dying you will be merging your mind with that.

You will need a calm environment to facilitate your final letting go. People should not cry out or disturb you in any way. If you could be surrounded by other practitioners that would be a great support.

Many people report that physical contact such as hand-holding actually has the effect of preventing one from passing. You may have heard that some people can only let go completely when their loved ones have left the room to go for a cup of tea or a short break. Remember, it is difficult to allow death to occur.

Your last breath will be a long, calm, exhale. With that, the masters say, we can send all our love and compassion to those around us and to all beings.

Once your body appears to have died to others, they should be aware that there is still consciousness and you still need the right atmosphere in the room and even *in the minds* of those around you. Afterall, you will still be doing your practice and, now liberated from the physical body, you are quite clairvoyant and super-aware of what others are thinking and feeling. If they are thinking 'How awful. I can't cope', that will disturb you and keep you from passing on completely. They should be at peace and sending you their unconditional love. If they can achieve such equilibrium, *they* will sense your all-pervasive presence around them in the room, until even that has peacefully passed away.

You should feel no sense of being pulled backwards into the body. You will therefore be free to focus on reuniting your mind with the mind of all the buddhas.

It is not necessary for us to obsess or plan too much around what happens to our corpse afterwards. Especially in the West, it's just not practical for ordinary people to have extraordinary expectations.

However, the body should ideally be left untouched for as long as possible, to facilitate a graceful exit. We are told the natural exit point for our Buddha Essence is the crown of the head. So being touched or held could mis-direct the exit as it might draw the consciousness to some other spot instead. Similarly, we don't want our mind to be called back and tempted to try re-entry once it is out.

At this stage, the corpse should be seen be all as a shell from which the mind has been liberated. In a few hours it will literally look like a shell and loved ones can rest assured that *that* is all it is.

Once it's appropriate, the washing and so on can begin.

Personally, I don't favour embalming or fancy coffins. I have provided for my body to be cremated and the ashes scattered soon afterwards. However, it doesn't matter very much *what* is done to the body. Man, I will be *so* out of there by then! In fact even donating our body-parts to benefit others could be our final act of compassion in this lifetime.

Buddhists talk all the time about practice. But many actually meet their deaths unprepared.

The word *practice* is so evocative of other things in the English language. We may recall the drudgery of practising the piano - maybe so we could play something if we were ever asked to. We tell our kids *Practice makes perfect*, but do we ever stop to think of what that could *really* mean?

In spiritual terms, we practise for enlightenment – the reunification of *our* essence with the *universal* essence. If that hasn't happened yet in this lifetime – and sadly it apparently hasn't – then what we are actually practising for is the next major opportunity for it to take place. We are practising for the moment of death. Our rehearsal will prepare us for that final chance, this time around, when practice hopefully *will* make perfect.

Delusion

Some of us think we are OK and others think they are not.

Either way, according to the Buddha, *this* is The Great Delusion.

Poor sentient beings! We live our lives completely in the dark. As long as we just scratch the surface of life, swept along by whatever thoughts and emotions wash over us, we miss the essence of our existence. We are so caught up in superficialities, we don't even have the faintest idea that there *is* a core to our being.

As long as we allow our Buddha Nature to go unrecognized, and for as long as we continue to fool ourselves into thinking that's alright and that thoughts and emotions are all we have, then Delusion will persist.

But the enlightened ones have vowed to work tirelessly against that ignorant pattern. Some are inside space-time with us, all across the multi-dimensional continuum. Others work from outside for the benefit of beings, remaining formless and limitless in their power to liberate us.

However we encounter the teachings, the important thing is that we *do* encounter them. It will be the greatest gift we could ever lavish on ourselves. We may realize our true nature, and everyone around us will benefit too.

But perhaps the most important thing about meeting the teachings is that we should connect with an enlightened master. Just to be in their presence, if we have an open heart and mind, will enable us to experience first-hand the radiance of their Natural Mind [and maybe even our own].

We are not talking here about an *instructor* at a meditation centre, or someone wearing monastic robes – unless they are also enlightened of course. What we need is to connect, on the deepest level, with a *realized being* – an enlightened master who can guide us along the path, a torch to dispel the darkness of delusion.

We do not have to *become* a Buddhist. There is nothing to become. We do not have to hang out and travel around with the master, to receive the teachings. There are usually too many *disciples* and *dharma-bums* already. We must remember that it is *we* who must transform our own minds, so we don't need the master on hand 365 days a year.

However, if we are open to it, occasionally being in the master's presence can have a hugely transformative effect on our mindstream and greatly boost our growing confidence in our own Buddha Nature. Furthermore, one of the kindest, most compassionate things offered to beings by masters of certain lineages is the *Introduction to the Nature of Mind*. In these traditions, the master is a veritable powerhouse, constantly radiating their own true nature to those around them. It is quite easy to perceive it when you are close to them or especially when you practise meditation together. These now-rare teachers can also send bursts of that enlightened essence out into their environment. It is like a mind-to-mind transmission, an electrical jump-start intended to jolt our dormant Buddha Nature into action.

One important principle to contemplate at this point is that *wisdom seeks wisdom*.

Our own Wisdom Nature [the Natural Mind itself] is yearning to wake up. And the Wisdom Mind of the master is devoted to bringing this about. So the *Introduction to the Nature of Mind* is an extremely powerful method – you might even say shortcut – to achieving that awakening.

To connect with an enlightened master on *any* level is an incredible blessing and can only result from your positive karma. In a sense, you might say all your previous lives' work has lead to creating the right conditions for this spiritual meeting to manifest now.

But be warned. If this is meant to happen for you in this lifetime, you will have to reach out and play *your* part too. The master will not just show up at your home and ring the doorbell. You have to find them. Many genuine, mainstream Buddhist lineages don't even advertise their existence or whereabouts. Buddhist masters, paradoxically, never look for new students. They know, for the teachings to be truly transformative, we must be ripe for them and ready to do the work. When that time comes, and we have suffered enough, we will go find the antidote.

Remember ego? Well, it comes along with us as we skip down the spiritual path in search of our teacher. The ego will really lap up the newness of the experience – the lovely cushions, the bells and smells, the colours, the music, becoming an expert in something new! But when it comes to the master... well that's another thing entirely. Maybe the ego won't like them one little bit. The more progress we make the more the ego will rebel and try to convince us to get out.

Dzongsar Khyentse Rinpoche says the Master is a highly trained assassin we've hired to completely destroy our ego. So naturally enough that's gonna hurt the little darling.

Because ego comes along with us for the spiritual ride, we have to remember we are still dwelling in the mists of delusion. So that means we don't see things as they really are. We continue to see ourselves incorrectly. The struggling ego almost prevents us from perceiving any spiritual progress. We may even feel *we* don't actually have a Buddha Nature. Furthermore, we continue to perceive phenomena impurely and the floundering ego will surely use that too. In this case what we may be perceiving incorrectly through a veil of delusion is the Buddha [and the master], the Dharma [teachings], and the Sangha [community of practitioners]. Always try to be mindful when obstacles arise on the path it's usually our ego-driven, impure perception that is at fault.

That said, search for a teacher we must. But even *that* won't be plain sailing. A truly realized master would never claim to be enlightened. Those who do, usually aren't. And we need to shop around a bit for a teacher whose tradition and personal style appeals to us. But the ego, sensing immanent demise, makes us too picky and prevents us from settling anywhere – the same old story.

We get so close to actually embarking on the path, but the Great Delusion persists. The best advice is to embark regardless. Accept that the ego remains, for the time being, and dive in.

Always remember, the ego is not an entity in itself. We are not possessed and we do not require an exorcism. Ego is the superficial by-product of Delusion – and even that does not really exist.

Consider the Natural Mind is like a light switch that's been left in the off position. The darkness is not an entity that must be removed somehow. Delusion is merely the absence of light.

Have courage and faith. Never give up on your true nature. It is your constant companion and best friend.

From time to time, with the blessing of the master, the light will be switched on but it will unfortunately slip into the off position again. However, an unstoppable process has been set in motion. Sooner or later, maybe in this very lifetime, the light will come on permanently. Then, as if the darkness never had any real substance or hold over us, The Great Delusion will have been dispelled forever.

Dharma

The truth that pervades all phenomena has been glimpsed throughout the ages. Many prophets, world religions, and philosophers have pointed towards it. There are doubtless many paths for revealing that universal truth for oneself. But the essence of the truth remains the same no matter which path we take.

The Buddha discovered that the nature of *everything*, the very meaning of life itself, can be revealed through *meditation*. By looking within, one can penetrate the many layers of the mind and experience directly its true essence.

Buddhists call this *truth* the Dharma. The word has many facets.

Dharma is the *truth*, the *discovery* itself. But it is also the *path*, the *method* by which we arrive there.

Dharma can also mean *phenomenon* thus hinting, if we experience the true nature of ourselves, we will also have revealed the true nature of *all phenomena*.

Therefore, we can say that the very essence of the Buddha's teaching, the Buddha-dharma, has twin aspects: The Buddha Nature, and the Meditations and Activities that will lead us to it.

In fact, all of the Buddha's teachings can be brought down to this heart essence:

Because there are thousands and thousands of types of beings, each with their own particular mindset and limited capacity for understanding the truth, traditionally we say that the Buddha expounded 84,000 Dharmas so that each and every type of being might be liberated.

This was an extremely skillful approach so all beings would eventually arrive at the same destination, albeit by a variety of different routes.

Even when you scrape away the various cultural layers that cover Buddhism as it has manifested around the world, it always comes back to the same teaching: *The Buddha Nature exists, and this is how you reconnect with it.*

But, that said, there is still a variety of different teachings and methods available that lead to enlightenment. They have appealed to a variety of people in various cultures at different times. It's as though the 84,000 Dharmas have been dispersed to the four winds and each has been taken up by different beings according to their suitability.

We are so lucky these days. Despite the dark age we live in, most of the main teachings and meditation methods of the Buddha are still widely known and practised to fruition. We only have to explore the various lineages and find the type of Dharma that may work best for our particular capacity.

Inevitably, there'll be a different emphasis and style depending on whether one goes the route of Theravada [for example Thai or Burmese], or the Mahayana route [such as Tibetan or Zen]. But one thing is guaranteed regardless of the lineage. The essence of the teachings is the same – The Great Perfection of the Buddha Nature and the meditations that will awaken it.

That is the Dharma core. Everything flows from there.

The first main teaching offered by the Buddha was in the beautiful deerpark at Sarnath, near modern Varanasi. It expands the primary truth of the Buddha Nature into four.

The Four Noble Truths

Because we do not realize our true nature, we experience *suffering* of every conceivable kind.

The *cause* of all suffering is the mind itself.

It is possible to bring about the *cessation* of all suffering, therefore, by working directly with the mind.

The *path* to the cessation of suffering is the Dharma.

From that last point springs the entire Dharma in all its glorious manifestations for the benefit of individual beings. Mostly, as we said already, the Dharma is concerned principally with *meditation* that works intensively and directly on the deluded mind, and *action* that brings benefit to others and, as such, is befitting of a buddha-to-be.

Now we can appreciate that the Dharma itself unfolds from there in a variety of directions, too numerous to cover here.

One commonly accepted expansion is the *Six Paramitas*: [generosity, discipline, patience, enthusiastic diligence, meditative concentration, and wisdom].

Or the *Noble Eightfold Path*, which offers teachings on the same topics but subdivides them into eight sections [correct view, correct intention (or thought), correct speech, correct action (or conduct), correct livelihood, correct effort, correct mindfulness, and correct concentration].

Whatever formulation the Dharma takes, ideally it should always encompass all three core aspects: Disciplined Action, Meditation, and Wisdom. This approach ensures that the three codifications of the Buddha's teachings are included.

The *Vinaya* is the code of *discipline* by which a practitioner may wish to live. It has clear guidelines and challenges for lay people and monastics alike in the form of precepts or vows.

The *Sutras* are written records of teachings the Buddha gave, mostly concerned with *meditation*.

Finally, the *Abhidharma* is a collection of *Wisdom* teachings and philosophical commentaries that have emanated from the Buddha's original teachings.

As a student of the Dharma, one may easily become distracted by the variety and depth of it all. The danger is we literally might get lost in studying it – perhaps for the rest of our life – and still be no closer to enlightenment. Inevitably we will no sooner have completed learning one section than, without putting any of it into practice, we're off on some other *fascinating* tangent. Maybe we hear of some strand of the Buddha's teachings preserved only in one isolated monastery in Cambodia. Or maybe we're off to Tibet in search of *secret* teachings of the Buddha, only shared with an elite chosen few.

Far better to have the personal guidance of a master who knows us and who we can trust completely to keep us focused and moving in the right direction.

Thanks to our samsaric, deluded ego-mind, we have allowed our true nature to remain obscured. We must resolve to do everything in our power to ensure the Buddha-dharma doesn't end up distracting us too. We don't have to understand it *all*. We don't have to accept it all. You might even say, most of it is beyond our capacity to understand right now anyway. What we *do* need, however, is to begin to understand and practise *some* aspect of it to start with. And, with expert guidance, take it from there.

For most people, meditation is the key that unlocks the rest. In time we can receive teachings on the Buddha Nature ... on Change, Impermanence and *Shunyata* ... on Compassion, Enlightened Action and Engaged Buddhism ... Sadhanas, Samadhis and Tantras ... *whatever*.

But, for now, we must start where we are. And to find where we are, as the Buddha taught that very first day in the Deer Park, it all starts with the mind – so we meditate.

Dream Yoga

Dream Yoga practices are usually taught to quite advanced students, when the time is right. Even though you can come across many books related to it these days, most of them are *new-agey* in origin. Some are published by respected *mainstream* Buddhist masters but they avoid going into too much detail, and with good reason. Therefore we will not be going into great detail here either.

Buddhist practices related to sleep and dreams require that the meditator has already done quite a bit of transformative work on their minds. Their minds should be quite stable regardless of whatever phenomena they perceive. And they should be capable of approaching *all phenomena* as illusory and dream-like, whether one is awake or asleep. Therefore these are considered to be quite high and profound teachings, yet eminently practical and wise.

Most people experience dreams as a vivid, almost cinematic *event*. It feels real at the time. We become wrapped up in the drama of it all and are usually so emotionally involved that we are quite swept along by its fake momentum, out of control and powerless to write the screenplay for the final reel.

On the other hand, there are some people who seem – without any meditative training at all – to be able to manipulate their dreams. They say they *know instinctively* the dream is not real. It is like playing a computer game or watching TV. Many report an element of carefree *fun* about dreaming. Even if it is a nightmare, they say they can change the plot at will or simply change channel and watch something more interesting!

Whether we can control our dreams or not, we all take dreams far too seriously. Only in very rare cases – usually with dreamers who are clairvoyant – do dreams actually *mean* anything at all. So why wake up exhausted or frightened? Why look for meaning in something that's essentially just our brain firing, its energy fizzing as thoughts and emotions?

There is one particularly appropriate *slogan* that comes to mind in this context. It is to be found in the teachings called *The Seven Points of Mind Training* [Tibetan, *Lojong*].

In post-meditation, be a child of illusion.

Once we are already well on the path of training the mind and opening the heart through meditation, we are well-advised to view all phenomena as illusory and dream-like. Everything that arises in the mind must be accepted with a spaciousness and openness that surpasses all concepts. We accept, and let go. That is the path of spiritual awakening.

Our formal meditation training in mindfulness and awareness facilitates the development of spaciousness and equanimity of mind during sleep too. In sofar as we respond at all to phenomena, it's always done with compassion and the strong desire to benefit beings.

The test ground for putting this mind-training into practice is the mind itself. So it is said that *we ARE the practice*, since our mind is always with us and always switched on.

For some practitioners, it is easier to try being a *child of illusion* while we are awake. For others, it's easier to try during the dream state. Either way, the cumulative fruition of meditation is to *slow down* the speed of our habitual reactions. The masters say: *There is a gap*. We gain more time and more freedom of choice regarding exactly *how* we are going to respond. This is the *view* we must cultivate.

It is good to do some meditation as we are falling asleep. The peace and stability it brings is very conducive to dream yoga.

More experienced practitioners may do particular practices as they fall asleep. They may imagine merging their Buddha Nature with the mind of their master who embodies the enlightened essence of all the buddhas. This union is imagined as *clear light,* which is brought down into the heart centre where it resides throughout the night glowing cosily and radiating benefit for beings.

This kind of *yoga* sets the stage for sleep and produces the correct environment in the mind for spiritual practice *during* the dream state. We hold to that vast expansive view while we are dreaming and actively remain conscious of our mission to remain stable, open and of benefit to all the beings we encounter there.

In time, we gradually overcome our long-ingrained tendencies of self-protectiveness, anxiety and primal fear. The antidotes we practise while dreaming are *compassion for others* and *resting in our true nature.*

Accepting we're just beginners in all this is very important. We don't judge ourselves by how we appear to have success or failure in the practice. We just continue on the path to enlightenment, undoing ancient ego-patterns and sowing newer, more sane ones.

Even though the beings and scenarios we meet in dreams are not real, we still create *karma* and deepen our ego-patterns while we sleep. This is why we must eventually learn to have pure perception and open hearts even when we dream.

You might say, the trick to becoming *a child of illusion* is to view our dream life as a *real* opportunity for spiritual growth, and our so-called *real life* as an illusion.

Drugs

It is a fact that all beings are basically the same – we just want to be happy and we don't want to suffer. The problem is we don't always get what we want.

Most people do not see this as a huge problem. They don't have unrealistic expectations of life and are therefore not particularly shocked when their day isn't filled with champagne and roses. When you travel a bit outside your comfort zone – especially, for example, if a European travels in Asia – the first thing that hits you is how different *everything* is. Then a gradual realization slowly dawns on you ... *Oh my God, this is how the vast majority of the world lives!*

Most human beings are not like us. They live simple, frugal lives. Struggle and suffering is part and parcel of everyday life. Although they have healthy ambition, especially for their children's future, they also have the wisdom to accept the things they cannot change. For the most part, they are content.

In Europe and America, on the other hand, it has to be said the story is quite different. Our privileged, neurotic lifestyle has created a particular mindset.

When happiness does not come our way, instead of accepting it as yet another temporary life situation, we become dreadfully *unhappy*. Furthermore, when suffering comes our way, we struggle against it, wallow in ego-self-pity, and generally make a bad situation much worse. In fact, as our so-called *First World*, Western values have spread to the East, and South of the equator. The neurotic mindset that goes with it is taking root there too.

They have given us all the major world religions. In return we have given them the culture of the ego-mind and a comparative sense of shame and disappointment.

The human quest for happiness and an end to suffering – rather than leading to global spiritual awakening – has brought about an enigmatic crisis of the heart.

We live in a psychological realm of paradoxes and polar-opposites. We want to be happy yet we make ourselves unhappy. We don't want to suffer yet we run headlong towards it. Ours is an era of apathetic expectation, high-speed inertia, tree-hugging self-centredness. Our whole *culture* is identified by a profound superficiality, pseudo-spiritual consumerism, and a huge sense of being intelligent but numb.

Call it *post-modern malaise*. Call it the *dark fruition of the ego-mind*. Whatever we call it, society has become sick and tired. Many many people are suffering great psychological pain and are reaching out for help. Suicide rates are increasing exponentially, but go largely unreported for fear of creating utter chaos.

However, what is even more shocking is that many people who can afford to are turning to drugs [including prescription medication and substance-abuse] to dull the pain ... housewives, children, royalty, policemen, ordinary people like you and me.

Some people do drugs to anaesthetize themselves *against* life. Others do drugs to *enhance* life.

Society shames drug users and drives the whole situation underground, thus creating a furtive sense of being *cool*, *naughty* and *rebelliously illegal*. We don't want to face up to drugs, as a society, because we don't want to accept some major truths.

Life sucks. Drugs are everywhere.

Life sucks because of the *samsaric* nature of our suffering minds. Change our minds and everything else changes too.

People take drugs either because they feel great [at least for the first few times] or because drugs dull the brain and take the edge off life. This possibility scares us – terrifies us – as a society, so we pretend it isn't true. We can't begin to allow for the possibility that drugs may actually help temporarily. At best, however, all drugs do is cover our mind with yet another layer of poo that will have to be undone at some later stage.

But the saddest flip-side to the euphoric-pacifying truth about drugs is *addiction*.

It is only human nature to become attached, grasping and addicted. That is the starting point of the entire spiritual path. So never believe someone [or maybe even yourself] – not for an instant – when you hear those all-too-mortal words:

"*I* don't have a drug problem. I'm not addicted. I can quit any time I want!"

The truth about drugs is that they chemically alter and damage the brain, which is itself essentially chemical in nature. And they merely add one more layer of murkiness and denial to the mind, which experiences suffering. Drugs make the brain think and feel a spectrum of things. But that's not real. Worse of all, the substance itself obstructs the mind from experiencing its own true nature.

There are various psychedelic plants that have been used since pre-antiquity by shamanic cultures. They are said to bring on strong hallucinations that deliver certain insights about the human condition. But a lot more comparative study needs to be done to ascertain the value of modern humans going that route. Realizing we are beings of light who need to save the planet is one thing. But there are many ways to get that profound insight. The real issue is how to respond to that information.

However that may be, the drugs we are considering here mostly are the ones that dull or agitate the chemicals in the brain. Of course, people will do whatever they want with their own bodies anyway. But what of the harm they are doing to themselves and others? If you don't have any personal experience in this field, ask a mother whose son is on heroin how great it is. Or go to a trendy bar some night and hang out with the 'beautiful people' out of their heads on coke and dope and a cocktail of so-called party drugs. If you remain sober yourself, you'll soon see how mindless and insensitive that whole scene is. Very messy indeed. They may even turn on you for not joining in. Neurotic aggression alternates with lifeless zombification all around you. So sad and useless. Anything but cool.

But the good news – the ultimate truth – is that our core being, the Natural Mind, is not touched or stained in any way by drugs *or* suffering. It is already perfectly blissful. When we begin to explore the profound essence of our Buddha Nature, we find the true key to lasting happiness.

The path is difficult yet truly joyful. It's not for the apathetic or those looking for a quick fix. Most people will not embark upon it in this lifetime. However, it is said that once we have become sufficiently exhausted with suffering we will all eventually walk the same path that leads to its cessation and the ultimate truth of our being. Therefore, we must not judge others. We identify with them. We help where we can. We understand that we are equally deluded.

The fundamental question is, *Just how un-deluded do you want to become?*

If we wish to become just *slightly* less deluded than we are now, then we might consider getting sober, getting *clean*, and maybe doing a beginner's meditation course at a good dharma centre.

If we wish to end *all* delusion, *forever*, then we need to get sober, get clean, get meditating, and get enlightened!

Either way, the entry point is clearing the mind of intoxicants.

Intoxicants create a barrier between the mind and reality. Maybe that is our intention. They smear our senses with a layer of chemicals. Anyone who has ever kicked a habit – say smoking – knows that you feel that murky coating dissolving as the senses become clear again. This can be a painful, overwhelming process. But the result is worth the effort. The mind becomes clear again and ready for even more profound transformation.

Therefore, the Buddha urged his [monastic] disciples to adhere to the *Five Precepts*, the fifth of which is to *Avoid Intoxicants*. Most masters today tell their students it is not possible to attain full enlightenment otherwise.

Ecology

The Buddha himself said almost nothing specifically about caring for the environment. This is hardly surprising as, in his era, *nature* was not seen as separate from humanity. And there was no 'climate change' crisis as we have today.

What precious little the Buddha did say, however, speaks volumes.

The essence of the Buddhist moral code – if we can call it that – hinges on three directives: *Do nothing negative, Only do positive things,* and *Achieve all this by training your mind.*

Therefore, it's clear that *Non-harming* is the very foundation of what it means to be truly human. In this regard, the Buddha laid down some specific rules for his first monastic disciples to follow.

The *Vinaya*, as it is called, directs monks and nuns not to defecate in nature without feeling sure it will do no harm to that place. Human waste should under no circumstances destroy the delicate balance that exists in the natural world.

Furthermore, the Buddha instructed monastics to ensure they had a minimal impact on the environment through which they walked. This embodied the practice of mindfulness as they moved from place to place through the countryside.

Beyond these specifically ecological concerns, the entire Buddhist approach is thoroughly based on *non-duality*, which guarantees the protection of the environment.

There is no separation between this and that, you and I, human beings and the natural world. The intricate web of inter-dependence, or *inter-being* as Thich Nhat Hanh says, implies we remain mindful of the effect every individual action has on the whole. This fundamental tenet of Buddhism goes far beyond ecological issues, but encompasses them all.

We know, therefore, that whatever we do, say, or even think, has far-reaching consequences. Yet we continue to ignore this at our peril. The current crisis we are facing with regard to climate change and the misuse of the earth's natural resources is partly due to that continued ignorance. It is also due in part to the *collective ego*; perhaps we actually understand the harm we are doing, but do it anyway because it benefits us in the short term. Maybe we don't believe in reincarnation, so we think we will never have to face the consequences personally. Maybe we don't care about the next generation either; human beings are the only species who destroy their own children's future lives. It could even be that, in the back of our minds, we actually believe it's too late for mother earth. We have raped and killed her. The damage is done. Our only option now is to face extinction or find another *M-Class* planet to colonise ... start afresh, then defecate and trample all over that one too!

The Buddha Nature we embody is the same as the essential nature of all phenomena. We are inseparable.

By virtue of this common essence at the centre of our being, we have no choice but to remain connected with all that is. We cannot choose to separate from nature and then treat it in a harmful way as if the consequences would never rebound on us.

Moreover, neither is our True Nature in any way passive. We cannot simply *allow* global catastrophe to unfold. The Natural Mind, rather, is an *active force*. And this force must work *within nature* - whatever we may understand about the *origins* of the Buddha Nature lying *beyond* space and time, we must also realise that it has manifested within nature, in the here and now.

When we gaze into the natural world, we are also peering deep into our true selves.

The Natural Mind has three aspects:
Shunyata/Empty *Essence*
Cognisant *Nature*
Impartial *Compassionate* Energy

In the same way, the ultimate *activity* of the Buddha Nature [in relation to the environment, and everything else] is also threefold:
Remain *open and connected* to it
Be *mindful and aware* of its True Nature
Be *healing, nurturing, cherishing and caring* without exception.

An extremely broad view of the scope of history enables us to accept that things come and go on a global scale. There have already been many cataclysmic periods during which almost all life on earth became extinct – always due to external forces of nature. But this is the first time one species has actually had the power to destroy it all.

The West, of course, was the first to develop *industrial* technology and, therefore, was also the first to destroy the environment. But now the East, and nations of the Southern Hemisphere are rapidly catching up and are causing the same chaos. China and India, in particular – ironically, the *birthplace* of oriental spirituality – are the biggest culprits. They defend their anti-environmental behaviour by stating how much their countries need to develop. It's the same old story: *Money matters most!* But they also make an interesting point about the 21st Century being *their* time to shine. After all, they're only following in the footsteps of the West. And whenever the East finally manages to become equal, technologically and economically, with the rest of the world then and only then can Asia begin to talk seriously about the environment. It is, they say, the price we all have to pay for progress.

Hopefully it's not too late, and we can find deep within us the wisdom and the compassion to avoid that. But, given that doing what suits *us* is precisely what got the planet into such a mess, one wonders if we'll actually have the courage to fully implement the solutions – especially if they don't suit us at all.

Who knows if it will be enough? But the solution at this late stage might entail extremely unpopular measures. How would it feel to be told that, with immediate effect – and for the next 100 years – we had to relocate to areas around the globe that would be less troubled by extreme climate change or rising sea levels? Or that we would have to farm for ourselves there, eating a totally vegan diet free from all animal products and based on local crops in season? How would we react to the news that society was no longer allowed to use fossil-fuelled vehicles such as scooters, cars, trains, boats or planes? No more travel, only emigration on foot?!

It might just come to that. Some experts are pessimistic and claim, even if the whole world adopted *Green* policy and practice overnight, it would not be enough to save the planet!

But Buddhism is the ultimate optimist.

In the face of universal delusion and suffering, the Buddha teaches the existence and supreme power of the Buddha Nature within. All the teachings and practices point to the absolute *power of one* to affect positive change.

May things change rapidly for the better.

May transformation flow like a vast, refreshing river across the face of the earth.

May the hearts and minds of all human beings awaken to this noble work.

And may it begin with me!

Ego

The ego does not actually exist.

Giving it a name is misleading, but we have to talk about that strong habitual tendency somehow.

When we call it something like *ego-mind*, we may be elevating the status of the ego. Worse still, we may actually lead people to believe there is a *duality* going on within the Mind itself. Those from a Judeo-Christian background may easily jump to the wrong conclusions. There is *not* a divine battle going on within us. It is not a question of light versus dark, good fighting evil for control of our soul. When we talk about the ego, we do not mean we've been *possessed* by something sinister. We do not need to be exorcised. In fact, the ego is not a separate entity at all. It is not something we have to *get rid of*.

Ego is a state of mind.

The word evokes a misguided quality that has emerged within us. It's the habitual tendency of falsely thinking ourselves separate from others. This mistaken sense of being separate creates a pre-occupation with clinging to that idea of a separate self, with self-cherishing, self-protection and aggrandisement.

Ego is a Latin word meaning *Me, myself, I*.

It literally encapsulates the way we compound the many words for I when we want to emphasize something about ourselves: *As for me myself, personally speaking, I think ...*

We now know, thanks to modern science, that the full potential of the *physical* brain is largely unused. The Buddha discovered that the same is true of the *Mind*. We operate very much within the realm of the mind's surface layers. The innate radiant quality of the mind produces activity on the surface. You might imagine this to be like the fizzy bubbles rising from deep within a bottle of champagne. When the bubbles break on the surface, we experience thoughts and emotions. As long as we continue to limit the activity of the mind to superficialities, we conclude that surface thoughts and emotions are all we really *are*. By identifying so strongly with that miniscule portion of the mind, we develop a false sense of self. We think that is what we are. Thoughts and emotions arise and we say to ourselves: *I think such and such, I feel this and that*. Our view has become limited and self-obsessed. The self-cherishing ego-tendency has taken hold and *Delusion* has been born within us. From then on, we experience disconnection and separation from the universe and our lonesome, isolated mantra becomes *Me, myself, I ...*

The greatest tragedy of all is that we actually *believe* our false assumption of a separate self to be true. We become like an agoraphobic. Feeling under siege and unable to reach out to the unknown, we run for cover. Not satisfied with remaining indoors, we bolt all the doors and windows of the house, blocking the light from outside. Then we retreat to the cellar and curl up in one corner of its womb-like darkness. The ego-tendency is like this. It drives us to be over-protective of ourselves and creates the *illusion* of safety.

Everything we think, do and say after this state of mind is created is directed toward the goals of the fledgling ego-mind: the pursuit of happiness and the avoidance of suffering. These objectives are unattainable and futile endeavours, however, so long as the mind is frozen in that self-cherishing position. Only when the mind's True Nature is realised, and our hearts are directed towards the ultimate benefit of *others*, will the ego dissolve and disperse. Like a rainbow or a mirage disappearing instantaneously, we will understand experientially that the ego never really existed at all, and how misguided we were to have devoted so many lifetimes to its false agenda.

Thich Nhat Hanh writes about the moment of enlightenment being like a prisoner who finally realises that the prison never actually existed. The man had been free all along! The jailer, it turns out, had been his own ego. And once he revealed the absolute truth of the situation for himself, the entire nightmare crumbled around him and vanished into thin air forever.

Ego-Buddhism

I have coined a new term here, *semi-humorously*, to give expression to a serious concern. No offence is intended, only a fervent aspiration to uncover the truth.

We all embark upon the spiritual path for a variety of different reasons. We remain on the path for equally diverse reasons. But all practitioners have at least two factors in common: we all wish to be free from Delusion and, until that happens, we are accompanied on the path by our ego.

Our strong ego-tendency continues to drive us. Some of us indulge our ego by writing books on Buddhism. Some of us just love all the esoteric chanting and exotic ritual that some traditions have. Even becoming *good at* the meditation posture can be appealing to the ego.

But at least those forms of ego-buddhism are harmless and hopefully inspire ourselves and others to go deeper along the path that leads us to our Buddha Nature.

When it comes to ego on the path, the ideal solution is to have an appropriate master keeping it all in check.

For those students who actually have a personal relationship with their spiritual teacher, working with the ego may become a very hands-on and intense affair. We have to start where we are, and the ego is the main problem. So some masters – depending on their lineage and tradition – zoom in on the ego of their student and work directly with that tendency. The master may adopt a variety of skillful approaches. They might devote their precious attention and energy to naming, challenging and squashing the student's ego whenever it manifests. Or they might provoke and stir it up so that it manifests all the more, and hopefully burns itself out. Either way the master must have that special kindness and ability to safely guide and teach their student in such a way, and the student must consent to this often difficult training. I dare say few Western students would be up for it. Anyway, such kind and devoted masters are unfortunately very rare nowadays.

So, for most of us, the problem of how to work on the ego remains. We don't have the direct training of the master and often the Sangha – the community of practitioners – are unwilling or unprepared to work with the egos of its dharma brothers and sisters. So individual students themselves may be ill-equipped at first to control their own egos, or to deal with the egos of others.

A meditation or retreat centre, therefore, is *at worst* made up of a collection of uncontrolled egos. This is written only partly tongue-in-cheek.

At best, the Sangha can support, guide and encourage our practice. They literally love us back to sanity. But make no mistake about it – *we* must do the work on our own minds ourselves. Otherwise no transformation can take place. We must take full responsibility for the progress of our own practice. In this spirit, we should not deny the existence of problematic egos in the dharma. They must not become an obstacle on the path. On the contrary, we acknowledge them and work with ego *as* the path. For samsaric beings such as ourselves, ego *is* the path. If there was no ego, we would already be enlightened.

We must enter the Sangha, therefore, in the clear knowledge that we and everyone else at our meditation centre are psycho-spiritually unwell. Otherwise none of us would be there! We are simply trying our best to get well again.

Those who feel well and have no problems don't go to hospital. So why feel so shocked when *you* show up at *Accident and Emergency* only to discover the place is full of sick people?!

Most Buddhist Meditation and Retreat Centres *do not* have a living Buddha in residence to teach, guide and supervise the egos of the Sangha. Therefore, the quality of the experience we have at a Dharma centre depends largely on our ability to cope with the egos of others and how they provoke *our* ego.

This is not a negative criticism of Dharma centres. It is the truth that will set us free. The realised masters who direct centres – albeit from afar – have actually set them up *so that* egos are gradually ground down by being in continued close proximity. This is the beauty of Sangha and, once you understand that in advance, the process should not be unpleasant.

However, there are Sanghas who are not so lucky. Maybe they do not have a realised master directing them at all. Or maybe there *is* one but they are so far removed from that particular centre they have no chance to check or guide what goes on there. In these Sanghas when ego goes on the path, unsupervised, it can create havoc.

The ego of the *meditation instructors* at such an unfortunate centre may become inflated and they may take on the role of a *guru* [in the most negative sense of the word]. This would be harmful to all concerned and possibly create a culture of ego-massaging. That spreads to the more experienced students who, in turn, may develop *expert minds* [as Suzuki Roshi put it]. A know-it-all can create tensions with others. But worst of all, their false view of themselves actually stunts their own spiritual development too.

By coining this new term, I sincerely hope that *you* can identify *ego-buddhism* if ever you come across it. Then at least you have the choice of avoiding that particular Sangha altogether or remaining in it and hopefully changing that unhealthy culture from within. There will be tears before bedtime, even if you proceed with humility and gentleness. But you will have done them a great service.

It is not really Dharma etiquette to create disharmony by pointing out someone's shortcomings but I believe it's our duty under certain circumstances. If our motivation is pure and directed for the benefit of others, including the person we are trying to help, then maybe we can mindfully try to do it. Furthermore, we should try to minimise and diffuse whatever consequent disharmony may follow in the short term.

So, in the spirit of cutting through ego – in *all* its forms – let the message be heard clearly around the world:

'Self-proclaimed masters who are in fact not realised, instructors who act like gurus, and know-it-all students who have completely missed the point ... Beware!'

We're onto you. The game is up!

Emotions

One of the four *Challenges* of Buddhism is that '*All emotions bring pain*'.

This *is* an extremely challenging proposition, especially for us Westerners. We identify so strongly with our emotions. Even the language we use clearly shows this. In English, we say *I AM angry* rather than *There IS anger*.

We don't allow the emotion to pass through us and subside. Instead, we cling onto it and make it worse.

In the West, we are even so preoccupied with the pursuit of *certain* emotions we don't believe anything negative could result from them. For example, *Love* – whether romantic, sexual, parental, friendship, or care-taking – maybe we imagine *Love* particularly will bring us ultimate happiness and peace so we are reluctant to entertain the notion that something as wonderful as Love could ever bring more suffering. Of course, if we could love *unconditionally*, and love *every* being equally, then ordinary love will have been transformed into *Maitri* – the purest form of spiritual love. But, ordinary *Love* while being a *many-splendoured thing*, as the old song goes, is also a most complex thing. Another more recent song reminds us, *Love is a battlefield*.

Therefore, the Buddha taught on all emotions. The Sanskrit word is *Klesha*, and it is translated as *the negative, afflictive emotions*.

Traditionally, the Kleshas can be listed as 3, 5, 6, 20 or even 51!

The shorter lists are easiest to take on board as they cover some already-familiar territory.

The three main destructive emotions [or three mind poisons] are ignorance, attachment and aversion. When classified as five, pride and jealousy are added.

Even at this stage, things can get complicated as *ignorance* is also known as Delusion, *attachment* is sometimes called Desire or Clinging, and *aversion* can often mean Anger.

However, we list and subdivide the Kleshas, they can all be understood in the same way. The root of all afflictive emotions is *ignorance* – if we only realised who we truly are, nothing negative would arise.

But, since we don't realise – at least for the time being – *attachment* and *aversion* arise. *Pride* is said to be a mixture of *ignorance* and *attachment*. And *jealousy* is a combination of *attachment* and *aversion*.

That's as complex as we need to get for now.

A great Tibetan sage once said he was not the least bit impressed by advanced practitioners who could perform miracles or create magical illusions. But he willingly gave all his respect and devotion to someone who could liberate one single negative emotion!

That's the good news! There *is* a very positive thing about Kleshas. They can all be *purified*. The masters offer us a cunning suggestion about where to begin.

His Holiness the Dalai Lama has said there are three reasons for believing that the destructive emotions *can* be eliminated from our minds:

All destructive emotions and negative mental states are essentially distorted, whereas their antidotes, such as love, compassion and insight, are undistorted and based on how things really are.

The antidotes have the quality of being strengthened through training and practice.

The essential nature of the mind is pure and undefiled by the destructive emotions.

Ringu Tulku Rinpoche gives us a very handy tip. We might consider first working on our *Anger/Aversion* as that is perhaps the easiest place to start.

Granted *Ignorance* would be the *best* place to start because, if we could only cut through that, the whole tree of Kleshas would come tumbling down in one go. But our ignorance is said in the Sutras to be like the earth itself. It is so pervasive and goes so deep we might find it too hard to start there.

Similarly, if we could cut through our *attachment* we would eliminate *aversion* into the bargain. But the same sutra holds that attachment is like water. It spreads everywhere and, like water, takes a long long time to evaporate or be completely mopped up.

On the other hand, *Anger* is said to be like fire. Once ignited, it bursts into flames suddenly, as if from nowhere. It burns ferociously, strong and bright – almost out of control. It is said that *anger* has no positive qualities whatsoever. It only harms ourselves and others. But for all its fierce irrationality, anger will burn out once the source of its fuel is removed. Therefore, it is the least difficult place to begin *disarming* our ego-minds.

The mind training we have already begun, especially meditation practice, will provide us with the most essential tools to take on *anger*. Our ability to become stable and open to phenomena will stand us in good stead. It will literally stop the klesha in its tracks. But it is still there. Now we have created a gap, an opening through which we can safely and dispassionately look deeply into the very nature and source of the klesha. Undistracted, and without wishing to alter the anger in any way, we just look directly into it and its cause. This will have the effect of disarming and dispersing it ... but it will return another day. Eventually, after many such encounters with the Natural Mind, the klesha will lose its power over us and cause no further disruption.

Another element to *purifying* the kleshas is to employ their antidotes. Becoming expert in the ways of Patience and Love is the antidote to Anger. The spaciousness that results can be said to have arisen as a direct consequence of the anger. And so the klesha with no positive side to speak of has actually created something profoundly enlightening. Anger, by being transformed, has become pure.

Similarly, for all the other kleshas. Although there are variants regarding which antidote to apply to which klesha, generally speaking *Ignorance* is dispelled by Wisdom, *Attachment* by Insight into the unattractive qualities of that which we desire, *Aversion* [Anger] by Love, Compassion and Patience, *Pride* is averted by Humility, Generosity and the like, and finally *Jealousy* by Rejoicing.

It must be remembered that applying antidotes is a 24/7 activity and as such is quite advanced. It demands a high degree of mindfulness, awareness and spaciousness, which is developed *ahead of time* through the practice of meditation.

However, it wouldn't be very beneficial, either to ourselves or others, to reduce the path to enlightenment to a simple matter of obsessively watching our every move and neurotically *blocking* emotions with opposites. Done the wrong way, the path of applying antidotes to kleshas might just drive us crazy – or at least dizzy!

But properly understood and applied, training the mind in antidotes will empower us and deepen our confidence and faith in the ultimate strength of our True Nature to overcome whatever obstacles may arise.

Ultimately, delusion is cut right through and enlightenment revealed, not by always having the right responses to life on hand – like a clever bag of tricks – but by growing in Wisdom and Compassion.

Therefore, a pivotal *slogan* from *The Seven Points of Mind Training* warns us to avoid getting stuck in any one method: *Liberate even the antidote.*

We take ourselves so seriously. For aeons we have taken our emotions too seriously. Now, when the chemistry of our brains fires up, we perceive its *energy-in-motion* as *E-motion* and continue to get swept away in the drama of it all. Or we become Buddhist and learn antidotes, but tragically forget that the whole point of the path is to *go beyond* all *-isms* and concepts. We must use what is useful while it is appropriate, but without getting stuck at that stage. We have to *keep moving* in the right direction ... all the way over to the far shore. We mustn't fall into the trap of mistaking the boat-trip for the final destination itself.

Emptiness

Shunyata is the essential truth that pervades all of the Buddha's teachings. Therefore, it is very important not to misunderstand it. Of course, it is only a word, a concept. But it points to the ultimate reality of all phenomena, including ourselves. The ideal way to understand Shunyata is by direct personal experience. Hence the urgent need for meditation, which leads to the realisation of the Nature of Mind.

Usually translated as *Emptiness*, Shunyata can take on a negative connotation. As such, it may become a stumbling block for many. Right from the beginning, the Buddha sought to illustrate how the nature of reality is to be found on a *Middle Path* – somewhere between Eternalism and Nihilism, the two erroneous, extreme views held by his contemporaries. He was reforming the mistaken views that either everything lasts forever, or nothing really exists at all.

Therefore, it is of paramount importance to fully understand the Buddha's teaching on Shunyata. If we infer anything nihilistic, we have completely missed the point.

Some masters translate Shunyata as *Fullness*, or *Openness*, in a genuine effort to avoid this pitfall.

But even this translation can't fully explain the *Ultimate Truth*, which is by definition beyond all conceptual understanding.

It could be said that all of the Buddha's teachings are approaching this Truth from every conceivable direction. Similarly, the skillful teachings of a realised master adopt the same approach.

There *is* a lot of justification, however, for exploring the use of the word *Emptiness* even though we may not like it.

Simply put, *Shunyata* means that everything is *empty of* intrinsic existence, *empty of* permanent existence, *empty of* any real substance whatsoever, and *empty of* individual, separate identity. This is why *Emptiness* was used in the first place as a useful term.

The genesis of *Shunyata* as a philosophical conclusion is built on the following progression: Change, Impermanence, Interconnectedness, Emptiness.

Everything changes; nothing remains the same from moment to moment. Therefore, we say everything is impermanent; nothing will last forever. In the meantime, everything exists in relation to, and in connection with, everything else. When we examine *anything* close up, including ourselves, we clearly see it is made up from many other elements; so we say that Emptiness is the nature of everything since nothing has an intrinsic existence or individual identity of its own.

The newer translations of *Shunyata* help clarify this further. Take the *self*, for example. Because of impermanence and interconnectedness, it can be said that *I* am *empty* [of any intrinsic self]. Therefore, it becomes useful to understand this also in terms of *Fullness* or *Openness*.

There is nothing in me that cannot be subdivided into its constituent parts. Furthermore, I am a compound of elements that also exist throughout the universe. Even the elements I am made from are not unique to me. So, we come to understand that we are *interconnected* with everything that is, we are all *interdependent*. Our essence is not fixed. It is *open*. We are *full* of all that is.

Like a mirage or a rainbow, *we* appear because of various causes and conditions. Remove any one of them and we cease to appear.

There is a profound double-paradox at work here. We should contemplate it again and again until we begin to experience the truth of it for ourselves:

Everything is Empty, yet it appears. Even though things appear, they are Empty.

Nothing is real, yet things really *do* manifest. We can touch them, break them, use them. But nothing that appears to exist is real.

A summary of these enigmatic phrases might read:

Reality is the Union of Appearance and Emptiness.

This is not just true of the physical elements that co-emerge and coalesce to make up our bodies. It is also the nature of our spiritual essence, the Buddha Nature, to be empty of intrinsic individuality. *Shunyata* is also our True Nature. There is no separation. Our Buddha Nature is connected to and dependent on the True Nature of *everything*; I do not possess a soul separate to your soul. We are both manifestations of the one Buddha Nature that pervades all appearances.

But this is not a paralysing truth. We are not rendered powerless or apathetic by it. On the contrary, it means we are not alone. The aspiration to benefit others is potentially shared by all beings. We are all united by our common nature in this pursuit. It also means we are *free*.

There *is* a great stillness about our True Nature. But that shouldn't be misread as inertia or being frozen somehow. The highest Buddhist teachings show how there is *movement in stillness*. Our Buddha Nature is always active, dedicated to the unfolding work of awakening for the benefit of others. There is no limitation on what we can achieve.

Thich Nhat Hanh teaches, *Thanks to Emptiness, EVERYTHING is possible!*

We should have unshakeable faith in our own empty nature and its incredibly *full* potential. Furthermore, we can rest assured that the Empty Essence is not a cold, unmoved, indifferent state. Its nature is to be *Aware* of the ultimate needs of beings. And its *Energy* is to show Impartial Compassion for all.

Energy

Energy is a word that is over-used nowadays. From a Buddhist perspective, it has been mis-used and ab-used by a variety of parties interested in spirituality, mostly by the New Age movement and other Western quasi-religions.

The result has been for genuine spiritual masters to shy away from using the term altogether. However, *energy* is the perfect English word to describe the movement and activity of our True Nature. It has a dynamic, inexhaustible ring to it which evokes the drive of beings determined to benefit others.

Buddhists use the word specifically in relation to the Compassionate Energy of the Buddha Nature that is impartially and limitlessly working to liberate all beings from suffering.

The *surface* display of the mind's energy, its unbridled radiance, manifests as raw thoughts and emotions. These two are considered to be gross by-products of mind's energy and, if they are to be useful at all, must be tamed and retrained by the meditative process.

Once this process begins to find increasing success, a practitioner can work with their mind's essential energy at a deeper level, because the surface has become less chaotic, more settled ... more *natural*.

Advanced Tibetan practitioners continue to use ancient Indian Buddhist techniques that would certainly have been lost altogether had they not taken root and been preserved in Tibet. Their basis is not secret. It is the existence, within the physical body, of a subtle *energy body*.

However, these practices are withheld from novice practitioners until such time as they can directly experience and influence the subtle energy body themselves. The Tibetans are *experts* in this particular field and are willing to teach it to students once they are ripe for it.

The main points, however, are very much in keeping with the present context, which is essentially a dharma discussion on *energy*. So it is appropriate to explore the basics a little further here.

The subtle energy body is described as having three components. The original Sanskrit terms are *Prana, Nadi,* and *Bindu* [Tib. Tsa, Lung, Tiglé]. In English they are *Channel, Wind, and Droplet [Essence]*.

The human physical body is mirrored by an energy body, which comprises a network of subtle channels running throughout the body and all feeding into the *central channel*. This runs in a straight line from between the legs all the way upwards through the centre of the body, exiting at the crown of the head. En route, it runs through seven main *chakras* or energy hubs.

All the *channels* are routes through which energetic *winds* move, carrying along the *essence* of our Natural Mind, the Buddha Nature.

There are blockages and points of sluggishness throughout the entire system. Advanced practitioners can heal and repair everything so it flows naturally again. They even perfect the practice of gathering all their essential essence into the central channel. Thus they concentrate their essence and can better focus and direct their compassionate energy.

The aspirations of this practice are to obtain an unobscured connection with our True Nature and to direct its compassion for the benefit of beings.

An interesting side-effect occurs at the moment of death. Familiarity and expertise in this practice may enable a practitioner to affect and guide the quality and outcome of their passing out of the physical body.

The essence is gathered into the central channel and concentrated at the Heart Chakra. Then it is brought upwards and popped out through the crown chakra where it merges with the essence of all the Buddhas. If perfected, this technique guarantees an unattached, sane, undistracted passage and may even result in enlightenment itself.

The Tibetan tradition preserved those particular sacred, semi-secret yoga practices. However, that does not mean other traditions lack something or are somehow inferior. On the contrary, other traditions *do* place a huge emphasis on working with *energy*. They just present the relevant teachings in their own way. The *Vipassana* meditations of the Burmese Schools come to mind. Likewise, the *Energy* of Mindfulness in Zen. Both of these sacred Wisdom Traditions come from the mind of the Buddha and, as such, lead beings towards enlightenment by working with the energy within. We should never be deceived by simple, straightforward language into thinking it is not teaching us something very profound.

The amazing beauty of the Buddhadharma is its poetic simplicity. It is perhaps Buddhism's greatest strength that it can express the most complex concepts often in terms that are profoundly easy and direct.

Too often, we fall into the trap of assuming that the *Truth* – if we could only find it – would be far too esoteric and complex for the likes of *us* to understand. It never occurs to us it might well be something quite simple yet profound that sets us free. The simple Truth, it seems, is often hiding in plain sight.

When it comes to *energy*, maybe things don't have to be so complicated for the uninitiated like you and me after all. Maybe we don't need to trek up the Himalayas in search of hidden yogis.

Why assume that $e=mc^2$ means something head-wrecking and mind-numbingly beyond our comprehension?

Maybe it embodies a simpler truth – perhaps something as outrageously uplifting, refreshingly democratic, and eminently useful as:

Energy is ... mindfulness multiplied by lots of compassion.

Engaged

All Buddhism should be Engaged Buddhism. Otherwise it's not Buddhism at all.

Action must play a large part for anyone embarking upon the Buddhist path to enlightenment. It is through our own activity that we emulate *enlightened* activity. The more Buddha-like we behave, the more Buddha-like we become.

Our spiritual awakening happens in two ways, simultaneously. The Wisdom teachings and practices of the Buddha enable us to recognise the essential Buddha Nature of all beings, including ourselves. By working with our minds, we first glimpse, then come to realise our True Nature, the Natural Mind, in which we continue to rest. The Compassion teachings and practices actually help us to benefit ourselves and others. The Buddhadharma is a *practical* path whose fruition is the cessation of suffering, for all.

This is why the Buddha's teachings are built around various things we can *do* to liberate ourselves and others. As well as various meditation techniques, the Buddha taught his followers how to *engage* with the world and its inhabitants. Depending on one's level of commitment to the way of the Buddha, there are many useful guidelines we can follow. Needless to say, we must enter into detailed study and contemplation about the methods of engagement at the same time as putting them into practice. These words we are sharing now merely constitute the beginning of that process.

In the simplest terms, we can *Avoid doing harm, Only do good,* and *Train the mind.* These are general moral principles, the details and application of which are to be decided by the individual according to their conscience and level of realisation.

A more specific path is contained in the *Six Paramitas*: The Transcendent Actions of Generosity, Discipline, Patience, Enthusiastic Diligence, Meditative Concentration, and Wisdom.

Another common approach for monastics and dedicated lay people alike is to explore the usefulness of committing to certain precepts. We may wish to become more engaged by avoiding specific negative actions, which harm ourselves and others such as Lying, Stealing, Killing, Sexual Misconduct and Intoxication. When we look deeply into each of these Five Precepts, we may see how far we are willing to take things. Obviously *Not Lying* could be taken to imply, by extension, that *all* negative speech is to be avoided, ideally. Similarly, *Not Killing* could also have consequences for what we are prepared to eat, and whether we are prepared to allow others to kill on our behalf. Our *sexual life* offers us a way of non-harming and expressing love. Avoiding *intoxication* helps us keep a clear head, behave consciously, and greatly reduce the layers of delusion separating us from directly experiencing our Natural Mind. We remain free, undistracted and *unaltered.*

The Five Precepts can be further expanded to fourteen. In his book *Interbeing: Fourteen Guidelines for Engaged Buddhism*, Thich Nhat Hanh – using the Buddha's own teachings – inspires his most courageous, revolutionary and committed lay students to engage with the world in quite a detailed, challenging and ultimately rewarding way. Sometimes referred to as *Revised Pratimoksha Vows*, they are easily found online at www.plumvillage.org.

You will immediately notice that some deal with the engaged actions of the mind, others with the speech, and the rest with the body [including sexual conduct]. The fourteen headings are:

Openness.
Non-attachment to Views.
Freedom of Thought.
Awareness of Suffering.
Simple, Healthy Living.
Dealing with Anger.
Dwelling Happily in the Present Moment.
Community and Communication.
Truthful and Loving Speech.
Protecting the Sangha.
Right Livelihood.
Reverence for Life.
Generosity.
Right Conduct.

So often Buddhism is misunderstood as a passive, non-engaged path. That couldn't be further from the truth. A real follower of the Buddha's teachings must engage directly with the world, not avoid it. Activity, rooted in the gradual fruition of Wisdom and Compassion, is precisely what produces Buddhas. Meditative progress alone, does not.

Engaged Buddhism is not just a modern trend. It has been the core principle of the Buddha's teachings from the start. Without being party-political, Buddhism is by its very nature a *political* activity – it is *ultimately* concerned with the welfare of people. Engaged Buddhism includes and surpasses current political concerns such as equality, human rights, non-violence, economics, and caring for the natural world and all the beings who share it with us. However, the scope of the Buddha's teachings goes further still. Our *ultimate* concern is a spiritual one. We work for the spiritual awakening of beings. We acknowledge that famine, poverty and war are destroying people's lives and must be eradicated. But, removing the suffering of beings goes much deeper than the realm of the physical. Similarly, while we acknowledge the necessity for people to have good mental health, we do not stop at longing to bring short-term happiness to beings. We must go even deeper than the surface realm of thoughts and emotions.

On the most profound level, Engaged Buddhism is concerned with helping the Buddha Nature of beings become fully manifest and active. When we accomplish that, we accomplish everything else.

Enlightenment

Many people think about Enlightenment. Some have written about it. But the ones who have actually become enlightened themselves have rarely, practically never, spoken about it. They don't even acknowledge in public that it happened.

Profound peace, natural simplicity free from complexity, uncompounded luminosity ...

This is how the Buddha spoke of his own experience of enlightenment. But, he wasn't sure if trying to describe the indescribable was actually useful to beings. So the Buddha is said to have withdrawn to the forest just after his awakening to contemplate just how to proceed.

Eventually, he went to find his old friends, the ascetics. Since they had meditated a lot and were already close to the ultimate breakthrough, the Buddha taught them what he had discovered and they quickly became enlightened.

When it came to teaching more ordinary people, the Buddha preferred to start with the most basic principles such as the Four Noble Truths and Meditation, and work his way up from there.

However, his first utterances after awakening encapsulate everything the Dharma contains. He described both the fruition and the qualities of the path that leads to it.

Profound peace, natural simplicity free from complexity, uncompounded luminosity ... these are not only describing how it feels to be enlightened but also the spiritual qualities that bring it about. He was also describing the perfect way of life, one which embodies the healthiest view of all phenomena. Even more than this, deep peace, uncomplicated simplicity, and unfabricated wisdom actually describes the *Natural Mind* itself. It is not a question of us having to evolve *into* enlightened beings. On the deepest level, we are *already* perfectly awake. We do not have to change or alter the essential fabric of our minds in order to *become* peaceful or compassionate. These natural qualities will be unlocked in limitless abundance once we realise our True Nature and cease to be deluded.

Realising that one has been enlightened all along, but just didn't know it, is a common factor in many of the famous [usually anonymous] accounts of the moment of awakening.

Frequently we hear of masters who felt such unfettered release that they simply laughed out loud at their previous naïveté. What is sometimes described as *carefree abandon* is often accompanied by the question, *How did I not realise this before, how on earth did I miss it?!*

The 14th Century Tibetan saint, Longchen Rabjam, put it this way:

Since everything is but an illusion,
Perfect in being what it is,

Having nothing to do with 'good' or 'bad',
Acceptance or rejection,
One might as well burst out laughing!

Thich Nhat Hanh famously described the moment of enlightenment as being like a prisoner who, seeing the entire jail dissolve around him, suddenly realises it had never really existed and he had always been a free man.

It is very inspiring to read such uplifting words. But *our* path to awakening, we must remember, begins right here and now in this present moment. We must not become distracted by concepts about how it would feel to be enlightened. Better to focus on the steps that will undo the ego-tendency in us right now and put an end to Delusion for once and for all.

The best thing about enlightenment, it has to be emphasized, is not that it would feel great, but that we would then be able to lead others out of suffering.

Apparently, there have been many cases where a person becomes enlightened and they simply can't – or don't know how to – be in the world afterwards. There is a wonderful book by Jack Kornfield called *After the Ecstasy, the Laundry* that explores this very phenomenon.

The need for spiritual guidance from an authentic master never goes away. The blossoming of the mind is not just about finding personal happiness. Complete awakening leads to enlightened activity, which is Compassion. To take away the suffering of beings is why we are here.

Environment

We must learn to live in harmony with our environment.

As soon as we hear the word *environment*, we think of the natural world and the ecological dilemma we are facing on this planet. But I would like to recycle the word and reclaim it in a Buddhist context.

The *environment* in a spiritual context can also refer to the external space in which we do our spiritual practice. Similarly, it refers to the internal environment of the mind that is practising. Due to the interconnection of *all that is*, we recognise that the external and the internal environments are not separate. They influence, inspire and *co-create* one another.

Therefore, as beginners, it is very important to create a suitable environment for our meditation practice. Without getting too elaborate, or even too *spiritual*, we can create an inspiring space for ourselves in some quiet corner. The qualities of that space will arouse the same qualities in the mind that meditates. Consequently, we aspire to a sense of comfort and ease, openness and contentment, a spaciousness that is entirely *natural* ... unfabricated, such that it allows our mind to remain undistracted and unaltered once the Natural Mind dawns. But we must avoid trying to create the *perfect* place. It will never happen and we will never get around to doing any meditation there. Neither should we become dependent on that particular space in order to be able to meditate.

The initial purpose of meditation practice is to soften the mind and allow it to become ever-more flexible and open. Therefore, we begin the spiritual path with that mindset.

Our short-term goal is to learn to meditate. Our mid-term goal is to be able to meditate anywhere, under any circumstances. Our ultimate goal is to rest in the Natural Mind all the time ... without using any meditation method, and without having any personal goal whatsoever except to bring ultimate benefit to all beings.

Attachment and aversion are the main obstacles to enlightenment. There is no path to enlightenment without obstacles.

Obstacles ARE *the path.*

Bearing this in mind at all times on the path to liberation, we apply it to how we approach the external and internal environment.

We must not become attached or averse to whatever positive or negative states arise within the mind. Neither should we become attached or averse to our external environment. We simply remain, open and flexible. If we do not adhere to this noble aspiration, we will only progress if external circumstances are *just so*. We will not be able to live a spiritual life in the real world, with all its distractions, busyness, sirens, people and problems. Seen in this light, any progress we make in the sanctuary of our meditation space or our Himalayan cave may be rendered useless in ordinary life.

The outer and inner environment of our spiritual awakening will only have true meaning if it eventually transforms us such that we become most beneficial to others.

In this context, we now return to the common meaning of the word *environment*.

The more awakened we become, the more we wish to benefit and awaken others. It is therefore a direct function of our emerging Wisdom and Compassionate Activity to transform the attitude we all have to the natural environment, which gives and nurtures this precious human life. It is said that without this miraculous life-giving planet, and the human ancestors that have evolved here, the particular being that I call *me* could never have existed ... and there would be no possibility for enlightenment to happen. So even from a purely selfish point of view, we should all cherish and heal the earth that we are currently destroying. From a spiritual point of view, moreover, the Buddha reminds us there can be no enlightenment without *non-harming*.

Always remember the words of the Buddha, *With our minds we create the world*.

As the Natural Mind awakens, *everything* gets better.

The masters teach us that spiritual awakening depends ultimately on the environment of our mind. When we practise, we can ensure the highest possible quality of mind by using the following three principles:

Before practice begins, arouse the Motivation of *Bodhichitta*. Generate Love, Compassion, Joy and

Equanimity. Pray from the bottom of your heart that the practice may bring all beings – including yourself – to enlightenment.

During practice, maintain what is called the *View*. The mind should be as *spacious* as possible. Experienced practitioners may be able to adopt the wide open mind of *Shunyata*, or at least a vast attitude that is *Non-conceptual*.

After practice, one should always make a strong *Dedication* of the positive merit accumulated through your meditation. Pray that all beings share in the merit and so attain complete liberation.

Equanimity

Meditation practice prepares us for life. According to the teachings, to be fully human, we must unlock our true potential. When we realise our Buddha Nature, we become a natural source of *limitless* love, compassion, joy and equanimity. These enlightened qualities are often referred to as the *Four Immeasurables*. Once they start to flow unimpeded, they will never run out.

As beginners and intermediate practitioners, we devote a large portion of our formal meditation practice to *sitting* mindfully. Many masters recommend this because we are developing equanimity. Once we have grown in that particular way, we can work more on unlocking the other three enlightened qualities.

Equanimity incorporates many things. We become more balanced and stable in our own minds. We become spacious and open to the world. Our openness, in particular, will be the very thing that allows us to love all beings equally. Like a cosmic mother, we will have love and compassion that is *unconditional* and *impartial*.

Unlocking equanimity is precisely that which enables us to arouse genuine Bodhichitta. Our desire to send love, and take away the root suffering of beings, must be impartial and unbiased. We do not have real equanimity if we cannot love our best friend and the world's worst serial killer equally.

If we feel, at first, it is easier to have love and compassion for some beings more than others, that's OK of course. We shouldn't have unrealistic expectations of ourselves in the beginning. However, as we practise more and gradually awaken, we will become more balanced. Our love and compassion will become more and more impartial.

The fruition of sitting meditation [Skt. Shamatha] is *One-pointedness*. We begin by learning to develop the delicate balance of being *focused* with being *spacious*. Starting by using the breath itself as our focus, we then train to focus on other helpful things such as inspiring, sacred images, mantra and visualisation. Training the mind like this eventually enables us to become connected to the Buddha Nature. As the heart and mind open, our equanimity deepens. We are able to remain stable and love all beings equally.

As the self-cherishing ego begins to dissolve, our lives open out and we become a living embodiment of compassion. We are no longer indifferent to strangers. We are no longer blocked. We are caring to all beings equally, whether they are loved ones or those who previously would have aroused fear and hatred in us, or those for whom we would normally have felt nothing. The glorious nature of Buddhist meditation means that something as simple and beautiful as mindfully observing our own breathing creates a profound transformation deep within us. A heart that was previously blocked and cautious, and a mind that used to be preoccupied with self-preservation, open up like a lotus blossom. We become willing and able to do the work we were born to do, the work of a Buddha. To love unconditionally and show compassion to all beings equally is why we are here.

Because we are interconnected with everything and everyone, as we progress along the path of transforming ourselves we in turn have a transformative effect on all beings. To liberate beings from their suffering minds emerges as *the* most natural aspiration in the world. We don't have to become someone else to do it, like a saint or a sage, a monastic or a hermit. We don't even have to become a Buddhist. The confused, deluded person we are now with all our baggage and issues, perhaps living a hectic life somewhere, *IS* the raw material for fully awakening as a perfect Buddha.

Starting where we are, right here, right now, we progress along the path *one breath at a time.* Encountering the Natural Mind, glimpse after glimpse, *is* the way to Buddhahood.

Evolution

In order for beings to awaken and realise their Buddha Nature, they must have the right kind of mind. Their mind must be capable of *seeing itself*, so to speak. This is closely connected to the type of brain they have. It is also strongly linked to their consciousness, and whether or not it is sufficiently *self-aware*. One final component is very important. For a being to become enlightened, it must have the right *karma* driving it in that direction. Based on one's past actions and aspirations, our karma will either enable or hinder awakening.

Therefore, we understand the ideal conditions for enlightenment like this: Awakening depends on several factors being present at the same time; without the right kind of mind, awareness, physical brain, and karma, we will not realise our True Nature in this lifetime.

In this regard, we need to contemplate *evolution*. Many of us have mistaken views of this concept. We understand enlightenment as some kind of *spiritual evolution* ... beings changing *from* one thing *into* another.

In Buddhist terms, Buddhas are not more spiritually *evolved* than us. It is not at all a question of evolving from one thing to *become* another thing. Darwinian Evolution has nothing to do with it.

A Buddha, quite literally, is a being – any being – who has awakened to their True Nature. That is why the Buddha taught that since we all have the Buddha Nature, we are *already* perfect Buddhas. We are just sleeping. We don't realise who we truly are or how to access our full potential. You might say we are spiritually dormant. We only have to wake up.

However as *physical* beings, on the other hand, we *are* part of an evolutionary process. We are evolving so that the brain, and the consciousness it is linked to, are both becoming more and more capable of *self-reflection*. The ability to turn the mind inwards and experience our own True Nature is precisely what enables us to wake up as Buddhas.

When you think about it, perhaps there are many other species who are capable of this too ... on this planet and wherever else beings exist in the universe. It could be that the Universal Buddha Nature, through the natural world itself, is busy creating species with just the right kind of brains to realise their True Nature. Maybe *that's* what the universe is all about. After all, if awakening were limited to just one planet, and only to human beings, then the process of universal enlightenment would be unnecessarily protracted, and uncharacteristically limited. It is the nature of the universe to manifest diversity from unity, complexity from simplicity.

Moreover, the underlying universal compassion that drives the gradual awakening of all beings, if it were to limit itself to such an extent, would be less than *Immeasurable* and therefore not true compassion at all. Simply as a point of logic, it is far more likely that suitable brains of all shapes and sizes, and in all corners of the universe, are evolving just so that as many beings as possible can realise their True Nature.

Note, the brain is not the generator of *Consciousness*. It is more like a radio than a transmitter. The brain receives and *tunes into* consciousness, both local and cosmic.

As well as the physical body, and the kind of brain it houses, another key evolutionary aspect is the mind/consciousness/awareness it feeds into. In order to realise our True Nature, we have to be able to look inside our own minds and experience our essence directly for ourselves. Whatever scientists may come to call this vital aspect – 'self-awareness', or the 'reflexive loop' – beings must have it in order for meditation and the consequent awakening to be possible.

So far we have been contemplating the role played by the physical brain, and higher psychological functions, preparing the way for enlightenment to occur. But it also depends on many other equally crucial, and interrelated, factors.

Because of past actions, and habitual tendencies, we've been propelled forwards through space and time. What we call the winds of karma have caused us to take birth in this particular body, in this particular family, in the here and now. There is a universal purpose to this. It is far from random that we have manifested as we have. It may be we have specific lessons to learn in this lifetime, or particular things we have to do for the benefit of beings. It could even be we've been born into the ideal circumstances to become enlightened.

Where *evolution*, understood in scientific terms, really does come into play is at this level. This is why so many Buddhist cultures revere their ancestors. Pictures or representations of a person's forebears are often found on Buddhist shrines along with a sacred image of the Buddha. It is believed, thanks to the ancestors, we have the precious opportunity in this very lifetime to awaken and become fully liberated.

Thinking of my ancestors in this way conjures up an image of a family tree sprouting from above my head and stretching back through the mists of time, ever-widening in its scope, until it embraces all beings everywhere. It's as if all the beings who ever existed procreated and loved one another, down through all the generations, just so that I could have *this* life. How fortunate then, how precious, how rare an opportunity my present life is!

Therefore, I will not forget them. Nor will I let them down.

In this spirit, we may wish to honour our ancestors and promise to attain enlightenment for all *their* sakes as well. It's thanks to them we are here now and have encountered the very path that will set us free.

We have also inherited many positive and negative genes from them. They come to the surface in our personalities and in our behaviour. We can be grateful to our ancestors for the positive qualities we have inherited. We must be grateful for the negative ones too. The current forms that attachment and aversion take in our lives – such as an addiction or a bad temper – may have come in part through our DNA. So, we can feel genuine, heart-felt rejoicing that we have something concrete to work with and transform. It may be precisely *because* of those inherited negative traits, and *how* we transform them through spiritual realisation in this very lifetime, that we actually become enlightened! You might even say, we have the chance to transform them, once and for all, on behalf of our entire family tree. *We* could be the ones to make good use of the negative elements of our DNA by purifying and possibly eradicating them altogether.

Another vision springs to mind of all the ancestors whose names are still remembered and the countless billions of nameless, faceless beings standing in the shadows of time. Perhaps they are smiling at us, nodding their approval. By virtue of our aspiration to awaken for the benefit of all beings, the ancestors fully appreciate that we have embarked on the spiritual path to benefit them too.

Family

We start out on the spiritual path by working on ourselves to release the power of peace and compassion in our own lives. Once we become more whole and stable we become more and more open. Then we must work for the benefit of others. We will need a safe environment to try out our newly acquired skills and put them to good use.

The natural place to start is where we are right now. Our personal relationships provide us with the perfect laboratory to exercise and flex these muscles. We bring *mindfulness, deep listening,* and *loving speech* into the life we share with our loved ones. Ultimately, we treat them with the love and respect due to all beings as buddhas-to-be.

The family is a wonderful place to bring much-needed peace and compassion. Different people have different definitions of exactly what a family is. It may be the family you were born into. It may consist of yourself, your partner, and your own children. You may be single, in which case *family* may include your circle of close friends and colleagues. It might even mean just you and your pet. Some people prefer to choose their own family and gather friends around them to share their life with. Whatever our particular set-up, we all have a precious opportunity to live according to the principles taught by the Buddha. The effect will be the same regardless. We ourselves, and those around us, become happier and suffer less.

Another important place to practise a non-harming, virtuous life is in a spiritual community of like-minded people. The *Sangha* is where we meet people who, just like us, have embarked on the spiritual path and have dedicated themselves to the ultimate benefit of others. Another family of sorts, with all its ups and downs, the Sangha is the perfect testing ground for us. Once our motivation is pure, the spiritual community is an ideal, safe environment in which to put the teachings into practice.

Wherever we are, we are surrounded by beings who all equally deserve our love and compassion. Living peacefully and openheartedly by their side can only make things better. Maybe our good example will even inspire them to change their lives for the better too. Some very courageous, strong people are capable of seeing the entire human race, or all beings, as their true family. Considering all beings to be like their children, or their mothers, they work tirelessly to help them.

Whatever our definition of family, we are missing the whole point of life if we *only* wish to make the lives of others better in physical terms. We often mistakenly believe we are showing love and compassion to others by trying to raise their standard of living or by giving them more *stuff*. Of course poverty is a huge problem in the world, but no one ever attained lasting happiness or true peace of mind by being rich. These things are only the beginnings – the basics – for a stable world. The real *revolution* will be a spiritual one. And it can continue today with us and how we relate to those around us. Depending on how we take the challenge of communal living, we could actually join something amazing that has already begun to blossom all across the world. It's not even about Buddhism or organized religion *per se*. There is what some have called a quiet revolution in the hearts and minds of people. Maybe it's happening because of global politics or climate change, but it is happening. Hopefully it will be unstoppable. Hopefully people's hearts and minds will continue to open and embrace others long after we have freed the world and saved the planet. Only then will the real work of peace, love, and compassion begin. In truth, the spiritual work of transforming our minds should not have to wait till then. If anything, we should be doing both in tandem. Saving the world and liberating the mind are not mutually exclusive. They are part of the same thing; one is actually a vital function of attaining the other.

Because of inter-dependent co-arising, the Buddha taught whatever we do in a small way really does affect the world. We know that too, from bitter experience. Global pollution starts with one individual. A truly unhappy person can destroy an entire family. Thankfully the reverse is also true. The solution can begin with one person too.

We should never underestimate *the power of one*. So we're not Mahatma Gandhi or Martin Luther King. So what! They were great people, but it doesn't help to compare ourselves to others too much. What each one of us has in our favour is the Buddha Nature. It is longing to be awakened and activated, and its power to benefit beings is limitless. Racism, slavery, or colonialism will not deter it, as we already know. Assassination cannot stop it. Nor can the one-step-forward two-steps-back dance of history prevent the Buddha Nature from realizing its ultimate goal. All beings have perfect happiness already within them, and they are already free from suffering to the very core of their being. Eventually, each one of them will come to realize this ultimate truth. It's only a matter of time, but *we* must play our part by really learning to love those around us.

Fear

Dwelling in the realm of ego breeds delusion. Not resting in our true nature gives rise to a vicious cycle of attachment and aversion, which manifests as afflictive emotions. These come in many forms such as addiction and anger, but they all boil down to the same disturbing forces: *I want ... I don't want.*

Also known as *Hope* and *Fear*, the chaotic emotions that spring from our ego-clinging are the very things that make us suffer. If we could even cut through one of them, the whole deluded house of cards would crumble and fall. Then we'd be liberated forever and enlightenment would flow like a river.

For this reason, the Buddha taught the mark of an enlightened being is *fearlessness*. Someone who has gone beyond fear is free from all the obscurations and obstacles that prevent us from manifesting as buddhas and ultimately benefitting others.

We are deeply afraid of so many things: fear of others, fear of the unknown, fear of losing our minds. We are all but completely paralyzed, not living to our full potential. This fear comes from our utter distrust of letting go and opening up – it is also a primal fear of the openness and the emptiness of our Buddha Nature.

In this light, the high point of the *Heart Sutra* is said to be the line:

There is no fear.

The full name of this sutra is *The Heart of Transcendent Knowledge*. By definition, it teaches that the key to full enlightenment is *fearlessness*. The whole theme of this particular sutra [Skt. *Prajnaparamita Sutra*] is *Going Beyond*. The preamble describes the Buddha Nature as '*beyond words, beyond thought, beyond description. Prajnaparamita ... unborn, unceasing, with nature like the sky*'. The essence of the sutra is its mantra:

> *Gaté, gaté, paragaté, parasamgaté, bodhi svaha.*

It is the perfect utterance of one who has already gone completely beyond all fear: *Gone, gone, gone all the way over, completely gone over to the other shore. Fully awake, Yes.*

The openness and contentment it describes is a total fearlessness that is egoless. Because of this earth-shattering breakthrough, one is freed up to focus on the ultimate welfare of others. Consequently, the *Mahayana* lineages call the *Prajnaparamita* the *Mother of all the buddhas.* Fearlessness is that which literally gives birth to a buddha. Tibetan Buddhism even goes so far as to depict the fearless mother of all the buddhas in female form as *Tara.*

In this way, we come to an understanding of the essence of the Buddha's teachings. The core message is not about elaborate philosophical treatises. Nor is it even about depicting the Buddha Nature in one form or another. All this serves a much simpler purpose. They lead us to a basic truth: Through meditation practice, we can awaken and connect with our true nature. By developing an unshakable conviction in our primordial purity, our aim is to *go beyond* all philosophies, all images, all concepts. Then we become completely free to lead others out of their suffering.

Forgiveness

When we do not experience true forgiveness, we remain closed. In order to move on and attain the ultimate state of openness and contentment, we must begin by accepting and letting go. If we have deeply wounded someone, or have been damaged by them, negative karma has been created. The spiritual path will be powerless to completely transform us unless we first engage fully in the preliminary practice of purification.

If possible, forgiveness should take place face to face. However, it must be genuine. Furthermore, true forgiveness must be experienced in one's own heart and mind. It is imperative to practise forgiveness deeply, and repeatedly, in meditation itself. Working with the mind in this way is what sets us free from the bonds of negative past karma. Without processing and purifying it, karma lies like a layer of filthy grime over the surface of the Natural Mind. Our view of our own true nature remains obscured until we purify it.

There are many formal practices of purification you can learn. One very helpful and powerful practice contains the following elements:

Begin by sitting quietly.

Arouse the motivation of wishing to benefit beings.

Meditate mindfully and simply. When you feel ready, proceed...

Imagine your Buddha Nature in the space above your head. Feel the presence.

Generate a heart-felt sense of regret for whatever specific harm you have caused.

Imagine a flow of nectar or light cascading from the embodiment of truth onto you, and through you, purifying and healing all of your blockages and obscurations. Imagine this process for quite some time. This is the main part of the practice. Really consider it is having a profound effect.

Finally, imagine you have accepted, let go of, and purified everything. Having resolved not to do the same thing again, the image of the Buddha Nature dissolves back into you and you sit in openness and contentment, glowing.

Your own well-being radiates out to all beings who also become purified.

Then, all the energy and light that radiated outwards returns and enters you. Ultimately, you yourself dissolve into a single point at your heart centre, which then completely dissolves too.

You finish the session by dropping all methods and simply sit. At the end, it is important to seal the practice by dedicating and sharing the merit with all beings to bring an end to suffering. Keep in mind there can be no spiritual development without a strong foundation of acceptance and letting go. This powerful practice might even become your main daily practice for some time.

The flavour of this practice should never be too heavy or emotional. Sit spaciously while one part of your consciousness focuses on the visualisation and the purification process. The main feeling, especially afterwards, should be a sense of being refreshed and renewed. In post-meditation, we bring into ordinary daily life our earlier pledge to avoid further harmful actions.

Friends

Good companions in life can be such an important factor of our happiness, well-being, and ability to remain on the right path for the benefit of self and others.

Many people who have fallen prey to terminal selfishness, or who have been unable for whatever reason to live happy lives, often lament how things might have been so different if only they'd had different peers influencing them.

Those of us who grew up in troubled places, and often despite difficult social deprivation, wonder just how *we* managed to grow up relatively sane, safe and sensitive while so many of those around us grew bitter and hard. While we say *only for the grace of God,* we also pay tribute to the qualities of the people we mixed with as we grew up. We know how things could very easily have turned out so different.

The friends we have play an enormous role in our continuing psycho-spiritual welfare. We must endeavour, while we are merely buddhas-in-training, to be careful who and what we allow to influence us. When we become enlightened, it won't matter so much. But for *now* it matters a lot.

Ideally our best friends are those who encourage us to live mindfully according to the *Four Immeasurable Qualities* of Love, Compassion, Joy, and Equanimity. Friends like that literally bring out the best in us. The worst kind of associates, by definition, are those who do not bring out our best side. As the saying goes: *With friends like these, who needs enemies?*

Hence the urgent need to exercise what is called the *Wisdom of Discernment* when choosing our companions in life. That's not to say we must immediately drop all of our awful so-called friends and run away to a Buddhist retreat instead. On the contrary. Who is to say we won't meet even worse types in the Buddhist place? Of course, this is just a joke. But the principle is sound. *Wherever* we are, as beginners we must be careful to protect and nurture our minds. If our aspiration is to arouse *Bodhichitta* and realize our true nature for the benefit of others, we have to start where we are now and work on our minds. At the moment, we are quite fragile little flowers. The outcome of our mind training depends precisely on the *environment* of our minds right now, including the company we keep.

Whether we reflect in this way about our ordinary friends or our Dharma friends, we face the same possibility that some of them – or at least some of their behaviour, some of the time – work *against* and sabotage our most precious aspirations. At those times, they are *toxic*. Not only do they not help us to awaken our Buddha Nature and benefit others, they actually make it less and less likely to *ever* happen.

Now we are faced with a mini-dilemma: Do we stay, go, change *them*, or change *ourselves*? One thing is clear ... something has to give in order for progress to be facilitated.

If I stay, nothing changes and no progress can be made. If I go, I will only encounter different people who might equally hold me back. If I try to change the people around me so that *my* life becomes easier, that is selfish and they would never agree anyway [assuming they could be changed at all]. The best and most achievable option available to us, realistically speaking, is to change *ourselves*. And that is what we work towards. That's what the Dharma is. We are opening our hearts and minds to such an extent that we'll be completely *beyond* influence altogether. At that time all negative peer pressure or bad influences will have no sway. But, for now, the question remains. What should we do?

Well, the answer is much the same really. We continue to work on ourselves, and become less susceptible to others. Maybe others will even be so impressed by our progress that *they* will become inspired to work on *themselves* too.

Of course, if someone is having a particularly toxic effect in our lives, we may have to take evasive action to protect ourselves. There comes a time in all our lives when discretion is obviously the better part of valour. In this spirit, without creating too much fuss, perhaps the best thing is to withdraw somewhat from those people. Their negative energy damages *them* too. So perhaps the friendliest thing we could do for them is to cut right through the cycle and nolonger enable them.

On the other hand, we should rejoice whole-heartedly in the love of those friends who are a positive influence in our lives. They cherish us and bring out the best in us. In the same way, the *Sangha* – the community of other practitioners on the same path – can be seen as our best friends. They actually help our true nature to manifest. In their company, and thanks to their many kindnesses and encouragements, we will continue to blossom and grow.

From the *Wisdom* perspective, however, the Buddha Nature itself is the greatest friend of all. It is always there for us, no matter how we ignore or distrust it at times. The Natural Mind supports and guides our every step on the path to full awakening. Ultimately, our true nature is closer to us than any friend or lover ever could be. It is inseparable from us in every way, always watching our back, leading us in the right direction. Could it be that *buddha* and *buddy* have the same Sanskrit root? ... Maybe not. But it brings a knowing smile all the same ... a glowing warmth inside that rests in a much deeper place, far beyond any concept of friend or enemy.

Fun

It is such a joyful thing to be alive!

We must *remember* to bring that sense of joy into everything we do. Spiritual practice, and the entire path, is no exception. We *rejoice* in the life we are choosing to follow. However, many of us take the practice far too seriously. Often, we approach it as something *holy* and so stand the risk of missing the point entirely. It could be we are dulling the en-*light*-ening quality of meditation. If the Buddha Nature truly is the *Natural* Mind, we mustn't forget that awakening it within ourselves should be *the* most natural thing in the world. We don't have to bring a heavy sense of becoming holy, or getting all *spiritual*, to the practice. The teachings say that awakening the Natural Mind is a *revealing*, a stripping away of the many *un*-natural layers that currently obscure it. Meditation is, therefore, revelation ... uncovering what is already there. While we are practising, and in the afterglow that follows, there should be a refreshing, enlivening flavour. We must learn to *lighten up* and experience the light-heartedness, the *fun*, as we blossom into the buddha we were intended to be.

We find this in life too. We take life *so* seriously – especially the difficulties. We lose all sense of the bigger picture. We forget we are buddhas-to-be and *nothing* can harm our true nature. Granted, we must live responsibly and sensibly. But we can do it all with a good-natured air of spaciousness about us. To live like this would certainly help us through the tough times. The good times, also, would bring us a deeper sense of joy.

If we're ever fortunate enough to encounter an enlightened or highly realized being, the one quality about them everyone seems to pick up on straight away is their joyous radiance. The more natural we become, the lighter we are.

In the English language we have a saying, *Laughter is the best medicine*. Maybe there's something to it afterall. Could it be that our physical and psycho-spiritual well-being is improved by having fun and enjoying ourselves? If so, we should really look out for every opportunity to rejoice, laugh and have fun. This is not to say we must become like bored teenagers always looking for something more interesting to do. Neither does it mean we should be reduced to grinning, giggling, guffawing morons. To be a *fun-junky*, whilst being hilarious and probably exhausting, is surely just another form of attachment afterall.

The sense of fun we can bring to and find in the Dharma is much more like a profound, lasting enjoyment... true contentment. It is an openness of spirit, a spaciousness that brings its own natural rewards. The natural high that comes from directly experiencing our true nature is the most powerful and beneficial bliss on the market ... and it's free!

May we, and all beings, reveal the natural, limitless joy within.

May it overflow into our ordinary lives and lift all those around us!

Gentleness

Some awakened beings are quite direct and strict with their students. Ever-watchful, they work tirelessly for the benefit of others in order to cut through their egos. But that is not how *we* should be in life with others. We are not awake and do not yet have the skill required to be trusted in such circumstances. Such masters are rare nowadays anyway. Therefore, to show a good example to their students, and possibly because of whatever monastic vows they have made, most masters of the Buddhadharma manifest as *gentle* guides.

There is a tremendous nobility, and an unassuming grace about a true practitioner. It comes easily to some. For others, it takes a while to calm down enough, and detox the ego-mind sufficiently, for real gentleness to emerge. Perhaps the vast majority of human beings came into this world relatively untroubled and gentle of spirit. But the speedy, often aggressive cultures we live in quickly teach us to be otherwise.

Competing with our fellow human beings is seen as a strength. We are taught that *survival of the fittest* is the natural order of things and the only route to inner peace.

Even as young children we are rapidly sucked into the rat-race. Struggle for survival and the search for success are our real religion. Always drawing our minds outwards, the delusion of a successful daily life relentlessly distracts us from our true nature. If we only knew our real potential, the masters say, things would be so different and so much easier.

To follow in the Buddha's footsteps is to become more and more gentle. We first minimize the negative effect we have on the world and its inhabitants. Then we care more and more for others. His Holiness the Dalai Lama says we must learn to *disarm* our minds if we truly intend to bring peace. This is done, initially, through practice and training. A wonderful opportunity to begin this process can start with *gentle speech*.

This is quite a challenge – one that may occupy us for all of this particular lifetime. The way we speak to eachother contributes enormously to the toxic energy of speed and aggression that prevails in the world. The antidote to speed is mindfulness. And the antidote to aggression is love. In terms of the essence of the Buddha's teachings, *this is it*.

Gentle speech is a commitment to bring *mindfulness* and *love* together in our daily lives in a way that's supremely practical and beneficial. At first, of course, it may bring difficulties. Those around us may wonder what on earth has happened to us. Maybe they'll think we are joking or have gone quite mad. However, they soon realize it's part of our practice. It is an external sign that things are changing for us. The inner transformation that has begun is simply beginning to have outer manifestations.

The more skilled we become at gentle, loving speech, the more open, content, and *disarmed* we will be. We pledge to ourselves *never again* to speak or react harshly. If we fail, we simply acknowledge and confess it, and begin anew in that very same moment. We can resolve never to provoke others or be drawn into careless aggression in the future.

Inner disarmament does not mean we become zombified. We should never lapse into becoming apathetic or disengaged from the world. Gentle speech becomes our way *of* engaging. It is perhaps the first outward fruition of our practice. Our *best side* is manifesting for the benefit of self and others ... plain and simple. Each time we live up to our resolution, we *remember to rejoice*. We become more and more gentle, as time goes by, if we celebrate all our small successes as they occur. Just as we gradually undo old habitual tendencies, we create positive new ones in their place. Remembering to water these seeds joyfully will help gentleness to make strong roots and flourish throughout our mindstream.

When we begin to practise meditation, we notice many important things about our own minds. One of these is that we observe how we *seem* to have a constant flow of thoughts happening. Then as we become more natural, relaxed and aware, we discover that this flow is not so constant. Sometimes there are perceptible breaks in the flow. They may appear as a kind of *gap*. It could be said that the initial purpose of meditation is to experience these natural gaps, then to make them last for longer and longer.

As we begin to integrate into daily life these small realisations – the existence of gaps – we develop a crucially useful skill. We come to *know*, by our own direct experience of the mind, that we can actually have more control over our actions and reactions; we nolonger have to be swept along by external events and the surface energy of our minds. Thanks to the Natural Great Peace and *spaciousness* that come from deep within, we have more choice.

Thanks to the open and content quality of the Natural Mind, we are truly able to shine the light of mindfulness on all the actions of our body, speech and mind. We discover that it really *is* possible to practise gentleness. Because of our strong intention to be so, we become gentle. And whenever others provoke or disturb us unexpectedly, we nolonger have to *react* in the old familiar ways. We have choices. There is a gap, a precious opportunity to bring a different energy to the situation. It is said, rather than *react* we should learn to *respond*. The former suggests one is being swept along by negative habitual patterns. The latter has a quality of self-awareness and control about it. By responding with gentleness we develop the innate, limitless power to transform ourselves and events that occur around us. We can even be a cause for transformation in others, both by becoming an inspirational example for them to follow if they choose and by preventing them from creating more negative karma for themselves.

It takes tremendous courage to over-ride the ego and be gentle instead. There is also an overcoming of primal fear that must take place. When thoughts and emotions arise such as '*What will become of me? Will I just be like some kind of doormat for people to walk all over? Isn't it better for my self-esteem, to be more assertive?*' ... simply do not go there!

Beware, it's a trap! Ego-mind, with all its self-cherishing, is precisely what got us into such a mess in the first place. It's time now – long long overdue – to try a different, more radical approach.

> May a gentle revolution erupt all across the world!
> May the hearts and minds of all become soft and warm!
> May we learn to cherish others more than ourselves,
> And may the timebomb of ego be diffused and disarmed forever!

Guru

The original Sanskrit word for a master is *guru*. Although it has been misused in modern times, properly understood it is the most beautiful of words.

Particularly in Buddhist terms, the guru has already worked fearlessly on their own minds and is now awake. He or she is a living embodiment of the spiritual path's fruition. They are proof that the direction we are taking actually works. As such, we can have full confidence in their ability to guide us along the path to awakening. With an ever-growing sense of faith and devotion, we take refuge in them. Their primary intention is to show us how to end suffering.

The *guru* is no ordinary person, although they may appear to be. They were once like you and me, but they have transcended their egoic limitations and attained enlightenment. They are an inspiration to all who wish to follow in their footsteps. The word *guru*, therefore, has the connotation of someone who is *full of* all good qualities. They are pure and trustworthy.

A guru, or master, has perfected the path to awakening and is not to be confused with someone who is still *on* the path. They are not *instructors* or facilitators. Neither are they self-appointed. Being part of a living wisdom lineage of awakened masters stretching back to the Buddha, our guru's own awakening has been guided and verified by *their* master. We can rest assured we are in safe hands.

It is *essential* when choosing the right master to look around and investigate them as thoroughly as possible. The responsibility for selecting well lies firmly with the student. Of course, one may not be able to test a candidate fully. But try we must, before making an informed decision. All the awakened masters of the past and present have said we must be as thorough as possible. Even charlatans suggest it!

And if we are not comfortable with a particular teacher, their style or their conduct? Quietly and politely MOVE ON. There is no point thinking they will change or turning a blind eye to what's staring you right in the face, what you feel in your gut, just so you can receive these teachings. There will be other teachers.

In this life, we may connect with more than one guru. But we are well-advised not to shop around too much. That may cause further distraction in itself. Buddha clearly instructed us to investigate, test, and chose our teacher carefully. But a decision must be made nevertheless. Once a good connection has been established, it's better for us to deepen that association and get on with the work of transforming our mind. The Buddha himself has passed away, as have all the masters that followed. Therefore, we come to see our own master as the kindest, most compassionate force in our lives.

The *outer teacher* embodies all the wisdom, compassion and realisation of the Buddha. He or she is a mirror. They show us how we are now and what we may become. The master is also full of the teachings themselves, the Dharma. With their guidance, we can't go wrong. There are many other ways we receive the guidance of the Buddhadharma. *Life itself* can teach us so much! We live and learn. We are constantly receiving the Dharma through our life experiences. Its truth is always being verified and confirmed from moment to moment. The natural world, our relationships, seemingly random events, all combine to show us the way.

The *inner guru* is the Natural Mind, our Buddha Nature. It is longing to fully awaken us. This Inner Teacher is the one who'll lead us to enlightenment.

Our true essence, nature, and compassionate energy are continually working away just under the surface of our scattered minds, trying every possible tactic to wake us up to reality. The outer guru penetrates and opens our mind while the inner guru simultaneously breaks free from the layers of delusion and self-cherishing that have obscured it for so long.

Ultimately, there is *no separation* between the outer and inner guru. They are the same. They have never been apart. Their work is the same ... to dispel the darkness that causes the suffering of beings. Once the process of universal awakening begins, its momentum can never be stopped.

Embarking on the spiritual path, with the guru as our *guide*, we become part of something so big and so powerful we cannot fail.

Habitual Tendencies

Unless we have already awakened, whatever we do, think or say during our lives is *out of control* and governed by our habitual tendencies. We continue to be the cause of suffering for ourselves and others, often despite our best efforts to the contrary. Our habits are driven by the ego-mind and have built up strength by being compounded over and over again during countless lifetimes. We react to life with strong attachment and aversion, maybe even indifference, whenever the appropriate buttons are pushed. We've been around the block so many times before that the many negative seeds planted deep by the ego only need the slightest drop of water to flourish. It's like the *real* us has no say whatsoever in how we live our lives – we are just swept along by our ancient habits. It is so exhausting and seemingly hopeless. Perhaps the greatest mercy is most of us don't even realize all this is going on. We are clueless and oblivious – a nice way to be if all you want from life is a *skinny latte* and the latest copy of *Vogue*.

A true practitioner, however, must have a keen sense of curiosity about how the surface mind actually works, and possess the courage to undo its many harmful knots. The main problem, according to the Buddha, is that all our bad habits create negative karma and this only leads to further suffering. Because of negative karma, the great delusion continues lifetime after lifetime and we fail to wake up.

Although we seek lasting happiness and contentment, our pursuit of short-term pleasure leads us further and further from the natural great peace of our true nature. Although we seek an end to suffering for ourselves and others, we run headlong towards the very thing that fills our hearts with fear and closes our minds to the natural beauty of reality.

We cannot experience something wonderful without grasping attachment, and without the dread of losing it. Neither can we experience something awful without paralyzing fear, and the sense of panic that it'll never go away. Both of these over-powering tendencies are ruining our lives.

The beginning of the solution is to recognize that there is a problem. Most of us never even get to this first stage. While we're willing to reject those habitual tendencies which obviously bring us pain, it is not so easy to see how habits that bring pleasure inevitably lead to more pain too. However, when you actually have a life filled with short-term pleasures, you come to realize that when pleasure ends there is a void inside and a longing for its return. Excessive pleasure, over time, actually leads to overload and burn-out. The things that previously brought us pleasure now cease to satisfy. We slowly come to recognize that *nothing* ever could.

Even now in the world's richest nations, our affluent culture is so misleading. We are like beings living in a kind of god-realm. Exhausted from continual pleasure, we are jaded and worn out. Nothing really satisfies us anymore and we have fallen into a stupor of indifference and cynicism. It could be that this is perhaps the most insidious habitual tendency of all. It's a sign of the times that all our selfishness has simply led us to where we just couldn't give a damn anymore.

No better time then to turn our minds towards the solution, which is the Dharma, the path to awakening. Only when we've come to a personal realisation that something is profoundly wrong with our life, can we meaningfully embrace the spiritual path. For this reason, mainstream Buddhism never looks for new converts to join. The masters always say, *'Leave them be. People need to discover the path for themselves. When they have suffered enough, they will come'*.

Healing

Many people first come to the spiritual path only when their life is falling apart. When we are struggling with serious illness, or facing death perhaps, reality often comes into sharp focus – maybe like never before. Sometimes, facing *that* particular truth actually enables us to consider the *ultimate* truth of everything. This is why the Buddha's first teaching was all about the nature of suffering itself. That teaching, *The Four Noble Truths*, paved the way for all the others the Buddha was later to offer.

The Jewel of the Dharma is surely those teachings related to our Buddha Nature. It is in that context that we now contemplate *healing*.

When we are extremely ill, or facing death, we suddenly become pre-occupied with our own fragility and mortality. Perhaps this is because we identify so strongly with the physical body we currently have. Contemplating our mortality in particular sometimes grips us with terror. *'What will become of ME, if I die?'*, we wonder. We don't even concede *'when* I die', so much in denial are we. The Buddha's teachings guide us to directly experience for ourselves the Natural Mind – that which never dies. Only by having such a realisation for ourselves can we truly *know* there is something within that's not affected by illness or death. According to the Buddha's teachings on *Shunyata* [or Emptiness] our true nature – the very essence of what we really are – is *unborn* and therefore *unceasing*. This body we cherish and protect so much is merely a vehicle for the real us, *The Unending Deathless Nature of Mind*.

However, as a vehicle for our Buddha Nature, the body is worthy of our love and care – not because we fear its demise, but because it is the means by which we have manifested, hopefully to awaken for the benefit of beings. This is why we have a duty to look after ourselves, both physically and mentally. Without our health we may not be so beneficial for beings this time around.

Healing is therefore something we approach from a non-egoistic point of view. With this perspective, it is said, anything is possible. Masters and some great practitioners can sometimes heal themselves of disease, but only if their motivation to do so is filled with love and compassion for others.

Different Buddhist lineages have different practice traditions for healing. Most of these practices are done by the person themselves and are augmented by the practice of other practitioners, or maybe even a master, all of whom wish to support our recovery. Some healing practices may be similar to the *Nectar Flow* Practice outlined earlier [see *Forgiveness*].

The Buddha understood the karmic link between past negative actions and present negative circumstances such as illness. Therefore it is with a view to purifying past karma that we embark on any healing practice. Physical recovery takes second place in this context. The most important thing is to fully use and transform this awful condition, which has arisen in the present as the fruition of past negative actions, and rejoice in the fact that it has finally come, has been purified, and is now completely done and over with.

Another aspect of the Dharma related to healing is the connection between the physical and the spiritual. The Buddha taught *'We are what we think'*. Because of our mind, everything manifests accordingly. Therefore the mind itself is also the route to manifesting good health. Spiritual practices for healing the physical body are not to be underestimated. They are done in conjunction with finding the correct medical healthcare. But, they are not merely *New Age* or so-called *complimentary* therapies. Awakening the connection with our Buddha Nature is the healthiest state we could have. It is primarily that connection that will see us through difficult times ahead when eventually, as it must, the body becomes sick and dies. The body can be returned to tip-top physical health many times during this lifetime, but one day it will not be possible.

Now we come to the simple yet profoundly healing practice of *Loving Kindness*. The Buddha himself taught this practice in the *Metta Sutra*.

It is not necessary to go into too much detail here, as this is only the beginning of a much longer practice intended for the well-being of *all* suffering beings. However, the self-healing preliminary section is really appropriate in our context.

May the healing practice of Loving Kindness return you to the best of health.

May you have the wisdom and the courage to face terminal illness and the body's eventual decline.

We simply rest in meditation. Although we are suffering, we are not blocking the experience from occurring. There is no struggle, only acceptance and letting go.

In the sky before us, we imagine a huge ball of healing light – the embodiment of the Universal Buddha Nature that pervades and connects all.

From deep within, we begin to silently repeat some short phrase that has meaning for us in the context of whatever is causing our present suffering. We can be as creative and as specific as we like. The phrases suggested by the Sutra are as follows:

May I be happy
May I be well
May I be safe

We could include whatever seems most powerful and appropriate in our particular case – *May my tumour reduce and disappear, May my illness be totally healed,* or *May I accept this terminal illness.*

The light's source responds lovingly. Rays of cool white healing light flow towards us and penetrate deep into the core of our problem, saturating our entire body with a transformative sense of well-being and good health. As we continue to use our phrases, almost like a silent chant, we really consider that healing is actually taking place. We carry on in this way for as long as possible, not getting distracted by the obvious emotional aspect of our suffering, but peacefully remaining.

Towards the end of the practice, the light slowly merges with us. Afterwards, there is natural, great peace and we simply rest in that state – open and content.

Some masters teach that, at times of inevitable suffering and pain, we should practise *Sending and Receiving* [Tibetan: *Tonglen*]. With the outbreath we send all our love to beings, thus making them happy. With the inbreath we compassionately take away their suffering. It's as though our own unavoidable suffering now has a more profound purpose. It has become useful. As we suffer our pain, we pray that the pain of every other being who is suffering is taken away from them; just like a buddha, we take away their pain and endure it ourselves along with our own. This doesn't mean our suffering becomes all the more excruciating, or that we have some kind of masochistic psycho-drama going on. Neither, for that matter, are we indulging a possible messianic complex.

This practice of healing through compassion is ideally undertaken without ego.

May it benefit all beings.

Heart

The word the Buddha used to describe one's true nature, our inner-most essence, is *Chitta* [in Sanskrit]. In English it is best translated as a compound of two words *Heart-Mind*.

There is a fascinating and inspiring nuance at work here. Ordinarily, Buddhist teachers use the word *Mind* [with a capital M] when referring to the Buddha Nature ... the Nature of Mind, the Natural Mind, Zen Mind, Big Mind, and so on. However, this only describes half the picture. If the truth be told, it's a very male way of speaking about *Chitta*.

A fuller way to describe our true nature must embrace both components, *Heart* and *Mind*. Those masters who have experienced directly the Buddha Nature for themselves have always spoken of its two essential qualities: Compassion and Wisdom. This is why *Chitta* is best translated as *Heart-Mind*.

Heart corresponds to the Compassion aspect. Until we are fully awake, it is experienced superficially as emotional energy. It appears all-important and engrossing, but it merely indicates the presence of something much more profound, pure and beneficial at our core. Similarly, *Mind* corresponds to our Wisdom aspect, traces of which emerge as thoughts on the surface.

World religions and philosophies have always been male-dominated. Buddhism too. Consequently, it has gravitated more towards the sphere of wisdom, thoughts, psycho-philosophy, belief systems and all manner of *isms* – despite the Buddha's admonition to the contrary. Vietnamese Zen Master Thich Nhat Hanh warns us against such pitfalls. In his teachings on the *Precepts*, in the very first line, comes the statement: *I am determined not to be idolatrous about or bound to any doctrine, theory or ideology, even Buddhist ones.*

It is long overdue that we retrieve from the Buddha's teachings the equally important realm of compassion and the heart, in order to maintain a proper balance and avoid all wrong views emerging.

Having said that, we also have to remember that even *Heart-Mind* itself is just a concept. As such it attempts to describe something essentially beyond all description. We must avoid the temptation to simply replace one system possibly preoccupied with thoughts by another system more interested in emotions. True Buddhism is about understanding and balancing both concepts, but ultimately about *going beyond* them.

But understand the concepts we must. Just as the word *Mind* doesn't refer to the brain or even our thoughts, the word *Heart* doesn't refer to the physical organ, or love [whether romantic or friendly], or to any other emotion.

The word *heart* is used because the heart of the enlightened mind is deeply rooted in compassion. If we allow it to awaken, we contain deep within us an overwhelming longing to love all beings and take away their suffering. This is not a fuzzy, glowing kind of love. It is very active and specific, and its strength is beyond any limit. The vision of the heart is vast. It understands the greatest way to alleviate the suffering of beings is to help them realize their true nature. It's not a question of getting sucked into the emotion of all the suffering in the world. We must go much deeper than that if we are to really benefit others. We must also remain stable and impartial. The awakened heart is open to all. It embraces all. Eventually it will even awaken all beings to their true nature.

If it truly is our intention to activate the compassionate heart within, we don't have to look too far for opportunities. We are surrounded by people and situations that will melt our hearts. We only have to switch on the TV news to allow empathy and loving kindness to flow. But the most important thing is not to confuse love and compassion with emotion. Our response needs to be so much more profound than the superficial, impermanent thoughts and emotions that arise when faced with other's suffering. 'Oh, I think that is really terrible. I feel just awful', as a reaction, is just not enough. The more emotional we are the less effective we become in benefitting beings – to say nothing of the constant spectre of eventual burnout and emotional meltdown. We are buddhas-to-be. Our wisdom aspect is driving us in that direction. As our hearts open, the compassion that flows is limitlessly capable of so much more than emotion could ever achieve.

When *we* awaken, we'll have both the Wisdom that knows things as they truly are and the Compassion that cares for beings. We will also have the power to liberate others. This is our birth right, our inheritance, our spiritual destiny. It is the meaning of life. This is why, guided by the Buddha, we follow the ancient path of training the mind and opening the heart.

Sometimes I reflect how since the Buddha's time so many historical periods have come and gone, great civilizations have risen and fallen – regimes, ideologies and isms – all gone. But the *Heart-Mind,* the path to awakening, has endured. It has been tried, tested, and followed to fruition down through all the ages by individuals, just like you and me. From the mountains of northern India, throughout the East, the *way* has flourished and beings have become self-liberated. And now the western and southern hemispheres are the Dharma's new home. Already, many many people have awakened to their true nature. They are in our midst – some obvious, some hidden.

> The heart leaps,
> remembering those awakened ones
> who have gone before,
> and those who shine today.
> The heart rejoices
> in its own compassionate radiance,
> And goes out to beings who,
> suffering in darkness,
> do not realize their true nature.

Hell

The way we perceive and respond to the world around us creates a unique internal landscape deep within our consciousness.

Even though we seem to experience the same phenomena as our family and friends, we do not. The world and events produce very different reactions in different minds. Some people suffer tremendously. Some remain quite numb. Others appear to have a happy, even blissful demeanour. The key to understanding these variants is the mind itself.

The foundation of the Buddha's realisation is that all beings suffer, and the root of that suffering is the mind. Almost regardless of external stimuli, it is the karma of the individual that has created the individual mind's predisposition to suffering, to a greater or lesser extent. In this light we come to understand that, to cut through suffering altogether, we need to transform the mind that perceives it.

Many beings perceive their life as an unrelenting *hell-realm*. Maybe they are living in the dimension spoken of by the traditional teachings on the *Six Realms*. Maybe they are sharing *this* particular realm here with us. Perhaps it's a friend or relative. Perhaps it's you. But we do know that the suffering experienced is the same. Perception is everything.

Even from moment to moment – so long as we are governed by the afflictive emotions – any one of us might perceive an overwhelming sense of hell on earth, however temporary. Similarly with euphoria. There are moments when we are all susceptible to being swept away by the highs as well as the lows. But for most of us, extreme emotion is not *so* extreme. And it usually doesn't last too long. Other people are not so fortunate. They experience unbearably extreme emotional states, often lasting for what appears an age. The lows are bleak indeed and bring with them unimaginable suffering of the mind, so profoundly dark and uncontrollable that suicide may seem the only release. The highs, on the other hand, are so fabulously euphoric that, while it may be enjoyable in the first instance, it inevitably spirals out of control and produces a kind of panic-stricken stop-the-world-I-want-to-get-off suffering all of its own.

Whether we experience emotional highs or lows the emotions bring suffering. Nobody wants suffering yet we imprison ourselves in an emotional quasi-hell-realm every day of our short lives. We chase and cling onto the nice emotions we want, and struggle to push away the ones we don't. We produce our own suffering by limiting our view. We lose our true selves in the superficial. To be free we must penetrate the hellish illusion we have created around us.

According to the masters, all beings are suffering needlessly in so far as we only have to wake up from the nightmare in order to be free. Furthermore, they teach that we human beings, out of all six traditional categories of beings, are best equipped to wake ourselves up.

The teachings also insist that *hell* actually does exist – not just as a state of mind within the human realm. This is undeniably hard for westerners in this particular era to understand – so much so that the idea of *hell* is possibly the least popular and most misunderstood element of Buddhism for some people. Many of us were threatened with the burning fiery furnaces of hell as children [and as adults too for that matter], but now feel we have left all that behind us.

Enlightened beings teach about hell, not just to scare us, but because they have experienced the suffering of beings there. As awakened beings, the masters have the wisdom to see things as they truly are and the compassion to free beings from suffering – *wherever* they may be. This means they *know* beings are suffering helplessly and wish to rescue them. We do not have that insight right now. There are several stories of masters, at the moment of death, requesting their closest students and other masters to pray that they reincarnate in the hell realm in order to liberate beings there.

Even if the majority of beings are not liberated from the hell-realms by compassionate masters, all is not lost. It is the nature of every realm that *things change*. This is a fundamental law of all possible universes and, sooner or later – even though it's perceived as an eternity – the hellish suffering of those poor beings comes to an end. That particular karma will have ripened and burnt out. A new chapter unfolds. We do not need the age-old coping mechanisms of fear or denial in order to begin to understand hell. The best response we could have is compassion.

In a way, it's just so typical of us poor deluded beings to imagine that something couldn't possibly exist simply because we haven't experienced it ourselves yet. Or to imagine that hell could only exist in so far as it might refer to some state of *our* mind. How ironic then that we've all been in hell so many times before, just as we have all been animals or hungry ghosts. The problem is we don't remember those incarnations, largely thanks to the mysterious amnesia that accompanies the seemingly endless cycle of karma-fuelled rebirth.

Just like the emotional spectrum mentioned earlier, there is a spectrum of incarnational realms we might inhabit depending on the winds of karma. Like the intense extremities of bi-polarity, these realms stretch all the way from unbearable, uncontrollable suffering ["hell"] to over-stimulated, euphoric intoxication ["god-realm"].

The difference in Buddhism is that ending up in one realm instead of another is not based on the idea of punishment or reward. It is a question of cause and effect [karma].

This begs the question: *OK, so who created the hell-realm, for example? If there's no God and no Devil in Buddhism, who made hell?*

The answer brings us right to the very core of the Buddha's teachings. Because we are driven by our karma, and our state of mind is everything as we die, we are propelled towards our next rebirth. The Heart-Mind literally *creates* the realm it will next inhabit. Then it becomes stuck there temporarily.

It is not merely a matter of a human being suffering so much they *imagine* they are in hell. Rather it is the continuing saga of a being whose mind creates the realm they inhabit.

We are what we think.
With our thoughts we make the world.

Humour

Far beyond the emotional extremes of tragedy and comedy lies an all-embracing approach to life that has stood the test of time. This wisdom approach is a kind of *humour*, a *light-heartedness* that is in no way governed by the afflictive emotions. Rather, it's a lightness of heart that dwells spaciously in the present moment. It is a supremely useful way of being *in* the world without being *of* it. It affords the practitioner a special predisposition towards removing the suffering of beings without getting trapped or bogged down by such suffering themselves.

Someone who actually possesses this kind of spacious, open-hearted humour is always more concerned with the ultimate welfare of others rather than their own. In fact, they often appear to have no self-regard whatsoever. This is not to say if we really wish to benefit others we *mustn't* care for ourselves. But if we do want to focus on and help others, we must begin by nolonger taking ourselves so seriously.

We need to develop a gentle sense of humour towards ourselves especially towards our ego-tendency, which is the root of all the world's problems. Taking oneself too seriously is *the* hallmark of an over-active ego.

When we help others we often do so with a tell-tale, egoic sense of reverence and saintliness rather than just getting on with it and doing whatever we can as one human being for another. Similarly, when we sit in meditation, the correct outer and inner posture is regularly accompanied by a feeling we are doing something extraordinarily holy or that we are partaking in some kind of esoteric, mystical rite. Really ... the ego is quite the joker. Unfortunately, though, the joke is on *us*. Even on the spiritual path we take ourselves so seriously it proves a sizeable obstacle to our making any progress at all.

Maintaining, in life, a relaxed half-smile on our face achieves two very important objectives. Externally, we become more pleasant and reassuring to others – especially those we wish to benefit. Inwardly, we become far less serious – everything has a natural lightness about it and there's a much greater chance of disarming the ego.

Similarly, sitting like this awakens a truly innate ability to rejoice in the positive. We become tremendously uplifted by the wholesome and virtuous actions of others, and we allow an internal spring of well-being and good humour to constantly bubble up within us.

Perhaps the funniest thing of all these days is we actually have to *remind* ourselves, even in the absence of any particular difficulties, to rejoice and be *happy*. But that is how it appears.

We have to rediscover the essential truth that our natural state is one of well-being and light.

Identity

As long as we remain deluded and un-enlightened there is a gravely wrong perception destroying our lives.

Fuelled by ego-grasping, we mistakenly divide the world we perceive into subject and object. We falsely assume there is an *I* that perceives, which is totally separate from all the various phenomena that are perceived.

For the time being we are unwilling or unable to simply rest in the open, empty essence of our Buddha Nature. Maybe the fluidity of its indefinable nature makes us feel uncomfortable and all at sea. We create an identity crisis based on the unreal duality of self and other. So we begin to construct a fake identity for ourselves to help us feel more secure – a misguided game that may well consume us all our life.

A skilled master can help us cut right through this dangerous delusion by constantly redirecting our attention to the nature of the *I* that seems to perceive phenomena. This process is backed up by intensive meditations that help us reveal our true nature.

The identity we create for ourselves might appear to help us feel more secure in ourselves: this is who I am, this is how I feel about such and such, this is my self-made personality, these are my habitual patterns... But in reality it just helps us put up a front to the world that says 'I know who I am'. Of course this couldn't be further from the truth and is even more dangerous than ridiculous. It heaps layer upon layer of delusion, which continues to prevent us from glimpsing our Buddha Nature.

Beings who have awakened still have personalities, opinions, emotions. But they perceive them in an entirely different way. They have a vast, fresh perspective on the nature of reality that enables them to see their own identity for the fleeting fabrication it truly is. Awakened beings have simply ceased to take themselves so seriously.

When we are introduced to our true nature by a master, or when we experience it ourselves through meditation, we come to *know* first-hand exactly what lies beneath the veneer of identity. In fact we glimpse the Natural Mind in such a profound way we realize how it is insufficient, futile and ultimately misleading to describe our true selves in *any* way. We come to understand how superficial the veneer really is.

The primordial purity and spontaneous presence of our Buddha Nature cannot be bound by or reduced to any concept whatsoever. It is completely liberated, by its very nature, and therefore we are free beyond limit to express the essence of our true nature by means of wisdom and compassion for the benefit of beings. The more we persist in identifying ourselves by personality, opinion, pattern, gender, or even by our humanity, the more we compound the delusion that prevents us and those around us from realising our true nature. We just create more suffering.

The Buddha taught about how the mind works. He discovered we create reality with our minds. So it follows, if we believe we're deluded and suffering that is what we will be. Conversely, if we realize we are perfect buddhas already, living this life for the benefit of others, then *that* will manifest.

Some advanced Buddhist practices actually use the power of the mind to imagine and create reality in this way.

There are contemplations to help us examine and deconstruct our identity. When we ask the question '*Who am I?*', or make the statement '*This is who I am*', we must go deeper and contemplate just *who* is saying this. When we look deeply, we acknowledge it is not the physical body or the brain that's saying these words. Similarly we enquire *who* is saying 'This is my identity'. The identity is the object of the statement, and *I* am the subject saying it. So now the question becomes 'who is this *I* ?' We take the process of enquiry deeper and deeper. Eventually we discover there is nothing we can point to and definitively say '*This* is me'.

Our experience of enquiring along these lines soon produces the realization "I am made ONLY of non-me elements." This is very profound yet simple. We have begun to touch the open, empty essence of the self. Furthermore, we have begun to understand the paradox of all reality:

Things appear, yet they are empty by nature... Although things are inherently empty, they appear anyway.

Take water, for example. I can drink it or wash in it, yet there is nothing called water that actually exists – only hydrogen and oxygen coming together temporarily to produce it. So water is empty of inherent existence yet it does appear; water is made only of non-water elements, yet there it is... water.

According to the Buddha, *we* are like that. There is nothing we can point to and say 'This is me', and yet we appear anyway – we *do* exist, in a way. In the famous *Heart Sutra*, this paradox – The Union of Appearance and Emptiness – is encapsulated in the following way:

Form is emptiness.
Emptiness also is form.

Applying this wisdom to the question of our own identity, we come to realize the truth of some interesting paradoxes in relation to who *we* are.

Although I am in essence a buddha, I am also a human being.

Although I have manifested in a human form, with a personal identity, I contain within me the potential to benefit beings as a buddha would.

Therefore, may I train and transform my Self, through practice and strong aspirations.

May I awaken to my full potential, in this very lifetime.

And may the Buddha Nature flow like an endless stream of wisdom and compassion, for the benefit of all beings.

Ignorance

Whoever said *'Ignorance is bliss'* was a fool.

Ignorance is not bliss. According to the Buddha, the definition of *ignorance* is someone who does not see the nature of phenomena as they really are, and that brings suffering.

Perhaps a better word for this ignorant state is *delusion*. Not only does an ignorant person misunderstand the true nature of reality, they make all sorts of wrong assumptions and life decisions out of ignorance – assumptions that bring more mental pain. Ignorance is the opposite of enlightenment.

When we speak about enlightenment or ignorance, the words we use are extremely important. Often *enlightenment* is also translated as *omniscience*, and that can create further confusion too. We end up thinking to be awakened means to *know* everything. We think enlightenment is a kind of *intellectual* understanding. Surely, awakening doesn't mean one becomes an insufferable know-all. The world is already full of them ... and look where that has gotten us. I doubt if the Buddha's awakening meant he *knew* everything there is to know. It is not a case of gaining access to a cosmic library of information. The Buddha probably didn't know the cure for cancer or even how to get from India to China. But what he *did* discover was so much more important. When the Buddha broke through that veil of deluded ignorance for once and for all, his awakening was so profound that he realized the empty, inter-connected nature of *everything*. Even more than that, he realized the true nature of all beings is capable of permanently rising above all mental suffering and, through love and compassion, capable of leading other beings to that same state. *This* is the true path to bliss. Ignorance only leads to more suffering.

Because of ignorance we are seemingly trapped in a vicious cycle of suffering. We don't want to suffer, we only want to be happy. But almost everything we do is so misguided we end up creating yet more suffering for ourselves and others. What we need is a precious opportunity to temporarily break through that cycle – a gap through which we may see the natural great peace and understanding that lies within each and every one of us already. The Buddha's teachings, especially those on the Mind and meditation, offer us that breakthrough opportunity.

We learn we *can* end our own suffering by unlocking those limitlessly good qualities within. But we must be patient and work with the mind in a systematic and diligent way. If we give up on ourselves we lose everything. All our hard work amounts to nothing and we end up being of little benefit to ourselves or others.

Ignorance, or delusion, has many layers to it. We can't afford to lose heart just because we break through one layer only to find another one beneath it. We must persist in our efforts to cut through all of them.

One traditional example of the multi-layered nature of delusion is encapsulated in this story.

A man goes into a darkened room. After a while his eyes adjust slightly but he spies something coiled round itself in the far corner. He doesn't know what it is. That is the first layer of his ignorance. We do not see things as they are. In fact, it is a rope but he doesn't see it clearly.

Almost instantly he leaps to the conclusion it must be a snake. This assumption compounds his ignorance – another layer.

Now his imagination runs riot. The man begins to actually *see* a snake, now he has decided that's what it is. Nothing could convince him otherwise at this point. By his own ignorance, he has created yet another layer of misperception.

Furthermore, he hates snakes. He's always dreaded coming face to face with one. And yet here it is, a *snake* ... lurking in a dark corner, poised to attack. The man totally freaks out and runs away screaming. He is out of control having tapped into a previously laid-down layer of delusion: a profound fear of snakes. He has created so much suffering for himself.

If he were to run for help, he might conceivably create suffering for others too. *They* will probably also see the snake when they approach the rope in the darkened corner. Layer after layer, the delusion goes on.

Mass hysteria ensues. Villagers are running for weapons. They have the monster surrounded. The bravest among them launches a frenzied attack with a machete. In his mind he has committed the barbaric but necessary act of hacking the snake to pieces. In the darkness he imagines he is splattered from head to toe with entrails and blood. Karmically, he *has* killed in a way – at least in his own mind – and that causes a tremendous sense of regret … more suffering. The whole village shares in the bad karma.

Although this is only a story, the message is clear. How much better it would be to see things as they are from the beginning. The awakening brought by the Buddha's teachings enables us to shine the light of awareness on all phenomena.

> May the Clear Light of our true nature shine brightly.
> May the darkness of ignorance and delusion
> be dispelled forever!
> May all beings come to see themselves and all phenomena
> as they truly are.

Illusion

We are living in the midst of a great illusion. Nothing is as it appears to be.

Like a mirage, or a rainbow, everything manifests yet it is empty of self. In our desperate attempt to make solid, dependable sense of reality we have created a dream-world for ourselves. Our ignorance blinds us so profoundly that sadly we have misunderstood *everything*.

Beginning with ourselves – the centre of the illusory universe – we falsely believe we actually exist as a separate entity. Even when we embark on the spiritual path we misinterpret the teachings to imply that we have a separate, individual, personal portion of Buddha Nature that somehow has taken root and now dwells inside our body. According to the Buddha, this is not the case; there is no separation whatsoever between ourselves and others, and there is no such thing as 'our' Buddha Nature separate from the Buddha Nature which pervades all.

Unfortunately, our gross misunderstanding has temporarily condemned us to dwell at the surface level of our minds, a realm where thoughts and emotions hold sway and we are constantly at their mercy. I *think* I exist, I *feel* separate, therefore I experience all the suffering that accompanies superficiality.

How frequently have we expended precious time and energy becoming attached to something or someone, or fearfully protecting ourselves, only to later discover the painfully temporary nature of phenomena? If only we could dispel illusion and embrace the true nature of reality. Then we'd find peace and happiness.

Our self-centredness creates a mountain of suffering. When we realize how fake and unnecessary the ego truly is, the great illusion will gradually dissolve altogether. We must come to learn, by bitter-sweet experience, that *we* are the root of all the problems in the world. By changing how *I* am, everything else changes. This can only happen precisely *because* there is no separation between self and other.

A famous Buddhist text [The Seven Points of Mind Training] implores us to '*Be a child of illusion*'. Even though we do not yet experience the true nature of reality, for now we can at least recognize that there *is* an illusion all around us. Our awakening will dawn when that illusion has completely gone. We'll cease to think we exist in our own right – we will cease to focus on ourselves altogether. Knowing there is no separation whatsoever between internal and external, we will live mindfully and for the benefit of others. We must continually remind ourselves ... *I* must continually remind myself ... all the self-induced crises of the world will continue to envelope us and blacken our horizon unless and until *I* awaken. The answer lies within.

Breathing in: I come back to the present moment.
Breathing out: I begin to see the great illusion all around.

Breathing in: The Buddha Nature arises.
Breathing out: There is no separation.

Image

For millennia, certain images have been used to help the meditative state to naturally arise.

Traditionally, an image is one of three commonly used methods: an object [including images], mantra, and observing the natural flow of the breath itself.

All these skillful means assist tremendously in creating the perfect conditions for the Natural Mind to become more manifest. In fact any one of the three, if properly used, can lead us directly to our true nature. Depending on how deeply we use these methods we may find different results. On one level they might serve as a refreshing way to gently return to the present moment. On a deeper level they may become an inspiration that calms the mind and opens the heart. However, on the most profound level, one of these tools could clear aeons of obscuration and reveal the Nature of Mind itself.

Similarly, we might look at an image – even a nice picture of something in nature – to set the stage, as it were, for meditation to occur. Or we could use a spiritual painting or statue of the Buddha, or a photo of an awakened master, to inspire the correct environment of our mind. But perhaps the best use of such an image, if we can relate to it in this way, is to see the image as a *mirror*.

The greatest wish of a buddha, or enlightened being, is to help *us* to wake up too. Therefore, it is entirely appropriate that their image should be used to that very end. We must never use such an image in an idolatrous manner, however. In fact the Buddha himself specifically forbade images of himself from being made, for that very reason, lest they be worshipped by misguided disciples.

We do not fall into that trap when we view the image as a *mirror*. In this mirror we see a reflection of our true selves – what *we* have the potential to be.

Therefore, when we gently gaze at the face or demeanour of the Buddha [or a master] we can be deeply transformed. Like an electric shock, the experience can jolt our own Buddha Nature out of its slumber. It might literally blow your mind ... at least the cobwebs.

On a simple level, looking at a beautiful painting of the Buddha teaches us *how* to sit in meditation. All the elements of the correct physical posture are there. We just have to learn and imitate the posture. Like *baby-buddhas*, we play act at being fully fledged.

But when we want to awaken the Mind of the Buddha within, we rest our eyes gently on the gaze of the Buddha or on the eyes of the master in the photograph who is smiling at us, reminding us of what *we* too can be. One can almost hear them quietly calling us, whispering lovingly across the oceans of space and time:

'*Wake up... Wake up, Sweetheart... Fully awaken for the ultimate benefit of self and others... If we can do it, so can you*'.

Imagination

The Buddha realized the incredible power of the mind to change and create reality.

Science has confirmed we only use a small part of the brain's capacity and Psychology is beginning to say something similar about human consciousness. Spiritual traditions have always held this fundamental principle. Buddhist masters in particular know, by experience, just how powerful the mind is and how little of it we are using at the moment.

But, because the ground and foundation of the mind is the all-pervasive Buddha Nature, the potential of the human mind is considered to be limitless. Most of us just don't realize we hold the power to transform ourselves to the extent that we can also change the world around us.

There is a bond that links all phenomena to oneself. This arises form the Buddha Nature that is inherently all-pervasive. Therefore, put simply, whatever we do with our body, speech or mind affects the entire inter-dependent web.

This may well be the most earth-shattering news we will ever hear!

What *I* do, say or think changes *everything*. When *I* meditate, the whole universe is affected.

Because of this power to affect both internal and external change, surely one of the Buddha's most favourite words is *IMAGINE*.

We all have amazing powers of imagination. Good or bad, we can imagine almost anything. Our imaginations have been misused lifetime after lifetime to create a mindstream polluted by seemingly endless patterns – all based on what I imagine I want or don't want. But the Buddha taught we can turn all that around completely. We must use the mind's own limitless capacity for imagination to bring about a new reality: '*With our thoughts we make the world*'.

Often called *Visualisation*, the Buddha taught practices using the imagination, practices that culminate in an alternate reality in which we ourselves are fully awakened. We are Buddha and we emanate love and compassion to all. The suffering of beings is removed completely. The world becomes heaven on earth. All beings themselves eventually become fully awakened buddhas. This is the cosmic vision of the Buddha, one that is gradually becoming reality thanks to the ongoing practice and activities of all those who have awakened eversince.

These imagination practices, sometimes known as the *Vajrayana*, only appeal to certain people. They are not everyone's cup of tea. Consequently they only flourished in a few places outside India. Furthermore, when Buddhism in India had declined and become extinct, these visualisation practices were preserved mainly in the remote, high Himalayan laboratory of Tibet – the Land of Snows.

Tibet is said to have preserved the Vajrayana because the tradition remained *alive* there. For over a thousand years, Tibet remained so isolated and closed to foreign influences that the power of the imagination practices was put to the test and developed by generations of enlightened masters and their students. Monastics, householders and yak-herders alike – special people who practised intensively in long-term retreats. Ordinary people like you and me who quietly got on with integrating a daily practice with daily life – in Tibet all sorts of practitioners realized their true nature using these practices and became living buddhas for the benefit of beings.

It is said the Buddha taught different methods of revealing one's Buddha Nature to different kinds of people and that accounts for the various categories of practice that exist within Buddhism today. Some say there were 64,000 Dharmas taught by the Buddha to ensure that every type of mind has the opportunity of self-liberation. *Visualisation* practice is one of them.

Curiously, at the time of the Buddha and practically eversince *in Asia* the Imagination Practices were not at all commonly taught or used. They were almost secret and were only offered to certain suitable candidates. However, these days *in the West*, ancient Buddhist practices involving *imagination* have caught on like wild fire.

Perhaps this is because the time is right for these methods to be widely used. Or maybe it's because Westerners have become so open to visual/imaginary stimuli such as computer games, TV and the internet.

Whether we approach these beautiful practices as *visualisation* or *imagination* depends on how strong our visual sense is. But there can be pitfalls on this path, like any other.

Some people have an extremely active visual sense; they only have to think something and there it is in front of them ... they actually see it. Good advice for them might be to tone it down a little. There's no need to get too *new-agey* or all *Star Trekky* with the practice. Beware the ego that accompanies us on the path. It could be that all those lights and visions we are seeing are just the product of an overactive ego saying: '*Hey, look at me. See what I can do. Special, huh?*' Sometimes we get so '*out there*', all caught up in our own projections, when we should be more '*in here*' transforming our minds *in* the practice.

A second pitfall when following the path of these practices is *trying your hardest to SEE something ... anything* ... but nothing comes! I myself, and my enormous ego, fall into this particular category. I had such incredible teachers and a really long period of stabilizing my *sitting meditation* practice before ever trying visualisation. Of course I was an expert in knowing what to do but when I tried to visualize not much happened ... *nada, niente* ... not even a microscopic buddha or a single light! I was devastated, and so surprised.

Afterall, me and my legendary ego had such a highly developed appreciation of the visual arts. [Once, in Paris, I was so moved by those huge paintings by Monet of *Water Lillies* that the museum's security guards had to take me outside ... they said my over-the-top weeping was scaring the other tourists!] But when I tried to visualize during meditation practice, in my mind's eye, a simple shaft of light ... nothing?! When I asked my masters and other Dharma teachers what I should *do* about my new-found 'spiritual handicap', they offered my the following helpful advice.

When visualising, *the* most important thing is not so much to *see* something but to *feel*. If you are visualising the Buddha in front of you or above your head, then *feel* that presence. Allow yourself to really feel their *presence* ... close to you, surrounding you. Come to feel that presence so authentically that it is inseparable from you. Maybe, in time, your experience will become more visual.

One thing that could block visualisation from happening might be you are trying too hard. Maybe that's pure enthusiasm, or maybe it's fear of failure. Moreover, the problem might be a simple misunderstanding of terms. The word *visualize* might be the problem. The moment I was advised to use the word *imagine* instead, everything changed very quickly for me and soon I was imagining – with the greatest of ease – lights and buddhas and pure lands. Even with your eyes open, you can come to imagine them around you clear as day!

Inertia

According to dictionary definitions *inertia* is one of the scientific laws of the universe, which states that *everything that exists resists change.*

Whether we are talking about an object or a being, whether stationary or moving, we all have a deep-rooted tendency to want to keep things the way they are. Inertia might also imply laziness or a perceived inability or unwillingness to actually get moving. It is a feeling of being *stuck*, albeit because of one's own negative attitude. Nobody likes change, yet change happens regardless. Every atom, every form of energy, is in a continual state of flux. Our biggest problem in life, and especially on the spiritual path, is we long for stability to such an extent that we fear even the very change that can bring that ultimate stability about.

Instead of trying in vain to avoid change, the Buddha teaches the wisdom of embracing it, letting go of our tragic resistance to change, and even learning to surf on its waves so that we actually use the energy of change to awaken the mind and open the heart.

The four great changes in a person's life are birth, old age, sickness and death. Just observe how we struggle against these momentous events, often creating even more suffering for ourselves into the bargain. But *all* change has the potential to bring suffering or awakening depending on how we respond. If we allow ourselves to have a habitual knee-jerk reaction like: '*No! I don't want it. Take it away*', then pain will surely follow. If we accept that change is natural, even changes we don't want or can't handle right now, then our life will go much more smoothly.

The principle of inertia manifests within beings as the *ego* and, as we know, it accompanies us on the spiritual path. Everything goes very well at first. The Dharma is more of a hobby than anything. The ego says: 'Dharma is *nice*, let's go a little further. What's the harm in meditating? It's *relaxing*'. But as soon as changes come, the first aspect of ourselves to feel the subtle shift is the ego. More often than not all hell breaks loose. The nature of the ego-tendency is to control and resist change at all costs. Before long we are having irrational thoughts about the process of meditation. It's all rubbish! Buddhism's a cult. The teacher's a manipulative fraud. I'm being brainwashed. Get me out of here!

Even though we may actually feel quite well in ourselves, and find the meditation refreshingly transformative, there is something in us that fears and resists it. This can manifest as a variety of interesting obstacles to our meditation practice. Some people become so hyper they can't sit. Others become so bored they can't bear it a second longer. There are even people who fall asleep the moment they hear the bell ring at the start of the meditation session. However, this is all natural and even *that* will change too. Take courage in the incontrovertible fact that *everything* changes – even the fear of change. Look deeply at it and we observe how it weakens or strengthens from moment to moment. If we accept the fear of change and let it go – give it space – it's power quickly subsides. The naturally greater part of our mind, the Buddha Nature, has seen through ego and will continue to help us little by little to find the lasting peace of mind we seek.

Sogyal Rinpoche reminds his students, when we are really filthy and stand under a hot shower we mustn't jump back out screaming in horror when we see the dirt coming off our bodies. It's far better to stay in and allow the dirt to get washed off and disappear down the plug-hole.

Meditation is a bit like this. Before we reach states of profound calm, it is natural to experience the mind's more turbulent baggage as it starts to get dislodged and stirred up a little. Once the state of inertia begins to shift, and we are moved in perhaps new ways, we need to let go – not hold tight. This is where the courage and conviction that comes from personal experience is so helpful. The more we get used to accepting change, the less uncomfortable it makes us.

Again, Sogyal Rinpoche reassures us. There is something that is *changeless*. The Buddha Nature that lies within each and every being is unchanging. Because this Natural Mind is unborn and unceasing it is not bound by the laws of change. Therefore, the more we make contact with it the better. We will not fear change so much because we have developed a strong conviction based on experience that the greater part of who we truly are – the *real* us – remains unchanged. We are perfectly OK on the ultimate level, regardless of what happens on the relative level.

Breathing in: I am accepting and open
Breathing out: I am letting go

Breathing in: I am perfectly OK
Breathing out: I am open and content

Breathing in: There is movement on the surface
Breathing out: There is stillness within.

Integration

"In a sense everything is dreamlike and illusory, but even so, humorously you go on doing things. For example, if you are walking, without unnecessary solemnity or self-consciousness, lightheartedly walk toward the open space of truth. When you sit, be the stronghold of truth. As you eat, feed your negativities and illusions into the belly of emptiness, dissolving them into all-pervading space. And when you go to the toilet, consider all your obscurations and blockages are being cleansed and washed away." [Dudjom Rinpoche]

The most important thing about the spiritual path is not so much to meditate, but to bring the fruits of that mind training into everyday life.

Although the fruition of the most profound practice is to experience the open, illusory nature of reality, we must continue to live and act in the world. Therefore, we should always be on the look-out for opportunities to be in the world in a way that benefits beings. If Buddhism is supposed to be all about action, then, we must ask ourselves exactly what awakened qualities our activities should embody.

The awakened qualities that arise as a result of our practice are said to be threefold. First, we develop a peaceful, non-harming, mindful way of life. Second, having tamed the mind, we open our hearts to others through loving kindness and compassion for all, without bias. Thirdly, we bring about a profound transformation that embraces the total purification of our past karma and our present perception of reality. In summary, we may essentialize all this into three awakened qualities that we must integrate into our daily lives: Peace, Compassion and Transformation.

Ever-mindful of the present moment, a true practitioner uses the events and circumstances of their life to practise peace, compassion and transformation for the benefit of self and others. In this spirit a simple breath, or a smile, can become an embodiment of peace that radiates to others. All our dealings with others are seen as a rare chance to show love and compassion. Even taking a shower, or going to the bathroom, are transformed into the most complete purification. Similarly, we can radically alter our perception. Difficulties and obstacles are perceived as precious life teachings – opportunities to put the dharma into practice. Seen in this way, we remain open to everything that occurs around and within us. Life itself becomes the manifestation of the Buddha's wisdom and compassion.

All that we do with our body, speech and mind really matters and we mustn't waste a single moment through mindless living. What we do, what we eat, how we speak, what we say, how our mind perceives – it all really matters.

By extension we must become a positive inspiration to others.

Few people ever lived a virtuous life because they were told how to live, or even because they imitated someone else. Real change comes from within. As we develop virtue in our lives, others may be inspired to look deeply at themselves too.

As we integrate the practice into our lives, we check our own progress as we go. We observe ourselves becoming more peaceful, compassionate and transformed. When we observe positive changes within, we rejoice without ego and keep going. When we observe a lack of progress, we do not beat ourselves up over it. Rather, we can acknowledge our short-comings, perhaps learn a valuable lesson, resolve to avoid making the same mistake again, and move on.

When it comes to integrating the practice we can be as creative as possible. Anything we can do to help ourselves remember our true nature will pay dividends continually. Anything that helps us remember the true nature of others will swiftly bear fruit.

Integrating everyday events and circumstances with the practice is the path to awakening. We have to remember, whether we are in a meditation session or on the street, our mind is the practice – not the technique we use. Since the mind is always with us, we can transform everything into practice. Therefore a wise person chooses to skillfully bring all circumstances onto the path. Why waste a single opportunity for enlightenment? Perceived purely, our next meal, poo or shower might just create the perfect conditions that lead to our liberation!

A famous Zen story reports a student asking his master how exactly to integrate meditation into daily life. The teacher says: "By eating and sleeping, of course."

The bemused student interjects: "But that's what everyone does! That's not meditation!"

The master replies: "Ah. But when I eat, I eat. When I sleep, I sleep."

The path of integration, therefore, is to carry out ordinary life with the mindfulness, awareness and spaciousness that comes from meditation.

Intention

It is said that *every* action of an awakened being has a positive outcome. Their whole lives, and all the activities of body, speech and mind, are directed consciously for the ultimate benefit of others. Because of the universal law of *karma* – cause and effect – the Buddha taught that the most crucial element of every action is the *intention* behind it.

For the time being, we ourselves are only baby *buddhas-to-be*. We are still at the all-important stage of training our minds and opening our hearts. Therefore, we must also train our mind to have pure intentions.

In formal meditation practice sessions, we *begin* by arousing the *Motivation of Bodhichitta*. We consciously *intend* that our practice will liberate both ourselves and others from all suffering. We pray from the bottom of our hearts that all beings will fully awaken their true nature.

This may take the form of a prayer:

By the power and the truth of this practice,
May all beings enjoy happiness and the causes of happiness,
Be free from suffering and the causes of suffering.

May they never be separated from the Great Happiness, devoid of suffering.

And may they dwell in the Great Equanimity that is free from attachment and aversion.

During our meditation, we hold that Bodhichitta Intention lightly in our hearts while spaciously maintaining the view of openness towards all phenomena.

After the meditation period, we *share* with all beings whatever merit has been derived from the power and the truth of our practice. We *dedicate* our practice for their awakening.

Together, these are called the *Three Noble Principles*. We generate a pure intention before, during and after our meditation. This is also known as *Good in the Beginning, Good in the Middle and Good in the End*. Our Bodhichitta, View and Dedication comprise the spiritual technology through which we most effectively benefit ourselves and others.

The next stage is to *integrate* the Three Noble Principles into *whatever* we do, 'post-meditation'. Because of our developing powers of awareness, thanks to the meditative training, we bring the same vast intention into all facets of our lives. His Holiness the Dalai Lama teaches that, when the heart-felt intention of Bodhichitta is combined with vast View of spaciousness, sparks will fly and our whole life is utterly transformed. We can move mountains.

We have already spent so many lifetimes thinking mainly of ourselves and those we cherish. And just look where all that small-mindedness has gotten us. Our heart-minds are consumed with hope and fear, almost to the total exclusion of everything else. If only we could broaden our horizons, and radically redirect our intention outwards. The whole universe and all the beings sharing it with us could benefit immeasurably.

When I focus mainly on myself, the best possible outcome is so limited – and I may still not be entirely content. When my intention is to liberate all beings from suffering, the outcome is profoundly more useful. This is known as the *logic of compassion.*

Once our own experience begins to verify the Buddha's teaching – *With our mind we create the world* – we come to understand that whatever intention we hold in our consciousness will become reality.

Thus, awakening to buddhahood and liberating beings *is* truly possible.

Inter-Being

One of the fundamental principles the Buddha discovered about the true nature of reality is the *interconnectedness* of all phenomena. It is essential that our path to spiritual awakening involves investigating for ourselves and verifying experientially the truth of this principle.

There are many ways to begin this investigation but they all lead to the same revelation. We may begin by analysing any given object. We may even use ourselves as the focus of our contemplation.

One master, Thich Nhat Hanh, encourages us to look deeply at a sheet of paper. We quickly realize that the paper is devoid of *self*.

Paper is a compound of so many other things that have combined to help it manifest: the labour of many people, trees, weather systems, natural elements that in turn find their own origins elsewhere in the universe. Therefore, we conclude that paper is *empty of self*, 'Shunyata'.

Its present manifestation is said to be *open*. Paper is comprised entirely of non-paper elements. It appears by virtue of the universal principle of *dependent co-arising*. Because of this, we infer that – like everything else – paper both appears and is empty. It is constantly subject to change, and it exists *in relation* to all other phenomena.

Thich Nhat Hanh has coined the term *'Inter-Being'* to point to this truth.

When I investigate myself in the same fashion I come to the same realisation.

I *inter-am* in relation to everything else.

We are not just connected in some vague way. We *depend* on all that is. There is a delicate balance that nurtures and sustains things the way they are. Disturb that balance and we run the risk of destroying everything. The web of inter-dependent appearance is always changing and shifting. Beings and phenomena arise and expire all the time. We are one of them.

But the one thing that links everything together is the Buddha Nature. All phenomena, including beings, are in fact never separated from eachother. We share the same essence.

It is not even a question of me having *my* portion of Buddha Nature separate form yours, or the dog's or the tree's. We have the *same* essence ... just different appearances.

When I become attached to the appearance called *me*, and think of it as a separate entity, I create suffering. When I rest in my essential nature, inter-being with all phenomena, I create harmony and well-being for myself and others.

To connect with the Buddha Nature in this way is the purpose of meditation.

Once inter-being is realized, we have a moral imperative. Now our consciousness has opened up to the consequences of our activity. We must decide for ourselves the actual details of how to be in the world.

The Buddha offered helpful general guidelines: Avoid all harm, Do only good, Train your mind.

May all beings inter-be in harmony.
May we awaken to our common essence.

Intoxication

The Buddha showed us how our deluded, superficial mind is shrouded in ignorance. We have no idea of our true nature – and that produces profound suffering.

The surface level of the mind is where our consciousness dwells most of the time. We are preoccupied with our transient moods, thoughts and emotions. Most of these are more chemical in nature, being produced largely by our brain. The more seriously and solid we mistakenly perceive them to be, the more deluded we become. Layer upon layer, we become more and more separated from the vast Natural Mind that lies within, just under the seemingly impenetrable surface.

Day after day, lifetime after lifetime – the Buddha says – we obscure our true nature with ever more layers of ignorance, habit and denial. Identifying so strongly with our largely chemically-produced thoughts and emotions leads us further from the truth of who we truly are. Could it really be that we are *already* perfect and complete deep down inside? Could it really be that simple?

The Buddha's challenge to us all is to systematically look deep within and see for ourselves.

The superficial thoughts and emotions seem so important to us at the time. Some are stronger than others. But, overall, they can be reduced to three basic categories:
1. Elation is good for me, I must pursue more.
2. Mental discomfort is unacceptable, I must avoid it.
3. Boredom is the result of feeling neither of the above. I must do more, be more, get more, in order to be fully human.

Given the closed small-mindedness of all three assertions, there is only one conclusion to draw – our expectations of life are simultaneously unrealistic and paradoxically limited. We do not seek enough from life and what we do seek is misguidedly self-oriented.

The temporarily imbalanced chemical makeup of our brain triggers instincts that try to redress that balance with other chemicals. Experimentation and trial-and-error steer us in the direction of an enormous variety of chemical sources. We are surrounded by a whole spectrum of them – foodstuffs, legal intoxicants of all types, medical drugs, alcohol, and illegal drugs. We develop attachments and cravings for certain stimuli because they, albeit temporarily, deliver what we want: [1] elation, [2] anaesthetic against mental discomfort, and [3] something to fill the boredom void.

Our strong habitual tendency has turned this into the hobby *par excellence* of a lifetime. We not only become intoxicated by the toxic chemical, we also become intoxicated by the craving, the search, and the ritual itself.

The problem with intoxication is that it *adds* to our essential problem rather than alleviate it.

Intoxication creates even more layers of murkiness to obscure our view of the Natural Mind within. It feeds our negative habitual tendencies, not least of which is the desire for self-satisfaction. Sooner or later we will have to unravel this extra layer of mess too.

If we are ever to break through to the perfect clarity of our true nature, we will have to achieve tremendous clarity of mind, sobriety and uncomplicated *simplicity*.

The sluggish, toxic, chemical goo produced by what we put into our bodies [and minds] virtually precludes awakening from ever happening. These toxins actually retard our minds and create an *extra* barrier, on top of all the others, between us and external reality.

Quelle surprise! That is precisely what we wanted them to do in the first place.

But the real tragedy is if we decide to follow the spiritual path, then we have to cut through this layer of toxic numbness too – and it won't be easy. Better not to have become addicted or anaesthetized in the first place.

The Buddha taught that, to become fully awakened, all our perceptions and sense gates must be completely opened and purified. For this reason, he advised against intoxicants [see: *Precepts*].

Just ask any ex-smoker or ex-drinker about the initially dizzying, almost overwhelming effects of quitting.

Clarifying the senses and experiencing the rawness of reality more directly, especially after so long, can be quite shocking at first. It is hard to believe we were not experiencing things properly before, and that *this* is how most people actually perceive things.

But we all have to start where we are.

No matter how difficult our struggle with toxins, the more we connect with our true nature through meditation the easier it is to abandon all superficiality.

Scratch the surface of every being and you reveal the already perfect buddha within.

Joy

The path to awakening is easier if it is a joyful one. We feel better about ourselves and are more energized by the transformation that is taking place within us. There is no benefit in focusing on our struggles or obstacles. By just getting on with life and watering the seeds of joy we swiftly become more beneficial to ourselves and others.

The teachings constantly remind us about the limitlessly positive qualities that characterize the Natural Mind. As well as Wisdom and Compassion, there is also immeasurable Bliss that bubbles away regardless of life's circumstances.

While we remain insufficiently connected to our true nature, and don't fully experience this blissful energy, we must however continue to move in that direction. Our practice should be conducted in a light-hearted, joyful way. We must never become too somber or bogged down by it. Meditation is meant to be a tremendous source of healing and a refreshingly joyful experience – one that energizes and opens us up.

We must rediscover the habit of *rejoicing* at the positive both in and around us. This will uplift our heart-minds and lead us in the direction of perceiving all phenomena purely. Anything positive we perceive internally, we rejoice. Anything we perceive externally, we rejoice. We especially rejoice in the apparently external if we feel we have nothing joyful in our own lives.

The majesty of nature, or the joy experienced by someone else, can become a limitless source of joy for *us*. We only have to shift our perspective and, seeing little or no separation between internal and external, rejoice in whatever good we see. You might say we learn to surf the waves of joy that we find around us. To this end, we may focus on a beautiful flower or a starling washing rapturously in the bird-bath in our garden. Rejoicing also in the positive energy of naturally joyful people around us is wonderful – even total strangers, why not?!

It is said in the teachings that the most joy we can generate vicariously like this, is when we rejoice in the spiritual liberation and enlightened activity of others – especially the masters. The positive energy generated by their awakening and their virtuous actions is a palpable, limitless source of joy for us too. We only have to recognize and tap into it – surf it – and *use* that energy to help us wake up too. We may even aspire and pledge to become equally beneficial for beings. Seen in this way, rejoicing waters the seeds of our own enlightenment and is a very skillful means of speeding up the process.

Some practitioners *do* experience inner bliss through their meditation. They have profound clarity and know the pure joy that emanates from within. They fully experience its transformative power and instinctively overflow and share it with others. They are *bodhisattvas* dedicated to liberating and awakening others.

Wherever we discover joy, we must have the presence of mind to recognize and rejoice in it. And ultimately we must make best use of it for the benefit of self and others.

We must maintain the stability of the big picture.

Why settle for becoming a stand-up comedian who merely helps others to laugh, when we could manifest as a living buddha and remove the suffering of all beings forever?

Just Be

The essential teaching of the Buddha, and all the masters, is to simply be in the moment.

When there is happiness and well-being, rejoice and just be present. When there is suffering, don't allow yourself to get swept away. Just be with it and know deep in your heart-mind that *ultimately* everything is still OK. Even these difficulties cannot destroy your true nature, your essential goodness, the natural great peace that lies within.

The practice of meditation, over time, helps us to establish a vast, open stability. It reconnects us to the Natural Mind so that we eventually become unshakable in circumstances good or bad, in situations high or low. By training to sit in meditation like a mountain, unperturbed by the clouds and weather systems that pass around us, we come to embody a kind of equanimity and spaciousness in our daily lives.

We learn to just be in such a deep way that the core of our very being nourishes and sustains us in every situation. If we can just be like this, we are free to abandon self-cherishing completely. And our liberation will empower us to live for the benefit of others.

When you think about it, to *just be* is actually the best we can do in life. The past has gone. The future has not yet arisen. The only time is *now*. To just be in the present moment is our only option, whether or not we accept that invitation.

When we focus only on ourselves we create struggle. When we care for others – especially if we bring them towards their own spiritual awakening – we are fulfilling the highest purpose of this precious human life.

If the insight of the Buddha is correct, and every being simply wants to be happy and not suffer, then the only time for that happiness and well-being to occur is in the present moment. The true source of that happiness is not to be found in the past or in the future. Neither is it found externally.

Meditation is said to be the greatest gift we can give to ourselves. It turns the mind inwards so it becomes stable and content, and it opens the heart outwards so we can share our inner peace and love with others.

Two simple words, *just be*, hold the key that unlocks all the wisdom and compassion of the Buddha's awakening. And by following that path, we can do the same.

> Dwelling in the present moment, I will just be,
> pure and simple.
> No longer prey to life's chaotic moods, I will just be,
> open and content.
> Awakening to all the selfless possibilities of each moment as it passes,
> I will just be, my true self, living for the benefit of others,
> In the here and now.

Kaliyuga

We tend to think of time in terms of moments, weeks or years. Sadly, we are even so small-minded that perceiving the particular lifetime we are now living as something of cosmic significance is somewhat misguided. We are currently so wrapped up in ourselves and our individual story. For true awakening to unfold, we must have a much broader view of space and time.

The ancient civilisations of India, such as Hinduism and later Buddhism, enshrined in the very fabric of daily life and their philosophical paradigms an overview of time that stretches out to embrace vast, enormous periods that literally make the conceptual mind boggle.

Just as we acknowledge the changing nature of all things, even from moment to moment, the ancients understood that time and space must be the same. There are highs and lows, discernable patterns and cycles, underlying everything. When applied to the present universe we now inhabit, these patterns are expressed in terms of extremely long periods of time. Time is measured in cycles of millions and billions of years.

These cycles express the periods of creation and destruction the universe goes through. There are peaks and troughs, and interim periods of increase and decline.

Buddhism applies this cosmic time-frame not only in terms of the development or decline of the material universe, but also to the *spiritual awakening* of beings. Thus, when we take the broadest possible view of time, we come to understand there have been certain periods when the spiritual life of beings has been more or less evolved, more or less nourishing and beneficial to others.

So, when Buddhism speaks – albeit on very rare occasions – about these spiritual peaks and troughs, it adopts the ancient Hindu terms for the four distinct periods that bring the cycle of renewal and awakening to completion. Similar to the four seasons we use to measure one year, the ancient time cycle takes us through four cosmic periods of time. They bring the universe, and the consciousness of beings, all the way from a so-called *Golden Age* era right through successive epoques during which this state undergoes inevitable decline. The last of these four eras before the golden age is once again restored is known as *Kaliyuga* – the *Dark Age* – and that is said to characterize the period in which *we* now live.

In terms of spirituality, *our* global civilisation is understood as a low ebb. Relatively speaking, there are said to be far fewer awakened beings [buddhas] living now. Therefore, the spiritual teachings that could otherwise bring awakening to beings are taught less and less. And when they are taught, these precious teachings are less likely to be understood or put into practice. We are far too intellectual nowadays. We want to understand a thing with our very clever brain, judge its apparent usefulness to us personally, and move on. Worse still, if we *do* actually make a heart connection with the teachings and have some degree of realisation, we are so lazy and jaded that we don't put it into practice.

The *Kaliyuga* is indeed a spiritual wasteland, a dark age, in which the lack of spiritually awakened beings becomes manifest in the actual space they inhabit. The era is identified by the abundance of warfare, famine and disease. The age of extreme wealth and poverty heaps mental suffering upon suffering, for rich *and* poor alike. The genuine, authentic *dharma* that brings peace, compassion, and transformation to the world has been rendered indistinguishable from pseudo-spirituality, 'new age' religion, and cults of the ego. Spiritually awakening meditation is easily confused with relaxation and stress-busting techniques. Bookshops stock mediocre *self*-help books alongside genuine spiritual books whose sole aim is to bring about the ultimate benefit of *all* beings, enlightenment.

While we are killing ourselves, eachother, and the planet that gives us life, all is not entirely lost however. When you look at the problem of living in a dark age from a more positive angle you soon realize that there is no better time to be alive and working with these teachings! The suffering of others is so widespread that, as awakening spiritual beings ourselves, *our* lives can have great purpose and meaning as we bring benefit and release to beings.

The more awake *we* become, our ego-tendency diminishes and the more helpful our life will be to others.

If the ancient teachings are true, the Kaliyuga is nowhere near its lowest point yet and things will get much much worse before they get better. We could try to live in a supposedly secure fortress and lock the world out completely. We could live on tins of baked beans and bottled water eventually to commit suicide out of despair or boredom. But where's the joy in that?

No. The only sane and heartfelt response to living successive lifetimes in this dark age is to *live joyfully* for the ultimate benefit of others.

Another positive side to all this is that the Dark Age can be **suddenly** brought to an end and the next *Golden Age* can flourish. But only if the people want it badly enough. We get so caught up in the bad times that we don't realize the catalyst for change is in our hands all along. To realize this is not simply about cheerfully looking on the bright side of life. The truth of change, and our power to affect change, must not be underestimated. Things change. Often very quickly.

Sometimes things can even change from one extreme to the other ... from total darkness to light, in an instant.

Karma

In life, there is a dangerous and naïve tendency to dismiss that which we do not yet understand. Maybe something is too alien to our own culture for us to take it seriously. Or we may have over-simplified the richness and many nuances of the thing we are trying to understand, reducing it to a point where it nolonger makes any real sense to us.

This is certainly the case with *Karma*, which in its truest sense means *Action*.

In our own inimitable, new-age way, we've reduced the word to a level where *karma* could mean literally anything or not much at all. Mistakenly using *karma* to mean something like *positive energy*, you even hear people say things like 'I have to rearrange all the furniture in my apartment to improve the karma in there', or 'I am wearing these particular colours because they bring me good karma'. Not only are we making an error when we misunderstand karma, we are missing a golden opportunity to find profound happiness and an end to suffering in this very moment, both for ourselves and others.

Another common misunderstanding – largely based in ancient Hinduism – is to imagine *karma* simply means that our present life circumstances are the result of our past actions. In this way it might be said, quite heartlessly and matter-of-fact, such and such a person is a deformed beggar living on the streets of Delhi because they must have done something terrible in their previous life. This is rubbish! *Nothing* is ever that simple. For all we know that very person could in fact be an emanation of the Buddha, manifesting for the benefit of all who pass by so our hearts open and we may be driven to practise the path of loving compassion.

Granted, a proper understanding of karma does involve the unavoidable yet very complex universal laws of *cause and effect* and *interdependent co-emergence*. But we must recognize that as long as we remain un-enlightened, unaware of the reality of phenomena as they truly are, we cannot claim to really know at all just *why* anything appears to manifest this way or that.

The wisdom approach of the spiritual path always brings us back to two essential things: the present moment, and *how* I experience it.

What we do – especially how we *are* – right NOW is what creates the future. It also literally *creates* the Present; how the Mind perceives the here and now actually *changes* it!

Therefore, we have control over the present according to the current *activity* [karma] of our mindstream.

It all depends on which aspect of the mind we manifest most strongly. Superficial Mind creates the malaise of

Samsara. Buddha Mind creates the loving compassion and bliss of Nirvana.

Ringu Tulku Rinpoche offers crucial pointers in this regard. *Karma*, he says, tells us more about how I *am* in the here and now than about my past. It best describes what I am like in the present moment, how I am in relation to phenomena around me – how I operate in the world.

If we find we're stable and content, loving and compassionate, present and aware, then we are doing very well indeed. But if we observe that the opposite appears to be the case, the most important thing to remember about karma is that *karma can be changed.*

It could be said the whole point of personal development through spiritual practice is to purify our karma and so reveal a new way of being in the world. Due to aeons of negative, ego-centred patterns and habitual tendencies it's no surprise really we have a lot of work to do if we truly want to undo all that and bring about the ultimate benefit for self and others. The practice enables us to start where we are and realize this goal little by little – one precious moment at a time.

The vital importance of training the mind to dwell in the present moment cannot be overstated. Our karmic habits are usually so strong that they propel our consciousness, often at great speed, towards the future – like a powerful wind blowing a leaf through the air. Only by being more grounded and deeply rooted in the here and the now can we hope to regain any element of control.

Only in the present moment can we find the stability and spacious peace of mind required to transform our karma. Only in the present moment can we awaken our true nature.

The past gave rise to the present, but it has gone. The future will be created by the present, but it has not yet arisen. Why, then, waste our precious time dwelling on faded memories or selfish hopes and fears?

The present – right here, right now – is all we truly have. But Oh, what a gift it is! The present moment is all we really *need* to completely transform ourselves for the benefit of all.

Our present *Action* ['Karma'] creates the present and the future.

> May the present moment grant me the opportunity to end all my harmfulness.
> May I cultivate a wealth of virtuous activity.
> May the here and now provide the perfect training ground for my heart and mind to ripen and flourish.

Let It Be

Perhaps my earliest memory of hearing pop music is the sound of *The Beatles* record *Let It Be*.

The sound of it was wafting through the locked door of our tiny front sitting room in my parents' house. I think one of my brothers and my sister were in there with some cool friends, trying to enjoy their latest purchase. They let the single play on the small stereo over and over. But, being young and childish, I was kept out of the picture.

This made me mad as hell and I wanted to have my way all the more. Although I was still only a very young boy at that time, I now recognize that the seeds of dogged selfishness had already been well-watered deep within me. I kicked that old door and screamed through the keyhole for an eternity.

They turned up the music to drown me out, *Whisper words of wisdom, Let it be...*

If I had only listened to those lyrics, and understood them fully, most of my problems in life – and the many problems I have caused others – could have been avoided. Eventually I was allowed to go into the room to listen to the record with them, just one time. The room was filled with smoke and the curtains were pulled to keep out the afternoon sun. I was welcomed into their gang momentarily.

Sitting on the sofa, wedged in between two big guys I'd never seen before, the record continued to play and we joined in with all the naivety and determination of youth, *There will be an answer, Let it be...*

If I had simply learned to *let things be* all that time ago, life could've been so much easier. But now I'm middle-aged, I am only beginning to put this wisdom into practice in my life. It sounds easier said than done. But it's a skill that requires mindful perseverance and enthusiastic diligence and will reap inconceivable rewards in the end.

More specifically, the ancient wisdom of the Buddha encourages us to respond to all that life brings us in the same way. In situations good or bad, in circumstances high or low, we must learn to have stability and openness. We must learn to surf life's waves rather than get swept away by them. Experience and practice shows us the benefits of *accepting* things rather than fighting against them; the wisdom of *letting things be* and *letting go* of our attachment and aversion to phenomena. Far from becoming a passive doormat, we adopt a much healthier approach to life. Our new-found equanimity allows us the space to accept and rejoice in the positive gifts each moment brings and the stability to better cope with the hard times.

Of course, there are many negative life circumstances that can and should be changed. Poverty, famine, war, injustice, these must all be healed and averted wherever possible. But even then, in order to be truly effective healers of the world, our best first response must be to accept the scale of the given situation and let go of our aversion to it. Only then does the world become a less daunting place. By lovingly preparing our own minds in this way, everything begins to appear far more fluid and workable than before. We have a much better chance of avoiding personal burn-out and, who knows, we may actually change the world.

The so-called *external* world, and the apparently *internal* realm of the mind are guided by the same essential principles. Allowing things to settle down completely brings a greater sense of happiness and a possible end to suffering. *Accept and let it be* is just the kind of mantra needed to spaciously bring the mind home and allow us the freedom to rest in the vast present moment. Once we arrive in such a place, *everything* is possible.

Dzogchen, the most profound teachings of the Tibetan Buddhist lineage, uses simple metaphors to unlock the most profound truth. In one such teaching, the master uses the image of a glass of muddy water. If you keep stirring it up, it will never settle. But if you just *let it be*, the glass of muddy water will eventually settle to perfect clarity. The true nature of the mind, it is said, is also like this.

It's the natural order of things that the continuum of awareness we call *'me'* carries with it karmic debris. It is also not unusual that this pure awareness, which we call the *Natural Mind*, radiates and manifests many things including superficial thoughts and emotions. They are the fizz of our own mind. Nothing to worry about or get rid of. Just a natural by-product of our own innate luminosity. But, like those particles of mud in the glass of water, all the apparent debris and fizz of the mind are *not* the mind itself. They are only a miniscule part of it. When we allow them to settle completely, our true nature – the Natural Mind itself, the awakened Buddha Mind – is revealed in all its glorious clarity and radiant simplicity. The Mind, you might say, becomes *self-liberated*, free from all its former entanglements and drama. The natural outcome of this personal awakening is a heartfelt longing and limitless ability to bring about the ultimate awakening of *all* beings.

It is not necessary to do something *to* the mind to make it settle and clarify.

All we have to do is simply *let it be*.

Love

Buddhahood is completely realized by first awakening deep within us *The Four Immeasurables*: Love, Compassion, Rejoicing and Equanimity.

Developing equanimity is an ongoing process; equipoise and openness are established through sitting meditation, it is the ground of everything else.

But when we speak about openness, we must remember it's the *heart* as well as the mind that is opening. Out of inner peace flows limitless love. The practice of *Metta* [Loving Kindness], therefore, is an essential training for unlocking the Buddha Nature within.

First we must love *ourselves*, completely. Not in an egocentric way. But in a way that thoroughly heals us and releases the innate capacity that lies dormant in our core being for loving others limitlessly and without bias. So much of the love we have right now depends on our mood and the circumstances we find ourselves in. The love of a buddha is impartial and unconditional. It comes from a much deeper place. It has no limit.

So, the formal practice of *Metta* begins with a session of developing Loving Kindness for oneself. This self-love is nourishing and pure. It prevents burn-out. It never runs out and is not conditional at all. Pure love flows effortlessly from the source of all, the Buddha Nature itself. If we didn't direct this healing love towards ourselves first, we would not be liberated to love fearlessly and our love for others would not be as effective.

After a period of sitting meditation,
Imagine the source of pure healing love, the Buddha Nature, manifests in the sky before you.
It should appear in a very inspiring way, perhaps taking the form of the Buddha, your Master, a saint – anything that represents for you the embodiment of Truth and Love. It may simply appear as a huge ball of pure healing light. With all your heart, request its help.
Now imagine its Limitless Love flowing into your heart in the form of pure white healing light as you recite the phrases: 'May I be happy. May I be well. May I be safe'.
Continue in this way until you actually consider yourself becoming more and more loved and healed, and for as long as this part of the session allows.
Eventually imagine, and really feel, the **source** *of that pure love enter you and merge with your own heart-mind, indivisible. Truly consider that you yourself now embody limitless, pure love. Remain in this non-conceptual state for some time.*

The next stage of the Metta Practice develops the ability to love others completely, and without bias or burning out. This process unfolds as you begin by sending love to people you know and love. Gradually you broaden your focus wider and wider until you have included people you hardly know at all, total strangers, even those you formerly hated or who hated and harmed you, then other human beings in all manner of circumstances around the world ... eventually including *all* beings wherever they may exist ... broader and broader ... to infinity.

Spending as long as possible on each category of being, sending love without attachment or aversion, we move from one phase of the practice to the next, without any bias whatsoever, and repeating the phrases *'May you be happy. May you be well. May you be safe'*. We really imagine the pure, white, healing light that we embody streaming out to those beings. And we really consider it is having an enormous benefit. We develop the conviction that our love truly *is* limitless.

Once the formal practice session is over, we gently drop the method completely and simply rest in the peace of our own sitting meditation. Finally, pray that the great benefit of practising in this way is shared with all beings and that they attain full awakening.

That is the practice of Loving Kindness.

In post-meditation, we integrate the practice into our daily lives by actively loving others... or sending Love and Light to others, random strangers, on the bus, in the street, on the TV... Without integrated, transformative action, there can be no genuine spiritual awakening.

Unlocking this immeasurable energy that benefits others, we build on the beautiful warmth of friendship, being in love with someone, or cherishing our loved ones. We completely transform that instinct altogether. We learn to love all beings as a buddha loves.

Magic

Something quite unique to the teachings of the Buddha is recognizing the illusory nature of the reality we experience in and around us.

This is not just heavy duty philosophical speculation. Buddha said this is how things really are. And we can experience the illusory nature, and penetrate it, for ourselves the more awakened we become through practice. The implication is we can and will identify the great illusion and have glimpses of the true reality that lies beyond it through our meditation practice, *right from the beginning* of our spiritual path.

Reflecting in this way, I remember how the Buddha insisted that his realisations are something people must experience for themselves, and not just a *credo* to believe in simply because the Lord Buddha has said this or that is true. So, we must come to see the spiritual path to awakening as *our* personal process – a sequence of revelatory experiences and realisations that *we ourselves* discover. Although we have the masters and our community of practitioners with us on the path, we are essentially going it alone and that is the only way it *can* be.

Since we are glimpsing directly for ourselves the true nature of reality, right from the start of the meditative process, we must never underestimate the capacity of the beginner's mind. In fact, in his simple yet most profound dharma book, *Zen Mind Beginner's Mind*, Suzuki Roshi advises us to maintain that *beginner's mind* approach throughout the entire path. A beginner's mind is considered to have a childlike purity that is always *open* and *ready* for realisation to occur.

An *expert's mind*, on the other hand, is quite closed and unwilling to consider anything that doesn't fit in with his preconceived theory. The illusory nature of reality remains an academic proposition to them at best. They may or may not agree with it and they are unlikely to directly experience it for themselves.

Beginner's Mind does not guarantee breakthroughs but vastly increases the likelihood. I am particularly aware of the importance of this beginner's open-mindedness because it is so crucial for any understanding or direct experience of this milestone on the path to full awakening.

The illusory nature of reality – *magic*, if you will – is such an important realisation. More than that, it is the way we must come to experience our reality.

The Buddha himself said:

Know all things to be like this -A mirage, a cloud castle, a dream, an apparition, without essence, but with qualities that can be seen.

Know all things to be like this -As the moon in a bright sky in some clear lake reflected,though to that lake the moon has never moved.

Know all things to be like this -As an echo that derives from music, sounds, and weeping, yet in that echo is no melody.

Know all things to be like this -As a magician makes illusionsof horses, oxen, carts and other things.

Nothing is as it appears.

It's vital to realize that the illusion we come to experience and penetrate, both within and around us, has *not* been created by external forces. Neither God nor the Devil, nor Big Brother nor some alien race is responsible. It is not even like that wonderful movie *The Matrix*.

We have created the magical illusion for ourselves.

While we remain deluded, suffering beings, we create a reality that is full of delusion and struggle. When we are enlightened, our Mind will experience true reality.

For the time-being, we must fully embrace the fact that our mind is creating the reality we perceive. We can even go further than that. The path can also involve being courageous enough to experiment a little with this magical quality of the mind to create its own reality. Through our practice, and even in our daily lives, we can be quite playful and daring by altering our perception ... No, I'm *not* tired. I am full of life ... I *refuse* to be drawn into an argument with you. I simply *won't go there* with you this time ... This Tokyo subway is not teeming with people and chaos. I am moving mindfully with grace and poise through an ocean of beings that I love ... This terrible weather is not getting me down. I am fresh and renewed.

Give it a try. Be a magician of the mind. The results might astound you!

Many Buddhist traditions actually utilize the magical ability of the mind to accelerate progress on the path. In formal sessions of meditation, students practise the many ways of *Visualisation.*

In the beginning we train in the skills of imagining ourselves becoming happy, well, and safe. Other practices enable us to experience healing and letting go of negative past karma. Whatever the practice, we fully enter into it. We begin to experience that well-being and healing *are* actually happening. We alter our reality from within. More intermediate visualisations evoke the Buddha Nature itself. We develop a very real and experiential personal awareness of it. Glimpse after glimpse, our confidence in the Natural Mind and all its power to purify perception grows.

Whatever visualisation practice we do, it always arises out of pure sitting meditation. It always culminates in us radiating immeasurable love and compassion to all beings, having first awakened those precious qualities in ourselves.

Higher visualisations involve allowing the Buddha Nature to arise within us such that we strongly experience our own Buddha-like presence ... we *are* baby buddhas-to-be, afterall. At first we are quite playful with it. Never over-serious or solemn. We are simply trying on the clothes, as it were, to experience how it might be. Later on, we truly begin to experience our own awakened heart-mind, and all its pure presence can bring to the world, as the *real* reality behind all the illusion. In such practices, we actually experience our environment in a completely pure way, and ourselves as awakened beings emanating transformative love and compassion to all beings.

The truth that lies behind these practices is so powerful. It is not just a question of *imaging* all this happening. It actually *is*.

The web of inter-dependent co-emergence that links all reality is a scientific reality. Whatever we do in our practice or in daily life *is* actually having an effect.

Whenever we break through the illusion of how things appear to be, we are deeply connected to reality. We have the power to change things and bring ultimate benefit to all beings. It's miraculous. Magic.

In this very lifetime, we are truly *the* most extraordinary of travellers and magicians. We are peacocks who can eat poison and transform it into the best of nourishing food. Alchemists turning cheap metal into gold.

Manic-Depression

Manic-depression, which is called bi-polarity these days, is a very challenging but interesting phenomenon to contemplate. It is a condition that affects the surface mind, the toxic realm of thoughts and emotions. Our true nature, the Buddha Mind, is not at all affected by chemistry.

The people who live with this condition have an instability in the chemical make up of their brains. They experience cycles of extreme elation and hyper-activity followed by the opposite, extremely black periods of inertia and profoundly grave depression.

The medical world cannot really offer an explanation as to why it occurs. Doctors just prescribe very strong drugs that numb the emotions and subdue the person to the extent that they complain of not feeling much at all. While many individuals are relieved to be nolonger prone to such extreme states of mind, more still secretly go off their medication altogether because they say they'd prefer to have the extreme highs – despite the horrendous lows – rather than feel nothing at all.

The periods described as mania are characterised by intense euphoria [however temporary], often accompanied by an overpowering drive to do things with their time and to grasp after objects of desire. It's said that many sufferers claim they cannot control themselves, even when they desperately want to stop. Total exhaustion usually follows.

Depression, on the other hand, is described as an overwhelming spiral downwards. Sufferers say it is like drifting way way down into a deep, black pit where the senses are totally burnt out and cannot kick-start their motors. The very thought of any further stimulation is repulsive. How awful this must be, having to push the world away and block it out, living in a dull state of dread and fear. No wonder so many people say they feel so completely hopeless and alone that it would be a great blessing for them to fall asleep and never wake up again. Unfortunately, an alarming number of people take their own lives.

Manic-depression is so heart-breaking. Yet it is also fascinating to consider from a Dharma point of view.

When we take away the extremes, the tendencies are exactly the same as the ones we *all* live with every day as human beings and which, according to the Buddha's teachings, cause us so much suffering.

We want so desperately to be happy that we grasp after whatever we think will help [attachment]. Likewise, we do not want to suffer so we run away from whatever we think will cause it [aversion]. We don't realize what we really are [ignorance]. We prefer the façade of ego to the great unknown, so we don't explore the matter any further. However, we don't just want to greet life with total indifference either. So the whole mess is exhausting.

Similarly, nobody relishes the prospect of experiencing *nothingness*. Maybe this is another reason we avoid the spiritual path? Our ego-centric self-grasping longs so much for existence that it keeps us from the dharma. We fear so much a path that leads to *spaciousness* and *openness* in case that might just be a clever way of tricking us into going headlong over some kind of cliff into the *VOID*. Of course, nothing could be further from the truth. However, thousands of people kill themselves every day because of the fearsome abyss they feel inside – and they are people who do *not* suffer bi-polarity at all!

Whether we consider ourselves to be quite ordinary, a bit on the fragile side, or full-on manic-depressive, the same essential truth applies. *Everybody* just wants to be happy and not suffer, but we don't realize how to achieve it. The reason is always the same, no matter who or what we are.

It's all too painfully obvious ... We have *no clue whatsoever* who the hell we are.

Materialism

A few years ago, I met a young boy in an internet café in a very small town in Northern India.

We chatted for a while and I could see he was really fascinated by me – this alien creature from a world he had only seen online. He couldn't take his eyes off me. Suddenly, and for no apparent reason, the boy's eyes welled up and tears began to flow down his cheeks. Some time passed, me asking what the matter was and him trying to save face and brush the whole episode aside. He finally blurted out that he was so upset because he had just realized, quite profoundly and perhaps for the first time, that he'd *never* own an authentic pair of *Nike* trainers, and he would never see the West for himself.

I was stunned. I also knew it would take me some time to digest what was really going on for this little guy. In the days and weeks that followed, as I moved further and further North into the foothills of the Himalaya, it dawned on me that we are *all* just like that boy. We assume that new things and fresh experiences will bring us happiness and relieve our suffering. And so our senses send out their searching, grasping tentacles far and wide, deep into an ocean of hope and fear. We don't realize that we already possess a wish-fulfilling jewel right here, right now. The answer to our prayers has been with us all along. The Buddha Nature, from beginningless time, is always there.

The more I reflected on that young boy, the more astonished I became. He was not hungry or dirty. He went to school and had a part-time job. He lived with his parents and family in a modest house on the edge of that little town. And yet he truly believed his life was so awful that trendy footwear or living in the West would be his salvation.

My contemplation went deeper. The crux of the issue wasn't whether actually possessing a cool pair of Nike eases or creates suffering. It is the *grasping* onto things that causes all the problems.

Neither Western nor Eastern kids nowadays appreciate what they already have. They are not content. It is common, it seems, to all human beings to crave and grasp after something *else* to fill the void. We create our own suffering.

Materialism is making our suffering even worse.

It's not so much that we *have* stuff that creates problems. Our suffering is amplified by our grasping tendency... *I want this. I don't want to lose that. This will make me happy. That will bring me inner peace.*

Chogyam Trungpa Rinpoche went so far as to point out that many of us travel the path of Dharma with exactly the *same* grasping for happiness and peace. He called this wrong view *Spiritual Materialism.*

We see the Dharma as a commodity just like any other: yoga, pilates, fashion, cocaine... Maybe we think to ourselves, *I'll just give this Buddhism thing a go. It might be fun. It might help me sleep better.*

Then, maybe when we've had some good initial results, we unleash our grasping in all its glory. Our attachment and aversion really kicks in as we throw ourselves head-first into the whole Dharma *thing*. The spiritual path itself quickly becomes an *object of desire*. We can't stop thinking about it. There is so much about it that fascinates and soothes us. It's like finding a new lover. We can't keep our hands off them. We are drunk on them. We can't get enough of them. Then something happens that we don't like. We are wounded. Eventually we develop a love-hate relationship with them. Who knows, we may even walk away from them altogether and never see them again. Or we may turn a blind eye to the things that don't exactly suit our purposes ... we might go so far as to see other spiritual paths on the side!

Sometimes, for many of us, we find we've approached the Dharma in completely the wrong way. Although we grasp after it for the feel-good factor, we find it does not really sustain our interest.

The true spiritual practitioner is like an athlete training for the Olympics. We should not give up when the going gets tough. If we allow ourselves to remain at the level of thoughts and emotions we are merely scratching the surface. What we think or feel about the dharma shouldn't really matter. We must go much deeper for real awakening to occur. American sports coaches say there is no gain without pain. Maybe they're right afterall.

The ego accompanies us on the path. It just *loves* all the exotic, esoteric stuff that Buddhism appears to be at first.

But later on, it rebels against the practice once the ego discovers it is gradually losing its grip. For *that* is the whole point of the Dharma ... the death of the ego tendency.

As long as we are in the honeymoon phase where we *like* Buddhism, because it is *nice*, we are missing the whole point and are doomed to failure. Just like going to the gym, when we feel the *burn* but keep on working those muscles regardless, the path of awakening is a matter of hard work and perseverance.

If I perceive the Dharma, with all its Eastern promise and paraphernalia, as something I can possess – something that will make me feel good – I have sadly fallen into the age-old trap of all *materialistic* pursuits.

Far better to have bought a red BMW or found a new lover half my age!

Meditation

The most effective way to learn to meditate in the Buddhist tradition is from an awakened Master. The liberating power and blessing of their presence is palpable and really ignites something in us that cuts right through to the essence of the practice.

Sometimes it's possible to find a Dharma centre near where you live that is under the direction and care of such a master. There, you will find an inspiring and nurturing support system for your practice. Under the experienced guidance of qualified meditation instructors – usually long-term students and disciples of the master – the community of meditators [the *Sangha*] provides the best environment for progress to flourish.

However, the value of physically being with your master as you learn to practise is incalculable. Awakened beings exude the heart-essence of meditation. The quality of their presence and their incredible awareness can actually *introduce* a student to their own Buddha Nature. By literally *showing* glimpses of the Natural Mind, the master can lead the student to recognize that quality of mind in themselves and rest in it for increasingly longer periods of time. It is crucial, perhaps above all else, to be introduced to and become familiarised with our own Buddha Nature in this way.

The *technique* of meditating is another matter. We learn exactly *how* to meditate so we can revisit our true nature by ourselves. Then the connection to it is strengthened and stabilised little by little, until the day comes when the awakened quality of mind is permanently [and irrevocably] switched on.

The Buddha himself taught many and varied ways of practising meditation according to the needs and capacity of beings. Depending on the lineage of the master you choose, you will learn one or other of them. We are actually advised by the Buddha to check around a bit before selecting the master, and the method, we connect most eaily to. Then, once a decision has been made, stick with it to the end.

But they all have certain key qualities in common. A genuine, mainstream Buddhist Master is a living saint whose only concern is to awaken beings to their true nature. They are the Buddha Nature manifesting in human form for the benefit of others. The most common elements of meditation practice taught by the masters include the following:

The correct posture which is most conducive [a straight back that is not too stiff is key]
The most beneficial thing to focus the mind on while sitting [gently observing our breathing is most common]
And, ultimately, the way the mind itself should be during practice [natural, open and awake]

This is perhaps the most important thing to be said about meditation. It's not so much to do with technique, but with how the mind *is*. It's all about *getting used to* the way our own mind works. It is also about getting used to working with distraction; when the mind drifts off into daydreaming or whatever, we gently bring the mind home again to observing the breath, the object of our mindfulness. A wonderful quality to cultivate in our meditation is how to remain *undistracted*.

But the mind should not be too tightly wound up during meditation ['Now I'm breathing out, now I'm breathing in']. A healthy balance between being *alert* and being *relaxed* is best.

In basic sitting meditation [Skt. *Shamatha*], our mind operates on three layers simultaneously. We are *mindful* of the breath, and *aware* of whenever we become distracted, but above all *spacious*. This open, relaxed spaciousness should, in fact, account for over fifty percent of our mind. This is why meditation should be refreshing and liberating not about closing down or blocking out.

We accept whatever arises internally or externally and allow it to settle again by letting go, especially with every out-breath.

All these qualities of the mind during meditation are about *training*. Remember, we are training the mind and opening the heart. This is the period where we begin to put some shape on this lazy, flabby mind of ours. It is not the end yet. It's not even the middle.

But the most important quality to remember when meditating in the beginning is to be as *natural* as possible.

The Natural Mind is unlikely to awaken if our meditation remains totally contrived and unnatural.

Many meditators report their practice having positive effects from the outset such as feeling centred, more open and content, and so on. Even at the early stages of development, practitioners may feel a sense of *bliss, clarity* or an *absence of thoughts*. These three states are very positive interim signs that *attachment, aversion* and *ignorance* respectively are temporarily dissolving.

But even if we feel we're enduring an avalanche of thoughts and emotions in our meditation it must be remembered that *all* meditative experiences, good or bad, are just temporary states on the way to ultimate awakening. They will pass and we should let them pass in order for more profound progress to naturally emerge. Experiences, it has to be said, are not realisation in themselves.

Resting in the Buddha Nature is so profound, it is completely beyond all concepts. What meditation can be at the deepest level is something so pure it cannot be fully described, only hinted at. One great master, Nyoshul Khen Rinpoche, said this:

> Profound and tranquil, free from complexity,
> Uncompounded luminous clarity,
> Beyond the mind of conceptual ideas;
> This is the depth of the mind of the Victorious Ones.
>
> In this there is not a thing to be removed,
> Nor anything that needs to be added.

It is merely the immaculate
Looking naturally at itself.

Mindlessness

The problem is not so much my mind. *Au contraire!* When I bring the mind home, my mind dwells quite naturally in the present moment. There is no problem at all.

Losing my mind is the *real* problem I face. The battle to live consciously is something with which I must become fully engaged ... every moment of every day, year after year.

Our *Real Mind*, the Buddha Nature itself, scarcely gets a chance to emerge as long as we're so prone to distraction and *Mindless Living*.

It's not even that we are *prone* to mindlessness. I think we actually *prefer* it. Like some primordial anaesthetic, our mindless blank state of mind helps us cope with the suffering caused by not realising our true nature.

Mindlessness feels comfortable to us. We are habitually attracted to its familiar embrace. The best form of contemplation we could do right now is to take a serious, non-judgemental look at our daily lives. It's actually quite funny for me to observe just how disconnected from the present moment I really am.

We have all driven or commuted from A to B, only to arrive at our destination with very little memory of the journey. It's our tendency. We switch off. We are quite capable of functioning normally, but the mind is mostly disengaged. Numb.

Mindlessness has become so habitual for us, we do most things that way. I have a check list of current favourites: Watch TV with vacant eyes glazed-over, only truly become animated when meeting new and interesting people but remain quite neutral around the ones I'm supposed to love most, eat an entire meal without ever tasting it, type *ad nauseum* on my computer keyboard... Sadly, the list is endless.

But all is not lost. I recall the method of meditation. The mind becomes ever more present by applying it consciously to daily life.

We gently bring around 25% of our attention to whatever we choose. This is called *Mindfulness*. Then another 25% provides an overall *Awareness* that kindly alerts us when we have become distracted. And the rest of our mind, perhaps even over 50%, simply hangs out in the natural state referred to as *Spaciousness*.

Just as we use the breath in our formal practice, we can now learn to make our *mindlessness* the object that brings the mind home. We recognize and observe it. Then it is cut right through. The pattern, in that moment, is broken.

Mindlessness is the antithesis of being awake. But we can miraculouslessly use it *as* the path to awakening. The essence of the Dharma cannot be realized without penetrating mindlessness. Only by cutting through that dull state can we awaken our true nature. Once the Natural Mind is liberated, little by little, all its immeasurable qualities are unlocked.

There is natural great *peace*, loving *compassion*, and powerful *transformation*.

The natural flow of the mind is *un-distracted* and *un-altered*.

We can dwell in the state of *Primordial Purity* that manifests as *Spontaneous Presence*.

We are free.

Money

Imagine, if you dare – even for an instant – a brave new world where money doesn't exist.

What would it be like? Would people be happier or more content?

So many of our anxieties and struggles are related to economic pressures. Developing a global society in which financial problems are consigned to ancient history may be the next great leap that humans take. And why not? The money system of being, along with all its inequity and suffering, was just an invention afterall.

The Buddha wasn't against money *per se*. He recognized that rich people suffer too. But at least the rich can also use their money to take care of the poor or offer support to the Dharma.

Moreover, money and the whole economic worldview is just as fake [and temporary] as stone age men worshipping the sun, or white people having black people for slaves. Things change.

Didn't the vast empire of Angkor Wat in Cambodia completely disintegrate? The people, having discovered their king was not a god and could not guarantee healthy crops afterall, simply abandoned him to his mighty, jewel-encrusted throne and disappeared back into the jungle from whence they'd come in the first place. The king was powerless in the end. The people showed that the real power had been theirs all along.

The ruling class generally hangs on to its warped paradigms right until the bitter end when they are forced by the previously silent majority to drop them. This may be the case with money too. If we took care of eachother properly, and with a compassionate heart, then there would be no need for it.

There will always be trade and commerce of one sort or another ... probably. The natural order of things is not a pyramid, but ordinary people self-organizing from the bottom up. But the enslavement of the vast majority by a tiny minority under the guise of employment [and the whole banking system] *can't possibly last* much longer, can it? How many more global recessions can there be before the people say *No More! This is just not working!*

Likewise with war, famine, epidemics and poverty. It's only a matter of time before ordinary people force everything to change, change utterly.

According to the Buddha, *All* systems that are created will eventually fall apart. So better not put our hopes in *ANY ism* whatsoever... even Buddhism. The path to awakening is not a belief system for worshippers of the Buddha to follow. It is a sequence of personal experiences that leads to the enlightenment and liberation of all from suffering.

If the money *ism* did remain for a few more centuries we would just have to learn to continue living within that system, but without attachment or aversion, and without losing our broader view of what really is important in life. But it's hard to imagine money would have any real meaning in a world that has run out of oil, gold, and water.

If the scientists are right, and that's where we're heading, then shouldn't we prepare ourselves and our children for lives with *completely* different priorities?

Mother

If the Buddha was right and reincarnation *does* exist, then it follows that beings have lived together countless times before. We have all previously been loving parents to each other, with everything that entails.

We've loved and cherished all others when they were our darling little babies. We have cared for all beings when they were sick. We have even laid down our lives for them.

By extension, we understand that every being has also been *our* loving mother too. This view, for Buddhists, is the heart of compassion. Once we recognize the suffering of beings we automatically respond with love and compassion, as a parent would. With gratitude and an overwhelming instinct to nurture them, we resolve to *act* for their ultimate benefit and strive to remove their pain. The drive to actually achieve this comes quite naturally when we truly consider others to be just like our aging sweet mother or our beautiful tiny baby when they are sick. We would do anything to relieve their suffering.

Even if we've had a turbulent relationship with our actual mother in this lifetime, we should nevertheless cultivate the correct view of compassion towards all beings as having been our loving mother at some time before. If our mother made terrible mistakes *this* time around, we must move beyond that and generate great empathy and profound compassion for her especially. It may even be helpful to consider her as our child instead. We do not abandon a difficult child just because they have problems. We love them all the more.

The worst kind of suffering witnessed in beings [including ourselves] is the pain caused by being ignorant of their true nature. Although we also must work for their physical well-being, the highest form of love we can give them is to bring about their spiritual awakening. Only then can suffering truly end, regardless of personal circumstances.

We can and must make the world a better place for all, but that is the job of politicians since they are supposed to serve the needs of the people. But healing the hearts and minds of people is a spiritual practice. It has the power right here, right now, to prevent suffering even if external circumstances continue to be incredibly hard.

We can work to change both the world *and* the minds of beings simultaneously. But it is the mind training, awakening the Buddha Nature that lies dormant within, that will yield the greater benefit. What good is a world where *everyone* can have champagne if people continue to experience intense suffering – but this time because the champagne has gone flat!

Better to work on the mind that experiences suffering, as a priority. But, we should proceed with caution. Sometimes it seems easier to work hypothetically in our practice rather than in reality. It seems easier to consider *all* beings as faceless ailing mothers rather than help the being who is actually right in front of us. Ego is a very strong tendency. It distracts us from our higher goals. It makes it difficult for us to have love and compassion for *real* beings. Maybe we feel this one is not deserving or that one is responsible for their own suffering so we shouldn't care for them. Whenever we remain disconnected or judgemental of others, we're following the ego and no good can come of it. We do not perceive things purely and we only water the karmic seeds that lead to more negativity for ourselves and others.

But beware of all this Dharma stuff! It just might change your life!

For how could we ever again walk past a junkie begging for money in the street? How could we allow babies to starve in Africa? Or would we still eat animals for dinner if we *really* considered them to be our mother reincarnated?

Natural Mind

Dudjom Rinpoche says this of the essential nature of mind:

No words can describe it
No example can point to it
Samsara does not make it worse
Nirvana does not make it better
It has never been born
It has never ceased
It has never been liberated
It has never been deluded
It has never existed
It has never been non-existent
It has no limits at all
It does not fall into any category whatsoever.

The Natural Mind, though it has many names, is said to be beyond all concepts and cannot properly be described. But, for the sake of inspiring practitioners on the path to awakening, the masters offer signposts, metaphors and similes.

I prefer the term *Natural Mind* because it implies that awakening is the most natural thing in the world and all the superficial, neurotic fizz of thoughts and emotions [though quite naturally occurring] are not to be taken so seriously.

We can call it the Buddha Nature, the Essential Nature of Mind, Big Mind, Buddha Mind, the Real Mind, Zen Mind, Shunyata ... The most important thing to understand about whatever label we give it is that it speaks volumes about its polar opposite – the superficial realm of egoic thoughts and emotions, and all the suffering that generates. Therefore, we can infer that this ego realm of mind is unnatural, small, unawake, unreal etc. We take it as real and take it so seriously, but we must break that habit.

The Buddha and all the masters describe the Natural Mind in the same way. They have directly experienced it personally. They have all realized it, made it *reality*, awakened it.

What they describe is most interesting and challenging for us beginners.

The Natural Mind is always described as *un-compounded* meaning it was not created. It is completely unlike anything else we experience. It is not bound by space or time. Therefore it never dies. But somehow it is said to have *appeared*, manifested *in* space and time. But why has it?

The key to this apparent mystery is in the other words and phrases used to describe the Buddha Nature. It has a *luminous* quality. It shines *clear light* and it does this for the benefit of all lost and suffering beings. Its luminosity is said to be like the sun. It brings light and warmth.

The light is a *wisdom* torch that illuminates the path to awakening for beings to follow. It clearly shows the true nature of reality so they may understand for themselves why the mind suffers.

The warmth aspect is the heart of *compassion*. Its sole aim is to work only for the ultimate benefit of others, not itself. It has pledged to remove the suffering of beings through the Dharma that liberates the mind.

The Natural Mind, it must be remembered, is *not* at all passive. It *acts* for the benefit of beings. Yet it is unstained and unaltered by the *samsaric* [suffering, deluded] world of beings. It is *in* the world, but not *of* the world. Neither is it swept away by the blissful states that accompany the higher meditative experiences. Therefore, this Natural Mind is said to be beyond both *Samsara* and *Nirvana*. Sogyal Rinpoche says the Buddha Nature is like *Teflon*. Non-stick.

Since it has not been created within the realm of space and time, the Natural Mind is free to move through it unobstructed for the benefit of beings. There is no complexity. It is the most natural thing ever. Whatever their particular brand of suffering, the best way to remove the suffering of beings is to help them to awaken. Since the Small Mind itself is the root of all suffering, the Dharma is the solution because it offers a way to completely by-pass the suffering ego mind altogether.

Another important point, Dudjom Rinpoche reminds us above, is the Natural Mind has *never* been deluded. It has never been un-awake. So we can't exactly consider enlightenment a matter of waking up our true nature. In that sense, neither are we *becoming* enlightened, although we use those kinds of phrases all the time. Awakening is more about *ceasing to be deluded*.

But we *are* in the dark about all this without the teachings; we don't realize the Natural Mind exists and we never discover how to awaken to it. Yet it's said to always be there, anyway. Constantly willing us to realize our true nature. Rumbling and stirring just below the surface. Always primed and ready for awakening. We only have to begin to work with our minds through the practice and the Natural Mind will rise to meet us.

Incredible to think that such a huge awakening, that will benefit so many, is potentially always available to us. It is literally just a breath away. The masters often say when you realize the proximity and ripeness for awakening that has always been just under the surface of the mind, *You might as well just burst out laughing!*

How stupid and ignorant we have been to leave our natural potential just lying there unexplored. And how simple it would be to gradually awaken to the very thing that can end all suffering, not only for ourselves but everyone else too.

No need to solve all the problems of the Surface Mind one by one. The purity and simplicity of *Mindfulness* is the medicine that cures all at once. It is the master key that opens every lock.

Mindfulness is often misunderstood as being just a simple practice for beginners to try. That view couldn't be further from the truth. Properly understood, and profoundly practised, Mindfulness *is* the entire path of awakening to the Natural Mind. Its power and its truth actually come from its direct simplicity.

How natural! ... Beautiful!

Neurosis

We think too much.

These days we all seem to be totally wrapped up in a small world, of our own devising, where thoughts and emotions – and constantly expressing them – is our main reality. The spiritual path is not about blocking out these things but seeing them for what they are. We must go beyond the superficial transience of that vicious cycle. Our age seems to be characterised by this trap. We don't realize there is so much more to us.

Neurosis is a term nolonger much used in clinical parlance. Perhaps because we all have it. But it still has a lot of relevance for Buddhists. It evokes an understanding of the Surface Mind and its essential impasse.

When I think of a neurotic person, Woody Allen springs to mind. Creative genius is often accompanied by a mind bogged down in its own thoughts and emotions. His movies usually bear the hallmark of a central character on a course for self-destruction because they're feverishly caught in a downward spiral of thoughts and emotions. This is often in conjunction with an internal running commentary of self-doubt and angst. The protagonist is usually either in therapy or explores their angst, ad nauseum, with some other confidante.

On another level, it's as though the movie itself is a kind of therapeutic vomiting for the director. A vehicle for expressing, but not necessarily working out, his own issues.

We must be careful if we play this neurotic game, for so many reasons. According to the Buddha, whatever we allow to occupy our mind is actually what we become. A mind filled with speediness and thoughts piling up one on the other makes a person feel lost and un-grounded. A mind full of darkness, inertia and dread leads to deep depression.

If we occupy our surface mind with the Dharma it also follows that its fruition, awakening, will follow.

Buddhism, Meditation, and Mindfulness have become fashionable buzz-words in the psychotherapy of today. And Some Buddhist masters are courting respectability by exploring the cross-over between Talk Therapy and the Buddha's teachings. However, it must be said, that the two paths are not at all in harmony.

Buddha's awaken by accepting phenomena and allowing them to settle; the glass of muddy water becomes clear by not stirring it.

Neurotics with the help of expensive therapists stir up and express, express and stir, and to what avail?

Granted, talk therapy can be essential and most helpful for some people – especially those who have endured great trauma. It gently assists them in the *beginning* process of trying to express and name what has happened to them. But the next step is the same for everyone. Accept, let go and move on.

We do not, says the Buddha, sweep our neurosis under the carpet or hide from it or block it out of our minds altogether. *Accepting* it is a long process that can begin with our next in-breath. *Letting go* may take our whole life, but it begins with our next out-breath.

A correct understanding of Attachment, Aversion and Ignorance is the key. It is what underpins all our problems.

The path of neurosis stirs up and expresses the problem. There is still clinging, pushing away, and a profound misunderstanding about our true nature; attachment, aversion, and ignorance run riot.

The path of awakening begins with loosening our tight grip – releasing the grasping – on the whole drama; wrong perception gives psyco-drama too much prominence and power... *This is MY problem. I must bear it and battle with it all my life. This is part of WHO I AM.*

Learning to release and relax in all circumstances – especially in difficult times – is the very foundation of the path. That is why we practise with the breath in sitting meditation. We gradually become familiar with the process of *releasing* all attachment and aversion. And our mindfulness allows us to cut through our former ignorance by bringing the mind home and *relaxing* into our true nature.

Therapists are often accused of engaging in a prolonged psycho-drama of their own. The roles of expert healer and helpless patient are subtly laid down and the longer the process lasts the better. It is a profession afterall. That's not to say there aren't many fine people working in the field. But shining the light of mindfulness on the whole process quickly illuminates the great limitations and traps involved.

On the other hand, the Dharma [although the Master is taken as a guide] must be done alone, through practice. A truly awakened being's only agenda is that all beings liberate *themselves* from suffering as soon, and as directly, as possible.

Anything that could be achieved by professional talk therapy could just as easily – and arguably more effectively – by done by really talking with a friend or loved one. Buddhists are encouraged to learn and practise *deep listening* and *gentle speech* together. This is not proposed as a way of learning a new skill that we can practise professionally. The Buddha teaches it as *the* way of being fully human in the world. Living for the benefit of others.

But actually practising the Dharma of meditation and contemplation is the most powerful path. It leads to total liberation from all baggage, obstacles and delusion.

Going beyond the problems themselves and cutting them at the very root of the mind achieves everything at once.

Not everyone is ready to walk this path, in this particular lifetime. Sometimes short-term strategies are the only option. But, when the time is right, a person is ripe for awakening due to a deep exhaustion with the suffering neurotic mind. There is a profound shift in awareness, and a determination to be free is born. Only then does the path of self-liberation arise as the true solution.

Nobody said it would be easy, but it has to be easier than the endless cycle of Samsara that is fuelled by neurosis.

Nirvana

When there is *peace, compassion* and *wisdom*, I am open and content. As the spiritual path unfolds around me, I yearn for these three.

They awaken openness and contentment deep within me. Not as the world gives, but as the heart-mind gives; everlasting, beyond concept.

As peace, compassion and wisdom slowly dawn, I am becoming my true self and all traces of ego and delusion gradually fall away entirely.

While we are still bound by the ties of the self-grasping ego and the great delusion that keeps us ignorant of our own Buddha Nature, we're said to dwell in the realm of *Samsara*. It's like an ocean of suffering whose waves constantly sweep us off course. In the chaos of Samsara we are reduced to panic-stricken wrecks driven to the extremes of hope for salvation and fear of annihilation.

Nirvana, on the other hand, is the opposite of samsara. Once a being has entered this final phase on the path, they have moved beyond such hope and fear forever. The ego and all traces of delusion have completely dissolved. That being has awakened to their true nature.

For Theravadin Buddhists, the term *Nirvana* is synonymous with *enlightenment* and *buddhahood*. It is the final stage.

For Mahayana Buddhists, however, there are said to be further levels of awakening to full, perfect buddhahood. From the Mahayana perspective, one who has gone beyond attachment, aversion and ignorance is called an *Arhat*. They have also realized emptiness or openness [*Shunyata*] and have ripened all their past *karma*. But they're not considered a fully awakened buddha until they have fully embraced the path of *bodhichitta*. Such beings are known as *bodhisattvas*. They have deferred their own full awakening until such time as all beings have attained the state of perfect buddhahood first. The boddhisattva path involves such pure aspirations and actions dedicated to the ultimate benefit of beings that a boddhisattva is paradoxically said to have actually attained full enlightenment already.

These great beings are nolonger so common, but they are not rare either. There are even some living and working amongst us here and now. They may well appear as saints or masters of Dharma. Or they may prefer to remain incognito, quietly getting on with their vast work unnoticed. Either way, fully awakened beings such as them will never again be reborn with a samsaric mind. So pure is their realisation, they do not even remain in the blissful state of *Nirvana*.

The highest teachings within the Mahayana lineage, especially in the Tibetan tradition, urge practitioners in these last stages of awakening to *go beyond both samsara and nirvana* in order for perfect buddhahood to be fully realized.

This profound advice recognizes the slight possibility that the subtlest temptation may still remain to dwell in the realm of Nirvana. The great bliss experienced there may actually hold us back.

Therefore another term is introduced for the ultimate stage of awakening.

Parinirvana describes the moment when full, perfect buddhahood is reached. This special word is usually associated with the passing away of an enlightened master, the death of a buddha. In some cases, after parinirvana, a master will choose to reincarnate for the benefit of beings still languishing in the darkness of samsaric mind. In other cases – for example Prince Siddhartha, Shakyamuni Buddha – the master does not return but continues to work from outside the confines of space and time for the ultimate benefit of beings.

It's said that such buddhas are *so* powerful and compassionate we only have to think of them and they are right there in front of us.

Non-Conceptual [Shunyata Lite]

One time, I made the long journey from my home in Dublin to the small town of Gangtok in the foothills of the Himalaya, to be with my master. From Ireland to India was an adventure in itself. I hadn't really been anywhere so far before, and never alone.

Of course, I'd planned the route I was going to take and booked all my flights to connect well with eachother. No point being anally-retentive if you can't get that kind of thing right, right? Dublin to Frankfurt to Delhi. Change from international terminal to domestic [what an adventure!]. Then North, North, up, up, up. Delhi to Bagdogra by plane. Pause for state-wide Communist Party demos and all-out strikes. Then, Bagdogra to Gangtok by helicopter [$20], no baggage allowed, so all my packing was in vain. Finally, I arrived in my room with a panoramic view of Sikkim – that ancient kingdom now part of India – and the high snow-peaks of the Himalaya, with a mournful sliver of Tibet lying dark and distant on the far horizon.

I realized my trip from Dublin to Gangtok, though arduous at times, was not really all that bad and had taken less than a day door-to-door. The next day I phoned Ringu

Tulku Rinpoche, as instructed, to get directions to his place. It would only have been a short walk but I got terribly lost and it took an age. Just when I thought my journey was over, it seemed it was only just beginning. But I got there in the end despite the seering heat and the almost vertical roads on the particular detour I had taken.

The path to awakening is like any long journey. It's vital not to get too distracted by the various landmarks we pass en route. I could have spent a lifetime in any one Indian city or small village. But no. Best to simply drink them in, let them go, and move on.

On the spiritual path there are many such momentous oases. We experience them both in our formal practice and in our daily lives. They are signs that the practice is working.

Just as we may experience an absence of thoughts while meditating, there is a later stage where we experience all concepts falling away. This *non-conceptual* milestone is very important for many reasons. It gives us a glimpse of what the complete openness of *Shunyata* will be like. We gain confidence in the truth of the path and the underlying power of the Natural Mind.

When we nolonger *react* to phenomena with attachment and aversion, even momentarily, we recognize the innate ability we all share to remain stable and open to life. We learn to *respond* spontaneously rather than react habitually. In this respect, we are free.

When our judgemental, concept-driven, animal instincts begin to fall away like this a profound shift occurs in our consciousness. Concepts like *grasping after* and *pushing away* are over-ridden. Even the very notion of *subject* and *object* fall away. In fact, all *dualistic* concepts are rendered redundant.

Non-conceptual and *non-dual* experiences are an essential staging post because they are so close to realizing the Great Openness, *Shunyata*.

Once we begin to overcome the tendency to have conceptual reactions to life, we generate an increasing amount of the openness and contentment that characterise awakening. Because there is also a non-dual component to our experience, we actually begin to realize for ourselves the eternal yet elusive truth that there is *no separation* whatsoever between internal and external, self and other, this and that...

We then work to prolong and broaden this outlook. By resting in our true nature like this, we become so open we can gradually train to pass entire days non-conceptually. We begin to recognize our ability to remain un-distracted and un-altered by the drama of phenomena yet we are free to engage more fully with it for the ultimate benefit of beings. The paradox is plain and simple. To be more fully aware, and therefore more effective, we must not get trapped by the superficial. A Formula 1 racing driver does not sit there saying to himself *Oh my God, I'm going to crash! Watch out for that corner! What's that strange noise?!* Similarly, to be most useful to her patient, a heart transplant surgeon quickly gets over the instinct to vomit as she slices through human flesh and cracks open the ribcage. To fully function, we must be in the zone of non-conceptual engagement.

Many practitioners who have this experience, or glimpses of it, unfortunately get stuck at that stage. But it is very important to keep moving towards the ultimate destination. Break through. Open up even more.

Non-conceptual living is not at all a zombie-like state. It is very much *engaged* with the world and is a truly beneficial time in one's life. But we must remember that we are merely drinking *Shunyata Lite* and not the real thing at all.

It's a refreshing relief from the heat of the day, but it's only a preview of even greater things to come.

Non-Harming

The foundation of the spiritual path is to practise non-violence.

We train the mind in *calm abiding meditation* [Shamatha] so that remaining peaceful becomes our way of being. We work on this quality until our resolve for peace and non-harming becomes unshakable.

But the meditation, as ever, is all about training. Real life provides the true chance to put it all into practice. The challenges are great. Perhaps the hardest part is not so much living from moment to moment without harming. That seems somehow do-able. But the whole idea that we should *never* again cause harm – with our body, speech or mind – seems like a tall order. So it's necessary to continue to use our daily formal practice to strengthen and reinforce our ability, moment by moment, to embody this core principle.

The more one contemplates non-violence and non-harming the more vivid the scope of the challenge becomes. The Buddha never laid out a detailed moral code, only guiding principles. It is for us to touch deeply the reality of that challenge and work out the details for ourselves.

Perhaps each person might come up with different solutions to the same issue. And we must respect that.

Given that each one of us is approaching our new spiritual life sincerely, and with a good heart, it's up to us as individuals to start where we are and see how far we can go right now towards perfect action.

Some people see this principle as mainly to do with anti-war or anti-nuclear peace movements. Some see it as a more person-centred challenge and they practise mindful living so they might never again get angry or cause harm around them. They are practising *inner-disarmament*. Others go the path of Mahatma Gandhi. Others still operate at extremely advanced levels of mindfulness and non-harming. They may be vegan and try to grow food that is produced in harmony with their loving vision. If our motives are genuine and we don't simply replace one neurotic obsession for another, every step we take towards perfect non-harming is a step in the right direction.

The more we apply mindfulness to something, the less likely it is to have a harmful outcome. In this way, practice makes perfect.

Ultimately, we are moving towards full awakening. We must accept that we're not perfect yet. As long as we all do our level best, however, nobody could ask more of us.

But when we *do* realize full liberation it's said we will cease to create new karma altogether. There is no negativity in our presence and we have no harmful impact on phenomena.

Until then, we can only do our best and – from time to time – push the envelope a little further, and maintain the challenge to grow more and more.

Always looking for the positive seeds to water, we don't dwell on the failings of ourselves or others. Rather, we rejoice every time we witness non-harming as it continues to blossom in and around us.

Granted, it may be unusual at first looking for the *absence* of harm so we may rejoice in it; we rarely notice the absence of such things. But with the right mindfulness and awareness we can do it.

This practice will bring us great bliss and will inspire us even further to live without harm.

Numbness

The *ignorance* that underpins attachment and aversion can itself appear to manifest in many ways.

In my own case, I found once the initial maelstrom of thoughts and emotions began to settle a little through meditation and mindfulness that I slipped quite effortlessly into another trap of sorts.

Whether sitting in meditation or trying to integrate the practice into daily life I began to notice that I wasn't really thinking or feeling much at all. Far from being a good thing, I felt I was descending into a state I can only describe as *numbness*.

If you experience this too, you may even think you are alert and relaxed but something is still not quite right. It's not like lethargy or feeling vacant. It feels something more like the mild shock you feel after being punched on the nose.

Of course, as with all phenomena, this state is only temporary and will pass. Even though it may return many times, it's only a phase and will eventually subside altogether. If it were more like lethargy, one could counter it by enlivening the practice. Chanting mantra or refreshing the posture would help. On the other hand if it were more like feeling vacant, bringing the mind home to each breath in the present moment would be a powerfully grounding antidote.

But feeling numb is another matter entirely. On the negative side, it might feel like being a little in shock, or like you were on some medication that kind of blocked your senses a bit. This sensation of numbness could be a real obstacle if we allowed it to become our new habit.

However, on the positive side, the sensation could be a real sign that the practice *is* working afterall. Another marker on the path. Things might actually be shifting to such an extent that feeling numb is just a stone's throw away from experiencing phenomena *non-conceptually*. In fact, we might even be experiencing non-conceptually already, and have just misread the signs. *Misperception* is at the root of so many of our apparent problems.

Rather than being a problem at all we should just view this new observation as another step on the path, nothing more. Since it won't last anyway, good or bad, we can just treat it with the same equanimity as always.

But we must remember we are not alone on the path. Everyone else experiences all the same stages sooner or later. As our sangha community of fellow-practitioners they are also our support system.

If we're lucky enough to have access to our master, this is such a great blessing. Our teacher may simply put our mind at rest and tell us not to take ourselves so seriously and keep going on the path. Or they may explore this temporary stage a little with us, shining the light of illumination on our path.

The higher teachings of the Buddha sometimes describe delusion like a layer of murkiness that appears to be smeared over the Buddha Nature, obscuring our view of it. This might be what we're perceiving, who knows?

Often called the *Alaya*, the ultimate paradox is that this perceived out-of-focus layer doesn't actually exist. Once the mind relaxes more naturally again, it can disappear and offer us a glimpse of our true nature.

Obesity

The Buddha said, *You are what you think*.

Western Culture says, *You are what you eat*. So what are we eating that's making us so obese?

It could be we've lost touch to such an extent with the natural world that we eat all the wrong things. Our bodies are rebelling and we're spiralling out of *control*. And control is the one thing we truly crave. Our digestive systems, of course, are driven by the brain. And the brain is driven by the mind. But our craving has manifested in a very particular way in relation to food. We crave sugar, salt and fat. It makes us feel better. We've evolved into a new sub-species who use harmful foods and toxins to temporarily pacify our emotional life. But what's so wrong with our emotions they need this anaesthetic?

For many generations, we have thought of food as comfort. The favourite meals or snacks we reach for bring a kind of comfort perhaps because they remind us of childhood – a safer time – or because their unhealthy contents release in our brains a kind of chemical euphoria. We use food to manipulate and assert control over life especially if we feel powerless in other areas.

When we look at the psychology of obesity from a Dharma perspective there is no special case to be made. Obese or not, we are *all* in the same boat. We want control. We crave happiness and shun suffering. Attachment and Aversion. When we don't get enough of what we want – or when we get precisely whatever we didn't want – we feel chronically let down by life. We need to get back in the driving seat. Disappointment and dissatisfaction are endemic in the World. We will try anything to regain control, if we ever had it, over our life. Perhaps the amount we eat is the only thing we feel we *can* control.

But most interesting, in relation to the present dharma context, is the way obese comfort-eaters appear to experience *Ignorance*. Granted, we may eat all the wrong foods or eat too much food. They're just bad habits caused by the culture of luxury and excess in which we live; culture is not your friend. But obesity caused by comfort eating *is* a special case. It's all about the mind. Because of *ignorance*, we've lost touch with our true nature. Consequently, we have lost touch with reality and therefore feel disconnected and isolated.

Many compulsive eaters describe an over-powering longing for comfort at times of extreme emotion or stress. They say it's like eating their own emotions; when suppressed, over-powering emotions surface they have to be swallowed back down along with the food in order to be digested or buried. Of course we know at the time that suppressing emotions like this just makes matters worse and leads to a dangerous cycle. But we still try it.

Another insight I've heard unlocks perhaps the deepest secrets of obesity. This comes from obese people themselves. When we feel lost, disconnected or overwhelmed we perceive a dark void deep inside. Like a gaping hole, this sadness feels like a profound emptiness that needs to be filled. It actually feels like the emptiness itself is located deep in the stomach. Food helps a little.

This is extremely important, psychologically speaking. If a problem appears to be solved or alleviated temporarily by eating something in particular then a pattern is established deep in the brain; there is a perceived *pay-off* as a result of our actions, otherwise we wouldn't bother. A pattern is created. Even if the so-called cure diminishes in effectiveness over time, we still reach for it because it's all we know. Food, alcohol, drugs ... the same old familiar story.

Although it's still quite difficult to understand, and it is extremely unpopular for Westerners to say out loud, the Dharma goes much deeper than modern psychology. When psychologists speak about the *psyche* or the *mind* [with a small 'm'], however deep or complex it seems to be they're still only referring to the superficial realm of thoughts and emotions. It is only scratching the surface of what mind appears to be. Western culture continues to operate on the level of brain chemicals and the swirling energies of our moods. Sadly our quick-fix mentality leads us astray. We pop this pill for that. We take such and such a vitamin supplement for something else. We are so pre-occupied with *feeling* better that we never get to the root of anything.

The vast insight of the Buddha's teaching comes at things from the other direction entirely. By virtue of our own *spiritual* experience, we come to know directly for ourselves the liberating power of the Buddha Nature within.

The healing, loving qualities it radiates can cut through all the superficial suffering of the mind. When we are blocked from that direct experience, we are ignorant of our true nature. And that suffering manifests as attachment and aversion in *all* its forms. Deep feelings of being empty and alone are worked on in a very different way.

Recognizing how we are all obese and craving a sense of *fullness* shines a wisdom torch on the whole human condition. It cuts through the superficial appearance of mind and leads to the innate wisdom and compassion deep down inside, the natural healing and boundless sustenance that flow without limit from the root of the mind.

OCD

Obsessive-Compulsive Disorder is a relatively 'new' form of Suffering Mind. Often baffling, and difficult to cope with, it controls the lives of those who have to live through it.

However, OCD is nothing more complex than an extremely painful manifestation of the underlying tendency towards habitual patterns that we *all* share as samsaric beings.

With OCD, people are driven to ritually perform a variety of everyday actions such as hand-washing, locking doors or flipping light switches, over and over again. This is usually repeated numerous times according to whatever 'magic number' their mind has fixated on. The ritual must be performed perfectly and the repetition is done out of *hope* for some small relief from suffering or because sufferers irrationally *fear* the dire consequences of not doing it. A person living with this condition is as ordinary as you or me, yet they have no explanation for how they slipped into this behavioural 'groove'. They're often ashamed to admit to it because they are usually very competent in every other aspect of their lives. They also become quite expert at 'managing' it and hiding the signs from the outside world.

If we remove from this distressing scenario the actual habits the people are so obsessed with, and the extreme ritual nature of their compulsion, they're not really all that different from everyone else.

We're all drawn into habitual tendencies of one sort or another because we imagine they will have a considerable reward. Take away the imagined 'pay-off' element and we wouldn't do them at all. Instincts are quite basic really. No pay-off, no action. Generally, we don't waste our energy.

So where *is* the pay-off? What is its *nature*? Answer these key questions and we begin to unlock the mystery of OCD and all other habitual tendencies.

Human beings are still quite animalistic. Add a tablespoon of primitive superstition and a clearer picture starts to emerge. We are still only beginning to evolve, as a species. It is early days yet in the grand scheme of things. Modern humans remain only a few important leaps beyond cavemen.

We tend towards habitual patterns of behaviour because we prefer the familiar. It brings us a certain miniscule amount of comfort in an existence otherwise filled with uncertainty, longing and dread. Stripped down to its most basic level, it becomes transparent that obsession and compulsion are all about *control*.

If we feel we have little or no control over our own lives this causes deep-seated anxiety and we grasp after something – anything – that we *might* actually be able to control. Whatever that turns out to be is of little importance, no matter how significant it may seem to the person who is grasping onto it. The primeval urge is the same in every case. It's like a drowning man clutching at straws. Hope and fear.

The author of this soap opera is the ego. We all hope for control, and fear annihilation. Our chaotic flair for the melodramtic, *compels* us to become further and further *obsessed* with ourselves.

Cut through the ego at the root and all our obstacles begin to crumble like a house of cards. Bringing *mindfulness* to our problems helps us to see through them. Turning our *awareness* more towards the welfare of others destroys the habitual tendencies of the self-obsessed ego. All that we search for is contained in our own true nature. Its openness and contentment bring an unfettered *spaciousness* not available in the realm of samsaric mind.

> May all beings be free from self-obsession
> and the compulsion to act habitually.
> May we all go beyond the limitations of hope and fear.
> And may the ego be dissolved for once and for all!

Ocean

Anyone who spends time by the ocean is aware of its majesty and power.

It always appears to be moving, especially on the surface. The sea can bring both tremendous joy and terrifying tragedy. It is also extremely useful as a dharma-metaphor for the mind.

Even though we look at the surface of the ocean and think how enormous it is, the surface is nothing compared to the vastness of its hidden depths. In fact, the surface could be more accurately understood as the energetic display of the greater reality that lies beneath. The paradox is how the surface chaos and the profound depths below coexist as one entity, of the same essence. There is the superficial appearance and there is the reality; movement and stillness co-emerging from the same source.

Most of the movement perceived on the surface of the ocean has been provoked by apparently external forces: non-ocean elements such as the wind and the pull of the moon. But in truth there is no separation between what seems to be internal or external.

Our own mind is like the ocean.

In reality there's no separation whatsoever between the mind and so-called external phenomena.

The Surface Mind appears to be all there is. It is beautiful and scary, and seems to have a life of its own. We don't feel we have too much control over it or how it reacts to circumstances. It's so easy to get swept away by waves of pleasure or pain. At this superficial level of mind, there is attachment and aversion all underpinned by basic ignorance of the greater reality that lies beneath. The masters of the spiritual path refer to this ocean of suffering as *Samsara*.

If we allow the focus of our consciousness to remain lost in Samsara, suffering persists. This is why we train in meditation to bring our focus elsewhere. We dwell on a deeper level of mind. We don't run away from the chaotic surface. We learn to see it more in perspective for what it is truly is. The vast layers of *Real Mind* that lie below the surface increasingly provide more and more of that spacious perspective we seek.

The deeper the focus of our consciousness, the more grounded in our true nature we will be. This releases a mind that is free and unburdened, healthy and happy. In time we reach a level of *Real Mind* that is the antithesis of Samsara. It is so blissful it is called *Nirvana*. The awakened nature of mind at this level is completely free of attachment and aversion because there is no ignorance. We directly experience for ourselves our true nature. There is nolonger any doubt. We dwell there and know all phemonema from that profound perspective. At the same time, we live fully in the world but are nolonger imprisoned by its mindlessness.

The deepest teachings of the Buddha encourage us never to become complacent about our mind or whatever *level* of mastery we have over it. In order to attain *full* liberation we must go beyond Nirvana too.

This is where the image of the ocean's hidden depths, and all conceptual analogies, begins to dissolve . There are levels below levels and eventually words cannot adequately express reality. There is such openness and spaciousness, words fail.

We can relate to the concept of *movement* on the surface, and *stillness* lying deep below. But even beneath these two, there is the mind that observes them both.

The teachings tell us this. *There is movement. There is stillness. Out of the stillness comes movement. Even in the movement there is profound stillness.* But, *both* movement and stillness come from a deeper origin, the Buddha Nature itself.

It is not for ones own personal well-being that we train to dwell in the innermost essence of the Mind. We do it for the benefit of others. Our aspiration as bodhisattvas is not to reach *heaven* and stay there praying for others. We must learn to exist in every dimension at once. It's by resting in our true nature that we become free to live and work in Samsara for the ultimate benefit of beings.

Wherever beings exist, it is our pledge and our life's purpose to liberate them from the suffering of Superficial Mind.

Openness

When we are closed, there is suffering. Openness is the key.

Until we have awakened to our true nature, we dwell in the darkness of Ignorance. From this ego-centric state arises Attachment and Aversion. Collectively, these three are called the Mind Poisons. They are toxic and cause our mindstream to paralyze and set into fixed habitual tendencies. We are closed to the true nature of all reality. Lost and blind, we don't realize we're the author of our own mini-drama. All the suffering, instability and self-doubt have been generated from within. Whistling in the dark, we cling to small comforts and dread the worst.

Even while we're in this Samsaric state of mind, how much easier everything would be if only we could relax and enjoy the good times and not worry so much when things go wrong. Even this Ocean of Samsara could be a much easier ride if we could just learn to surf.

Every time we manage to let go a bit, and relax into a more open frame of mind, we experience benefits that are way out of proportion to the initial effort we invested. Life itself is teaching us the greatest lesson of all: Openness brings Contentment. It's as if the Buddha Nature, through all its wisdom and compassion, is manifesting in the circumstances of our own lives to show us the path to spiritual awakening.

We are so used to the darkness of ignorance – all that grasping onto and pushing away – we just don't realize there's more to life. That there is more to *us*. Another way.

Even when practitioners begin to progress along the path, we seem to forget that the *way* to openness and contentment lies within. If our meditation cushion is not *just so*, or if we don't *feel* like practising today, we simply don't seem to have it in us to draw on the infinity of resources that lie dormant within. We forget the Buddha Nature. We forget all the openness and transformation waiting inside us.

Were we fortunate enough to make a stable heart-connection with the Wisdom Mind of a great Master, how glorious that would be! But what happens when the master passes away? Awakened masters are constantly introducing us to the true nature of our own mind. They're tirelessly showing us how to work on our minds and never forget our real potential. But how easily we forget the main point. The solution to Suffering Mind lies within.

Especially on the spiritual path, an expert mind is a closed mind. We believe knowledge is power, that we could somehow *know* the truth – possess it – rather than experience it. Better to remain open and ready like a child or a simple peasant than to be a know-it-all. Otherwise we might miss the point entirely and the truth could so easily just pass us by.

In the practice, there are said to be gaps – windows of opportunity – through which we can glimpse the Natural Mind. All the surface judgement, chatter and movement of the mind can drop away temporarily. If we don't consciously develop the Dharma habit of openness to phenomena, this too will pass us by.

Life itself and our formal meditation practice both show us how invaluable Openness is. It's not just a good disposition to adopt *on* the path; Openness *is* the path.

It is the Ground, Path and Fruition of the Buddha's favourite words.

Pain

Anyone who knows how to live with pain knows the secret of dwelling in the present moment without fixation.

In my own life, perhaps the first real Dharma training began when I was still a young boy. It was long before I'd ever heard the word Buddha. Thanks to a cycle of debilitating headaches that have stayed with me all my life, I gradually learned a lonely but priceless lesson about the nature of pain. These experiences were what brought me into the spiritual life and eventually to Buddhism.

Serious headaches may have many different causes and require medical investigation. But in some cases, like mine, headaches are just the way life is. Pain comes. It stays a while. Then it goes away again. It used to be triggered by particular things. But suddenly one day it was something else entirely that set off the pain and I was once again free to eat cheese, drink red wine, enjoy physical exercise and strong sunlight. The whole thing remains a bit of a mystery. But the nature of pain is no mystery. The insight it can give us into the nature of how the mind suffers – and how to work with suffering – is extraordinary.

Most people don't get to learn these painful lessons, at least not until they get much older and develop serious illness or are facing death. Pain is an incredibly skillful teacher of the Buddhadharma.

With painful headaches in particular, I quickly discovered it's a *very* bad idea to indulge or agitate pain; stirring things up only makes matters much worse. Similarly, if I tried to fight against the pain in an attempt to block it out or over-power it somehow, things could quickly go from bad to worse. Right there and then, I realized *experientially* that grasping attachment and pig-headed aversion only served to escalate suffering. I also understood, although the pain was a physical thing, my suffering was essentially of the mind. Any pain management strategy I adopted would have to work with the mind too. Underneath the whole issue of pain, my real problem was that I was ignorant. I had no larger perspective on things. The headaches were so blinding, I literally couldn't see any way out. In that moment, when pain seems to pervade everything, there's no hint we are actually greater than the pain. We are glued to it. We identify so strongly with it, we truly feel that pain is all there is.

Of course most pain requires medication or some other treatment to help relieve the intensity of the suffering. But even with strong medication, it is vital to learn to *release* and *relax*. We must *accept* the reality of the situation and *let go* of the pain. *Allow* it to pass. There has to be no sense of clinging onto it or pushing it away. Just let it be.

The attitude of the mind is therefore very important indeed. We can even encourage things to settle by gently imagining the pain subsiding as we swallow the medicine or a cooling glass of pure water.

But even the attitude of our body is crucial. When I was young, and only getting used to having headaches, I discovered that positioning my body in certain ways was more helpful than others. It was like there was supposed to be a particular flow of blood or energy or something. And that couldn't be established if I was all bent out of shape, obstructing the natural flow.

The third crucial point is to be silent and allow the breath to regain its natural flow too. We don't want to increase our sense of panic by panting or gasping. Neither, on the other hand, do we need to force a particularly deep kind of breathing to occur. Better to simply allow the breath to settle by itself into its natural groove, un-manipulated.

In my own case, I'd been working with acute pain in this way for many years before I found my spiritual home in Buddhism. When I realized I had been on the right track all along, I was actually quite shocked. I just didn't believe I could've discovered for myself anything so useful.

Our big problem is not pain at all. We just don't believe in ourselves. We don't believe that we are bigger in essence than *anything* we could be suffering. The teachings on the *Suffering Mind* and the vast power of the *Buddha Nature* guide us to experience for ourselves just how wrong that view is.

Depending on the intensity of the pain, or how awakened we may be, the Dharma has several other skillful means to offer us.

For example, practitioners train in the ability to apply awareness to one particular part of the body, then to move it around at will to another place, then another. This is helpful when pain occurs because, with practice, we can gently move our focus off the pain and onto another area or sensation instead.

More advanced meditators can train in the practice of looking directly *at* the pain itself. Without getting sucked into the sensation of suffering, we are actually capable of seeing pain for what it is. Although strong and intense, we can also appreciate the nature of pain. It is not all-pervasive. It is not greater than the Buddha Nature. Our true essence is so vast it's not even affected in the slightest by it. When we release our tendency to grasp onto this 'gripping' pain, we can appreciate its temporary nature. Pain has come. It will pass. Even if it never goes away entirely, at least it will not always be this bad.

Pain brings us all into the present moment. In that way it has been a great friend to us. It shows us that the only true reality is here and now.

Pain can even be a wonderful teacher, awakening in us immeasurable wisdom and compassion. It is said that great practitioners who experience pain passing through them actually use the opportunity to pray that no other being should have pain. For such yogis, the pain becomes an occasion for generating compassion and *bodhichitta*.

With tremendous courage, and confidence in the Buddha Nature's unstainable quality, a yogi who observes pain prays fervently that by virtue of their pain may the suffering of all beings be completely removed and may they all be awakened here and now to their true nature.

Paramita

According to the essence of the Buddha's teachings, regardless of whether we're in the suffering mind of Samsara or progressing along the spiritual path or already fully-awakened buddhas, all beings should try to embody the same enlightened qualities.

The fruition is not only better for *us* but for everyone around us too. These transcendent, perfect qualities are called *The Six Paramitas*. Ordinary beings, like us, are well advised to generate a deep aspiration to transform our minds thoroughly so we can gradually come to really *be* like this all the time. Living mindfully, we should actively look out for opportunities to put the Paramitas into practice. To embody these six is the path to enlightenment. It is also the fruition; the very mind and activity of a buddha. We must embark on a thorough study and practice of the Six Paramitas without delay!

1. Generosity (Skt. dāna): to cultivate the attitude of giving of oneself to others.
2. Discipline (Skt. śīla): refraining from all harm.

3. Patience (Skt. kṣānti): the ability not to be perturbed by anything, to become expert at peacefully remaining.

4. Enthusiastic Diligence (Skt. vīrya): to find deep joy in what is virtuous, positive and wholesome.

5. Meditative concentration (Skt. dhyāna): not to be distracted; at the highest level, to rest in our Buddha Nature.

6. Wisdom (Skt. prajñā): the perfect discrimination of all phenomena; to perceive everything purely, *as it truly is.*

Pilgrimage

All the great masters of the past and present recommend going on pilgrimage. Visiting the special places in India and Nepal connected with the life of the Buddha can be extremely inspiring for ones practice. Doing so is also said to purify past negative karma and clear away the obscurations of mind that currently prevent us from resting in our own Buddha Nature.

With the exception of the Buddha's birthplace, which is in modern-day Nepal, all of the major sites are located in northern India. It's not so difficult really to go there, especially if you organize a group tour. But travelling and even being in India is not always an easy experience. It can be an assault on all the senses. There's nowhere on earth really quite like it. But the rewards far outweigh whatever down-side you may encounter. India changes you.

In the West, the notion of a *holy* site often raises all sorts of issues for us. But, as far as Buddhist sites are concerned, we need to drop all that baggage and truly experience a place for what it is.

I once asked my master what made a particular place holy. He replied it was all about whatever originally happened there. And what happened in that place subsequently is also of special importance.

For example, Bodhgaya is the place where an ordinary human being named Siddhartha fully awakened to his own true nature, and became known as the Buddha. Even today, over two-and-a-half millennia later, the whole place still resonates with the auspiciousness of what happened there. A descendent of the original *bodhi tree* stands on the exact same spot. The awe-inspiring Mahabodhi Temple and the grounds around it provide a truly transformative environment. Ever since the Buddha became enlightened, most of the great beings and masters have journeyed there to meditate and bring the whole world a little closer to full awakening. That has maintained the spiritual purity and power of the site. So, when *we* visit and practise in a place like that, we can remember all this and benefit tremendously from it. We are actually said to accumulate great merit by being there in such a positive frame of mind.

In theory, a site could also cease to be a holy place if whatever wondrous thing that happened there was not followed up by practitioners keeping the energy flow pure. It's also possible that something horrendously inappropriate happened there at a later stage and the great blessing of the site was somehow extinguished. But this is not the case in relation to any of the major places connected with the Buddha himself.

What *we* can practise in these holy places is limitless. But the essential spiritual practice must surely be to connect with our own Buddha Nature – and to do that for the ultimate benefit of all beings. Learning the practice of *Refuge* and *Bodhichitta* before we go is invaluable. We visualize all beings by our side. We also include all the people who contributed to us ending up at such a special place: our parents, ancestors, loved ones, masters, instructors, sangha community, the bank manager ... and so on.

As well as rejoicing in the sheer joy of it all, we should allow ourselves to have great fun also. We're on holiday too, afterall. The Buddha wouldn't be too upset if we laughed ourselves sick, or if we even felt grumpy sometimes. We don't have to pretend to be too holy or solemn. Above all, we mustn't take ourselves so seriously. The path to awakening is paved with great joy, humour and a huge sense of release.

All the holy sites are still in really remote areas. There is a lot of poverty around. The towns and villages themselves are sometimes quite filthy and unhealthy environments for foreigners. But relax. It'll be fine. The spiritual path shouldn't be too comfortable or easy-going. If we think it *should* be, we may as well just go to Disneyland instead and receive all the blessing that Mickey Mouse can muster. At least our ego wouldn't be challenged at all there.

Since awakening is also about going completely beyond fear, we can use the conditions and circumstances we find ourselves in on pilgrimage to help us progress towards that liberated state.

It's not a good idea for the Indian pilgrimage experience to be too sanitized or safe. A blindfold or rose-tinted sunglasses won't necessarily help in the slightest. If we're to go there at all, then we have to *go there*. Personally engaging with the raw humanity of India, and the profound spirit of these particular places, is the only way. If we're moved, and are feeling creative, we could even personalize the prayers and aspirations in our formal practice so we actively share what is in our hearts. What joy to be there! How awful the suffering of beings, ourselves included. May we all reach full awakening!

Here is a poem I composed myself just after being on pilgrimage there with Ringu Tulku Rinpoche. Its structure has one section for each of the key places that were so important in the life of the Buddha: where he was born, the kingdom he renounced, the place of his eventual awakening, his first spiritual teaching, where he later taught the Heart Sutra, and the place of his death.

WALKING WITH BUDDHA

[Lumbini]
Buddha is born in the here and now.
The trees and the blossoms, the forest bears witness.

[Kapilavastu, the Royal Palace of the Sakya Kingdom]
The cocoon of the familiar, in time, is renounced
To wander and search in the vast present moment.

[Bodhgaya, under the bodhi tree]
After so many gurus, exertion and hardship,
Stretched almost to breaking, you chose a new path.

Oh what a release just to sit on this cushion,
The simplest of grasses, beneath a great tree.

As every day opens to night, into daytime,
From evening to morning, from dusk into dawn,

The Mind also opens and drops all delusion.
The Heart lotus blossoms, all grasping released.

The morning star dawning, sun's rays shine impartially,
Completely awake, free from all complexity.

So vivid and peaceful, in openness and contentment,
The true perfect Buddha is found in one's heart.

[Sarnath, the Deer Park]
The truth overflows and the parkland rejoices.
The deer all come closer to hear the good news:

The mind with its torments and all of its grasping,
Cut through by Awareness, for all time, is free!

[Rajgir, Vulture Peak Mountain]
A Song of Perfection is sung from the mountain
To valleys and hilltops, to trees, to the sky:

All things are empty and yet they appear,
Like so many rainbows, mirages, and dreams.

Remembering this, be a child of illusion,
With purest perception, beyond hope and fear.

Rejoice all who hear this, the plants and the stones,
The breezes that carry it in every direction.

The great panorama, the view, chants its answer:
Halleluia! Hosanna! Gloria! Amen!

Thus have I heard... Halleluia! Hosanna!
Thus it is my dear friend... Halleluia! Amen!

Gaté, gaté, paragaté,
Parasamgaté, bodhi, soha.

[Kushinagar]
Everything that is born also must die-
Kings, beggars, buddhas, and me.

A last sip of water, a few final teachings.
Oh child of illusion, remember these words:

You are the Buddha, remember, remember.
And you are Salvation, remember these words.

The deathless unending Nature of Mind,
Unborn and unceasing, with Nature like the Sky.

Sit like a mountain, reflect stars on the water,
Like the wings of an eagle about to take flight.

Rest in Natural Great Peace, my dear friend.
The Natural Mind is Pure Light, remember.

Lux aeterna, requiem aeternam,
Parasamgaté, bodhi, soha.

Pleasure

One of the most emotionally challenging insights of the Buddha is that pleasure is not always such a great thing afterall.

When the teachings speak of suffering, they refer to *everything* that threatens to de-stabilize us. Whatever keeps us living on the surface of our mind, by definition prevents us from realizing the depths and profound power of our Buddha Nature. It pulls us in the wrong direction and creates more suffering for the mind. For a practitioner, stability and openness are the most important things.

From a Buddhist perspective, suffering not only refers to the so-called bad things that happen in life. It includes the *feel-good* things too.

Pleasure, as well as pain, is truly capable of sweeping us off centre. We *feel* good, and that's a clear indicator we are operating at the superficial level of mind. Our emotions produce the attachment and aversion that cause so many problems.

However, all is not doom and gloom for Buddhists. We have to live *in* the world at the same time. And thoughts and emotions don't magically go away after we become enlightened. How we deal with them is the crucial point.

If we don't react to bad things with aversion, then there is no problem really. So too with pleasure; if we don't react with attachment or grasp onto the experience [including its source], then all will be well. We can even turn pleasure into a spiritual practice. By using it as an occasion to rejoice and live mindfully, we are actually contributing to the process of our own awakening. We can wish that all beings should be so happy, and that such happiness blossom into profound Natural Great Peace.

The problem with pleasure is its strong connection to the ego and our tendency to become addicted to whatever makes us feel good, however temporarily. Even though it's very superficial, pleasure appears to be so real at the time. When we look deeply into it, and shine the torch of mindfulness on the whole experience, another picture emerges entirely. People, experiences and chemicals that bring pleasure feed so strongly into our addictive streak that we want to have more and more of them. We cannot do without them. But, alas, the pleasure is never enough. Sex, drugs, rock and roll, soul-mates, friends and family are all dangerous territory depending on the reaction they bring out in us. But real life is all around us. If we live mindfully then we have a good chance of enjoying Life without getting swept overboard. It's also important to realize that pleasure is OK provided it doesn't harm us or anyone else. The moral principle of non-harming applies.

Anything done mindfully can bring profound illumination. Even something very harmful could provide the spark to wake us up to reality were the light of awareness to suddenly shine on the situation.

For example, imagine if the awful truth suddenly dawned on you while using heroin *mindfully*. You could have a profound realization of the nature of addiction and all the suffering it brings.

Similarly, shining the light of mindful awareness on our sexual life can reveal deep understanding. For many people, sex is the way they find the truth of all things; it can bring both pleasurable and harm, so it is like any other Dharma path that shows the nature of attachment, aversion and ignorance. Even loving relationships can teach us all we need to wake up; they may start out as paradise but can end up hell-on-earth. Our love for someone can sometimes cause us to try to possess and control them. In the end, maybe both lives will be destroyed. Pray strongly we all learn to enjoy pleasure without grasping or any harmful outcome arising.

If we only realized the ultimate happiness is already inside us, waiting to be unlocked and shared. It transcends the greatest bliss imaginable... and it's free!

Precepts

For Buddhists, morality is mainly a personal issue.

The great challenge laid down by the Buddha was to *avoid all harm, only do good,* and to *achieve all this by training the mind through mindfulness and awareness.* This *non-specific* exhortation to live a good life is very appealing to many people.

But some actually prefer a more detailed code of ethics. So the Buddha suggested five guidelines for things to be avoided. If a practitioner wishes, they can take a vow, or *precept,* in the presence of an image of the Buddha. This can also be done in the presence of ones master, or a monastic sangha member – either formally or informally. The precepts are as follows.

Avoid:

1. killing, or allowing someone else to kill on your behalf
2. stealing; taking what hasn't been given to you
3. harmful speech, such as lying or angry words
4. intoxicants; they impede clarity of mind from arising
5. sexual mis-conduct; anything that could harm yourself or others

Monastics take a whole series of precepts, sometimes hundreds. These vows cover a myriad of potential pitfalls.

But, for *lay practitioners* who wish to take the path a little more seriously, Venerable Thich Nhat Hanh suggests expanding the 5 Precepts into 14.

In order to go deeper into mindful living, the 14 Precepts [or *Pratimoksha Vows*] provide a more detailed moral code.

This path is quite challenging for some of us. But, even as an aspirational goal, it clearly lays out a path that leads to liberation from suffering, with non-harming and virtue at its heart.

1. Openness

I will avoid fanaticism and intolerance because they create more suffering. Therefore I will not be bound by any doctrine, theory or ideology, even Buddhist ones, in order to maintain an OPEN mind. Buddhism is a guide, which helps me open the heart of compassion and understanding. It is not something to fight, kill or die for.

2. Non-attachment to Views

Attachment to views and wrong perceptions creates suffering. A little knowledge is not Absolute Truth. I will remain open and observe the present moment, ready to learn from life, from others and from within myself.

3. Freedom of Thought

Imposing my views on others creates suffering. I will avoid it, even in relation to my own children and loved ones. Everyone has the right to be different. The only way to end fanaticism and narrowness is to open compassionate dialogue with others.

4. Awareness of Suffering

I will deeply observe the nature of suffering without flinching or avoiding it. I commit to being with those who suffer, helping them to transform suffering into peace, compassion and joy.

5. Simple, Healthy Living

True happiness does not come from wealth, fame or sensual pleasure. How could I pursue that while millions are dying from hunger and poverty? I will live simply and share my time, energy and resources with those in need. In order to do this, my body and mind must be healthy. Therefore, I will avoid toxins.

6. Dealing with Anger

Anger blocks communication and creates suffering. I will recognize and take care of it as it arises in me. I will also transform the seeds deep within me that create anger. Whenever anger comes up, I will not do or say anything negative but determine to practise mindful breathing or walking so I can embrace and look deeply at it. I will look with profound compassion on anyone who appears to spark off my anger.

7. Dwelling Happily in the Present Moment

Mindfully living in the present moment, I will bring transformation and healing to my mindstream. I will not become distracted or swept away by the past or the future. In the here and now, I will live happily without attachment or aversion. I will water the seeds of joy, peace, love and understanding deep within me, and see the wonder around and within me as a source of nourishment and transformation.

8. Community and Communication

Lack of communication always brings separation and suffering. So I will train in the compassionate art of Deep

Listening and Loving Speech. And in my community, I will avoid judgement and reacting habitually. I will never cause discord or a break in the sangha but bring open dialogue, reconciliation and a resolution to conflicts, however small.

9. Truthful and Loving Speech

The power of words can create happiness or more suffering. So I will speak with care. I will never cause harm and only tell the truth. However, even if my own safety is at stake, I resolve to speak out against injustice.

10. Protecting the Sangha

The essence and aim of a Sangha is the practise of Wisdom and Compassion. I am determined not to use the Buddhist community for personal gain or profit or to transform our community into a political instrument. A spiritual community should, however, take a clear stand against oppression and injustice and should strive to change the situation without engaging in partisan conflicts.

11. Right Livelihood

I will choose a livelihood that does not further contribute to the violence and injustice already being done to the environment and society. I will bring Wisdom and Compassion to my growing awareness of global economic, political and social realities. I will be a responsible citizen and consumer, and will never invest in companies that deprive others of their fair chance to live.

12. Reverence for Life

I will protect life and prevent war. I will not kill and will not allow others to kill either. Non-violence means bringing peace and reconciliaton to the world.

13. Generosity

I will practise generosity by sharing my time, energy and material resources with those who are in need. I will work lovingly for the well-being of people, animals, plants and minerals. I am determined not to steal or take what is not mine. And I will do my best to prevent others from exploiting and profiting from the suffering of beings.

14. Right Conduct

(For lay members):

I will not engage in sexual relations based on craving. It is not the answer to loneliness or suffering. And I recognize that the ideal situation must involve mutual understanding, love, and a long-term commitment. We should do everything in our power to protect children from sexual abuse and protect couples and families from being broken apart by sexual misconduct. We will treat our own bodies with respect too, and preserve our vital energies for our bodhisattva activity. Finally, we must be aware of the consequences of bringing new lives into the world, and what we can do to make that world a better place.

(For monastic members):

As monks and nuns, we have left behind the ties of wordly love, preferring to work for the benefit of all beings through wisdom and compassion. We are determined to support and protect all those who wish to practise chastity. They are preserving their vital energies for the work of their bodhisattva ideal. We understand that breaking this vow would destroy our monastic life.

Primordial Purity

The Buddha Nature manifests within space and time even though it's not bound by either.

The origin of our true nature is said to be *beyond* the confines of space-time. This Buddha Mind [Skt. *Tathagatagarbha*] pervades everything that exists but, because of its uniquely pure origins, is itself understood to be without beginning or end. It has not been born, and it will not die. Therefore, our true nature is *primordially pure.* This does not suggest the world is somehow impure. It simply describes the way our *Mind-Heart* is.

The Natural Mind has *never* been damaged or stained by anything that may have occurred during all our countless lifetimes. This is why *Teflon* is a perfect simile for our true nature. On the *absolute* level, we are non-stick.

It is so incredible to contemplate how we could never ever be damaged in the slightest by anything.

The teachings say, because of the primordial purity of our Buddha Nature, the Non-Stick Mind: *Even buddhas could not make it any better, and beings certainly couldn't make it worse.* In a time-space continuum where everything is constantly changing, the Buddha Nature can therefore be understood as the only thing that is *changeless.*

The teachings on the *Tathagatagarbha*, our true nature, are found mainly within Mahayana Buddhist lineages. To really come to realize their essence generates within us such a sense of nobility and a positive, healthy sense of pride in who we truly are. Recognizing our primordial purity is not an intellectual recognition. It's experienced through the practice of glimpsing then resting in the Buddha Nature. The overall effect is not just that we see ourselves in a fresh new way. We perceive the Buddha Nature in all beings. This is true Wisdom. And we genuinely wish to liberate them from the suffering of Surface Mind by bringing them back home to *their* own Buddha Nature. This is true Compassion.

Since primordial purity is something we *practise* rather than just think about, it is so vital to progress along the path to the stage where it comes naturally. I doubt if many Buddhist masters could run 100 metres in 10 seconds. That is not what they have trained for. Some Tibetan masters I know even find it difficult to drive or swim. But they *can* dwell in their true nature 24/7 and every activity they engage in is full of wisdom and compassion. Given the choice between training to run in the Olympics, to be a connoisseur of Samsara's trivial pursuits, or to rest in the Natural Mind ... well, there's no competition really, is there?

We've spent countless lifetimes training the mind to dwell in the superficial realm of the *ego* 24/7. And just look at all the suffering it has caused! The masters say, if we train well and are sufficiently ripe, we might actually awaken to perfect buddhahood in this very lifetime!

Quantum Theory

There will always be differences between Science and Buddhism.

Even within Buddhism there are different opinions about the nature of reality. But it has to be remembered that the various philosophical schools within Buddhism are only using different *words* to describe the same awakened reality; they are all just experimenting with language and concepts to point to the way things truly *are* from the perspective of the awakened state.

The era in which we live is very interesting from a scientific standpoint. Everything that appears and exists is now being looked at in such fine detail. First there was Biology. Then Physics, and now sub-atomic Quantum Theory. Soon there will be a *Theory of Everything*. But science is only just beginning to catch up, rather spectacularly, with the spiritual experience of phenomena that culminated in the teachings of the Buddha over 2500 years ago. Science and Wisdom are not the same. Science theorizes about reality. The Wisdom Mind experiences reality directly, as it truly is.

In many ways, Science and Wisdom are complete opposites. The dominant scientific theory presupposes the brain somehow generates consciousness. Whereas, The Wise Ones *know* experientially that Consciousness manifests all.

But there is a radical element within Quantum Physics right now that is on the cutting edge of scientific discovery. We could almost better understand this development as a branch of Psychology or Spiritual Wisdom.

All the foundation stones that form the basis of Buddhism are currently being verified by Science; There is a web of energy that pervades everything; All phenomena co-emerge in relation to eachother; They are interdependent manifestations that drift in and out of existence as the right conditions arise and subside.

Thus, even at the smallest sub-atomic level, particles are now known to be *empty* of independent existence. Their essence is described as being more like light rather than matter. Reality, is understood as *potential* energy that may manifest, however briefly, in any form.

But, perhaps the most fascinating aspects of Science today are the latest discoveries about the causal relationship between *consciousness* and phenomena.

In this regard, radical scientists speak of consciousness and awareness not merely as functions or products of the brain's chemical structure but as the generator of phenomena. Science is slowly catching up with Buddhism and is beginning to verify that *Conscious Awareness* – the Nature of Mind itself – is actually CREATING all that manifests.

'With our thoughts we make the world'
[Buddha]

This is so powerful not just because it's so challenging and shocking, or because Science is starting to verify Buddhist Wisdom. It's ultimate power lies in the simple truth that we literally create our own reality; to change the world just change your mind.

However, there is also a *collective consciousness* at work here. No man is an island, and we are all responsible for co-creating the reality we experience together. When enough people awaken to their true nature, the Natural Mind that underpins the whole collective consciousness will manifest a *new* reality for us to inhabit. But, if we ourselves do not purify our own perception, one person at a time, nothing else can change. For now, the cosmic process of awakening and changing for the better must begin with one person ... You.

I smile to think of myself in the past, when I was young and foolish. I used to think I was the centre of the universe. And now I am old and foolish, I'm reliably informed that I *am* ... just not in the way I thought.

Sure you might as *well* just burst out laughing!

Questions

Every dharma student will have questions. It's a natural part of learning and very much part of the 'modern' approach.

But the dharma is not simply a matter of *learning* something new. It is, as the Buddha himself pointed out, all about *experiencing* for ourselves. And about testing the teachings against our developing awareness of reality's true nature.

Occasionally, our questions just require clarification or slightly more information. These can easily be addressed by our teacher, qualified instructors, or the appropriate book.

However, from time to time, more profound questions arise in our minds. These confusions are an integral element of the path. We are, afterall, deluded and samsaric creatures. At least for the time being. Therefore, it's also quite natural that we can't understand everything yet. But our confusion is so great unfortunately that it's *not* actually possible [or indeed helpful] to have all our questions answered as they arise; they emerge at such a pace even if they were to be answered one by one they'd only be replaced by even more supplementary questions. It could be said that *not* having all our questions answered, as and when we like, is probably the best thing for us.

For it is *through* our confusion that wisdom dawns. You might say, confusion *is* the path. For the moment at least, we must *get used to* our confusion. We must *accept* that we have an insatiable desire to possess ever more knowledge. We don't like delayed gratification. We want everything right *now*. These are our habitual tendencies. The very things that stand between us and true wisdom dawning. Now, if we approach the dharma in the same old habitual ways, we may at best gain a mediocre *knowledge* of it. But we may never *experience* its truth at all. Most likely, transformation and awakening will not occur under those circumstances – because *we* ourselves have not really changed.

Sogyal Rinpoche often recommends that his students first recognize their tendency to over-question everything, and to be always in a hurry to understand. Sometimes, even if we have what appears to be a fundamentally urgent question, it can be more helpful to sit with it – literally *hold* it in our hearts – especially during the teachings. It's amazing how often these questions are actually answered by the teachings themselves if we just treat them with patience and an all-pervasive air of spaciousness.

As Zen Master Suzuki Roshi used to say, we should all have *beginner's mind*; a beginner's mind is an open mind. It is empty and ready ... a clean slate. It is not an anxious, needy, or a doubt-filled mind.

Working with the over-questioning superficial mind in this way *is* our path. If we allow ourselves to fall deeper and deeper into our old grasping tendencies, the path will not clarify much at all. We'll just get worse and perhaps develop serious *doubts* about the dharma, our teacher, and even about the very existence of the Buddha Nature within us.

Far better to avoid all that misery and *allow* wisdom to dawn within us as a result of systematically practising the Dharma. Its truth arises externally, both in the form of our teacher's guidance and in the teachings offered by life itself. It also arises internally, by virtue of our inner teacher – the Natural Mind – which constantly guides and nudges us in the direction of full awakening.

In our study and practice, we must pray strongly that we do not add in any way to our confusion.

The 11th Century Tibetan saint Gampopa was the main disciple of the renowned master Milarepa, who was himself later to become the master of the first Karmapa. This four line prayer, composed by Gampopa, is addressed directly to the Buddha Nature as it works tirelessly both within and without for our Awakening. It embodies everything we need in our approach to the questioning, exhausted mind.

Grant your blessing so that my mind may turn towards the Dharma.

Grant your blessing so that Dharma may progress along the path.

Grant your blessing so that the path may clarify confusion.

Grant your blessing so that confusion may dawn as wisdom.

Refuge

Poor Samsaric beings! Our biggest downfall is relying on all the wrong things in life.

If something brings us a little pleasure or apparent security we throw ourselves wholeheartedly into it without understanding its impermanent and unreliable nature. It's like we are running away from life from the moment we're born. We want to return to the womb. We overlook all the feelings of claustrophobia and suffocation we experienced there during those last days. We just want sanctuary. Somewhere safe.

The first step on the Buddhist path is to replace that primal urge to seek shelter in all the wrong places with something more wholesome.

We go for *Refuge* in the Three Jewels: the Buddha, the Dharma and the Sangha.

They are not like other refuges. They are not a place to hide *from* life. The Three Jewels represent the Buddha Nature itself in all its manifestations, both external and internal. When we connect with our own true nature – the nature of everything – like this, we unlock limitless sustenance, protection, well-being and profound inspiration. Instead of being safe *from* the world, we are completely *open* to all the wondrous possibilities of life.

We find our true *Sanctuary* in the Buddha Nature, in the form of the Three Jewels, because they embody the *truth* our souls are so longing to reveal. The Buddha Nature is the one thing we can actually *trust* in. So far, we've been placing our trust in so many things that have let us down. Now we need to finally recognize that the all-pervasive Buddha Mind is the only object of refuge truly deserving of that trust.

If we go for refuge in the Buddha Mind, our Dharma study and practice, and our Sangha community, we must also be careful not to bring our *clinging* habits along with us. We don't want to turn the Three Jewels into yet another comfort blanket that will ultimately let us down. Neither should we turn the precious teachings that liberate the mind into some form of ideology. If we do, we'll disable its true power to help us and the most golden opportunity for awakening will pass us by. The Buddha says:

> Sometime, somewhere, you need to take something to be the truth. But if you cling to it too strongly, then even when the truth comes in person and knocks on your door, you will not open it.

There are many wrong ways to go for refuge: With a selfish motivation, to escape the world, considering the Buddha as an almighty god who will somehow save us, considering the Living Teacher as a guru-saviour [like in a personality cult], mistaking the Dharma for some kind of dogmatic ideology that we can cling to or proselytize, creating a Sangha community which is more cultish than supportive of true awakening.

Refuge should be more like coming home. Like a child running into her mother's arms. Merging our mind with all the buddhas of past, present, and future.

Of course, we still love our family and friends as before. Maybe even more so. We must not allow ourselves become elitist or disconnected in any way from ordinary life or people not involved in the dharma.

We connect with our Buddha Nature, through the Three Jewels, not just for our own sake but for the ultimate benefit of all.

Remember

As we move through our daily lives, it seems Buddhists have to remember so much. So many teachings. So many crucial points. How could we ever hope to integrate the entire Dharma?

The answer is profound, yet surprisingly simple. We must train our mind to remember *one* thing. Never forget it. Always live it.

The one point to remember is the essence of all the Buddha's teachings:

WE HAVE THE BUDDHA NATURE.

Our true nature is always accessible in the present moment. By remaining open to it in the here and now, everything is transformed. The Natural Mind is awakened by *remembering* it. When we touch the very essence of our true self, we connect with the essence of everything.

As beginners, remembering our Buddha Nature may be fascinating and inspiring. However, it remains an intellectual remembrance until we begin to experience it directly for ourselves through meditation practice. Once that begins to happen, glimpse after glimpse, we are nolonger beginners. We are remembering and accessing something that we *know* is there.

We must live in the 'real world' *and* develop the stability to *rest in the Buddha Nature* simultaneously. The fruition will also be twofold. We will experience the peace, loving compassion, and power of our true nature. And we will *act* spontaneously in the present moment for the ultimate benefit of others.

So we train ourselves to *remember the Buddha Nature*. We do our formal meditation practice from the perspective of that glorious, spacious realisation. Furthermore, we train our minds to remember the *bigger picture*, while we are not meditating, by integrating that vast perspective into daily life.

Gently focusing on the breath will stabilize us in the present moment. As we breathe in we remember and experience our Buddha Nature. As we breathe out we bring peace, love and compassion to others.

We train ourselves to gently return to this whenever we become distracted from it: we have the Buddha Nature and we are bringing ultimate benefit to beings. We will be able to maintain this perspective, known as *The View*, for longer and longer periods of time. Eventually, there will come a time when we can enter into this pure awareness permanently.

We will have fully awakened.

Respond

It seems we spend our whole lives being driven along by forces that *appear* beyond our control: karma, instinct, genetics, culture.

Buddhism is not so much a religion, or even a nice 'way of life'.

It is a training, an experiential science of the mind that enables us to awaken the profound innate powers that lie within. By awakening our conscious awareness through meditation and integration we regain control over our own lives. The present moment opens up to us a vast, spacious world of liberation and choice.

The Buddha's teaching on *The Eight Consciousnesses* [see 'Consciousness'] clearly shows the technicalities of how the practice works. The more stable our mind becomes the more we dwell in the present moment. Once we have mastered that, we nolonger have to *react* habitually. We have created the space to *respond* as we choose.

As phenomena enter our mindstream, the impact is greatly reduced. We do not react with all the usual judgemental attachment and aversion. The 'non-stick' quality of the Natural Mind sets us free. Put simply, we replace the habit of reacting automatically with the openness of *responding* consciously. The power of our *intention* increases. If we truly intend for ourselves and others to be happy and not to suffer, then finally we have the power to bring that about.

Our way of being in the world has changed utterly.

We are free.

Retreat

It is never a good idea to hide away from life.

But from time to time many of us need to get away from it all and recharge our batteries. Meditators often take time out to focus more intensively on their spiritual practice, even though they may have already established a stable daily practice at home.

It is possible to do such a retreat in a variety of ways. One could set aside a day or a weekend to practise at home. Or our local sangha community may organize such events for us to take part in as a group. Some more experienced meditators go for longer periods to retreat centres or monasteries where they can practise quite intensively, without too much distraction. I know some friends who have recently completed a traditional Three Year Retreat at a Tibetan Buddhist temple in France. In Tibet there is even a tradition of advanced practitioners retreating to isolated caves for many years.

But, however we choose to organize our personal retreat there's one extremely important factor to embrace. The key to a successful retreat is to *drop samsaric mind*. Awakening cannot unfold otherwise.

Whether we're at home or in a cave, our confused and suffering mind comes with us. If we do not *renounce* our samsaric habitual tendencies, and practise resting in our Buddha Nature, retreat is meaningless. The mind is always with us, wherever we go, providing us with the raw material for awakening. In that way, every moment of every day can be a retreat if we practise dwelling in the present and touching our true nature.

With a sincere, heart-felt longing to drop our ego-driven, deluded aspects, our whole life can be like a retreat. Once that is cut through, the Natural Mind with its heart of compassion is awakened. We feel extremely well in ourselves, and we bring far more benefit to beings. The signs that a retreat, or even spiritual practice per se, is working is whether or not we have become more compassionate and present.

There is a wonderful Tibetan story of an advanced practitioner who entered solitary, long-term retreat for many years. When he came out, he went to visit his master to have his realisation and progress checked. He told his master his mind had become unshakably stable, and that all his Loving Kindness and Compassion practice had changed him permanently. He claimed to feel only compassion, nothing else. Without saying a word, the master took him completely by surprise and slapped his face really hard. The student totally lost all self-control and flew into a rage. The master simply smiled at him lovingly and said, *Where has your Compassion gone now?*

So even formal retreat, apparently under perfect circumstances, may not lead to the desired outcome straight away. We should not enter retreat with unrealistic goals or make outlandish claims of success afterwards. Granted, some rare and precious people have sat down as ordinary beings to meditate for the first time only to rise again as perfect buddhas. But, for the rest of us, there is slightly more work to do.

Some masters say that leaving home achieves half the retreat. Others say we should completely exhaust ourselves with samsara's nonsense before letting it go. Whatever our approach, the key is to drop samsaric mind for once and for all with a great sense of relief and liberation. Only then can we be fully alive and freely take part *in* the world for the ultimate benefit of others.

Intensive practice retreats may speed things along.

But every breath, wherever we may be, also offers us the chance to wake up.

Revolution

When we think of all the great prophets and spiritual masters of the past such as the Buddha, Jesus, and Muhammad, we often forget that they were revolutionaries and reformers as well as gentle, highly-realized beings.

It's a mistake to only remember them as sitting in prayerful meditation. True spiritual masters also shed the light of wisdom on the times in which they live. However we look at it, the spiritual path is a challenge – to say the least – to the socio-economic and religious patterns of the day.

If we really believe an individual can commune directly with God, or merge their mind with the Buddha Mind, without the need for an intermediary then that *is* revolutionary.

Furthermore, if we believe the ego-tendency must be overturned in favour of the ultimate benefit of others, then *that* is also revolution of the highest order. The path to spiritual awakening challenges everything. But not in a violent, ideological way. What's called for is a total turn-around; a *quiet* revolution of the heart and mind.

What could be more revolutionary than showing people they can find lasting happiness within themselves? It's unlimited, free and available to all. True happiness does not depend on external factors such as religious institutions, social status, or money.

The Buddha walked away from all the socio-religious norms of his day. What he established in their place was truly outrageous!

He overthrew the caste system that still remains so ingrained in Indian society. His sangha eventually welcomed all people: male, female, rich, poor, monastic, lay, kings, the 'untouchables', common criminals and even repentant serial killers like the infamous Angulimala; as far as the state was concerned, that was an act of treason in itself!

By teaching the path of meditation that leads to a direct, personal experience of the divine [the Buddha Nature], he was also abandoning the Hindu religion. There was no need for priests or shamans, temples or rituals. The path is already hard enough without all those extra layers of culture and superstition. For all its profundity, the path to enlightenment is plain and simple. And must remain free and accessible to all who wish to follow it.

The Buddha recognized that not everyone is ready to follow the spiritual path in this lifetime. And he encouraged those who weren't to support the practice and well-being of those who were. In his day, the core group of the Buddha's disciples were ordained monks and nuns. These monastics were celibate and devoted to spiritual practice. They had no money or food and were homeless. This Monastic Sangha relied on food offerings from villagers as they moved about together. They did not preach or try to convert others, although many came for teachings and meditation when the sangha settled temporarily nearby. During the rainy season, the whole community of practitioners would live in a special retreat that had been built for them by royal and wealthy patrons. In this way, there was no need for money and what few things the sangha did possess by necessity was held in common ownership. There was no personal property whatsoever; even the robes were given to them by others and the Buddha's own robes were sewn together from a collection of humble rags.

The entire way of life of the Buddha and his followers was a rebellious and courageous departure from the norm.

Nowadays, few of us want to be monastic practitioners and even fewer are willing to live our daily lives without money, possessions, security or status. But the challenge still remains – as a shining, guiding light.

Maybe there *is* another way. Perhaps our 'modern' way of life with all its outlandish priorities *is* misguided. Just look at the mess we've made of everything!

It seems, for all his revolutionary reforms, the greatest challenge the Buddha laid down was that we should try to live a simple life, free from unnecessary complexity – a peaceful, loving life lived without regret and leaving no negative impact. Not forgetting the spiritual work we do on our minds and hearts isn't for our own sake, ultimately we want others to find lasting happiness. That is our revolutionary priority.

So-called *Western Society* considers itself cutting-edge, the pinnacle of Human Civilization, based on revolutionary principles. But the best *we* could come up with after thousands of years has been The Magna Carta [*'The King must also obey the law'*. Who knew? And does he?], The French Revolution [*'Liberté, Égalité, Fraternité'*: Freedom, Equality, Brotherhood. Oh yes, and *Off with their heads!*], The American Declaration of Independence [*Everone has the right to 'Life, liberty and the pursuit of happiness'*. Well, where do I begin? The meaning of life is the *pursuit of ones own happiness*?!]

All joking apart, the Buddha's teaching is so revolutionary precisely because of this last point. It turns the whole thing upside-down. The meaning of life is that we should pursue the happiness of *others*.

To truly bring happiness and the highest benefit to others, the greatest act of love and compassion we can offer others is that they may experience complete awakening. To this end, we do not proselytize, however. We try to lead by example, especially within our own sangha community. We support newcomers whole-heartedly whenever they do join us on the path. But, apart from that, authentic Buddhists should not go out looking for new converts.

Our strongest aspiration is that Peace may break out around the world, and that Loving Compassion flow down like a river into the hearts of all.

Our greatest mantra must surely be this:

May the gentle revolution begin with me.

Simplicity

The *Pali Canon* contains the earliest collection of the Buddha's teachings, as memorized and later written by the first generations of his disciples. There you will find much of what we now know as *Theravada* Buddhism.

By the time Buddhism almost totally disappeared from India this form of it had already taken root in Sri Lanka and much of South East Asia and Indonesia. As well as a more monastic approach to dharma practice the emphasis was firmly placed on living a good and above all a *simple* life.

Avoiding harm is the keystone of the entire Buddhist path. And simplicity itself is the whole approach in a nutshell.

Simplicity [*ajjava* or *asatha* in Pali] is unfortunately so rare nowadays that it shines like a beacon in the darkness if ever you encounter it. There is a natural beauty and a grace about a person who needs no adornment or attention in their life. The collected Sayings of The Buddha [*Dhammapada*] and the first Sutras, such as the *Samyutta Nikaya* praise highly the person who lives simply, without complication or commotion. Gentleness [*maddava*] and modesty [*lajjava*] generate an attitude of mind itself marked by clarity and a distinct lack of complexity.

The Buddha's teachings may be lengthy and detailed or short enough to contemplate, but all of the main points can be summarized in a simple phrase or two. This is the hallmark of Universal Truth.

Attachment to one's image or material possessions often leads to suffering. Simplifying our life can bring greater and greater joy and stability. But, more importantly, a simplified mind generates great openness, contentment and bliss.

This is not to say we must have no thoughts or personal things. On the contrary, our simplified *attitude* is what brings peace. In time the more Mindfulness, Awareness and Spaciousness we manifest in our mindstream may lead to a totally simple and uncontrived life. We may nolonger require so much struggle and strife to support our new simplified life.

The Buddha himself in the *Metta Sutra* advised his followers to adopt such an attitude that they may be able to support themselves more easily [*subharo*] and thus live more happily without rushing around [*appakicco*] busily gathering wealth and possessions. And those who do require some support from the community will not be so much of a burden.

The Simple Life, as a way of being, brings great benefits to one's physical and mental circumstances. It also leads to a great self-liberation and clarity that makes a more *moral* life possible. Because simplicity can help us directly to focus more clearly on applying *The Precepts* from moment to moment, the Buddha called this natural ease a kind of "straightforwardness" [*uju* or *ujuka*]. It brings us straight to the place we want to be.

The *Six Paramitas* also become a real possibility for us as we naturally become more generous, non-harming, unperturbed etcetera.

However, it is always wiser to focus on your own mind and practice. Do not be judgemental or deceived by the appearance of other's lives.

I know a millionaire who lives such a simple life that his mind would not suffer very much at all if he lost everything tomorrow. I know a hermit who lives in solitary retreat in the Himalaya who struggles every day with his attachment to his prayer beads and lives in dread of the spider who shares his cave. The contradictory list is endless; the Buddhist master who needs constant pampering and a lavish lifestyle, the homeless woman who *is* a living Buddha, the guy who gave practically everything away to enter *Life Retreat* in his modest home but whose mind remains extremely bothersome and irritable.

At one time, I myself designed and built an amazing, minimalist home infused with a simple Zen esthetic. It was like living in a modern art gallery in New York, but with absolutely nothing on the walls whatsoever. There was even an incredibly inspiring glass meditation room in the garden.

Hilariously, the truth of the matter was that the meditation room was rarely used at all. And visitors never got to see the one room that was stuffed to over-flowing with all the clutter and chaos which facilitated the rest of the house being so uncluttered and light!

Sky

Masters sometimes use images from nature such as the sky to describe the profound yet simple qualities of the Buddha Mind.

In Ireland, most days when we look up we just see clouds. It's all too easy to forget that the sun even exists.

However, the clouds form only a tiny layer of the huge space we know as sky. When we go in a plane we are powerfully reminded of that fact. As we quickly rise above the clouds and pass into the vast expanse beyond, it's quite awe-inspiring to remember the sun is always up there shining impartially, regardless of the weather down below.

The image of the clouds representing the superficial *appearance* of mind, the layer of thoughts and emotions that so preoccupy us, is an extremely potent dharma teaching – especially for those of us who *know* how it feels to live with almost constant cloudiness.

But, beyond the clouds is the enormity and spaciousness of the wide open sky. And in that unobstructed space shines the sun. Some of the deepest teachings of the Buddha are embodied in this clear, bright image.

The Natural Mind, our inner-most essence, is said to be like the sky. The actual phrase in many of the ancient texts is often translated as the *sky-like nature of mind.*

The Natural Mind, or Buddha Nature, is further described as having *three* main components, each giving rise to the next:

Its *Essence* is infinite and empty of self ['Shunyata']

Its *Nature* is cognisant ['pure awareness of the here and now']

Its *Compassionate Energy* is impartial and all-pervasive.

Now, in order to experience a little of what the Buddha Nature is really like, practise in the following way:

Imagine a sky ... empty, open and spacious ... primordially pure ... Its **Essence** is like this.

Imagine a sun ... unobstructed ... clear light ... spontaneously present and aware ... Its **Nature** is like this.

Imagine that sun's rays shining on us, and on all beings ... impartially, and in all directions ... Its **Compassionate Energy** is like this.

Smile

When we look at a beautiful, traditional painting of the Buddha in meditation, we often forget what we're gazing at is intended to be a mirror.

We are looking at *ourselves*, what we can become.

We are looking at the embodiment of happiness and freedom from suffering. In the details of the perfect meditation posture contained within that picture, we also see the very path that will lead to lasting happiness. What we must do. How to sit, how to be.

It's as if the picture is reflecting our true nature back to us, across the vast ocean of space and time, saying *This is who you really are. This is what you are awakening. And this is the method for doing it.*

The posture being transmitted has three aspects pertaining to the body, speech, and mind of the practitioner. All this is spoken of elsewhere, but even when we look at the posture of the body we see just how much detail there is. Given that every *yoga* of the body evokes a corresponding yoga of the mind, we must therefore take all these details *seriously* and try to perfect them in our posture too.

Buddhism is a *serious* thing afterall. But it should never be so serious that it's uptight, minutiæ-obsessed, or solemn. If our practice ended up like that it would be such a great pity. And we would've lost much of the spacious spirit of freedom and refreshing joy that true meditation brings.

Now, just *what-the-Buddha* has all this got to do with today's keyword '*smile*'?

Maybe it's just a real male thing. But it's so typical of us to look at that picture of the Buddha sitting in meditation and garner what we think are all the most important elements of the posture while perhaps habitually overlooking the fact that the Buddha's lips are slightly parted and he is *smiling*.

How typical of us to ignore the smile as an integral component of good meditation. How typical to ignore the power of the smile in daily life too. It's like we dismiss the smile and cast it aside as a way of being because we just don't believe joy could be *that* simple. It's just too good to be true. Isn't it?

Well, as with everything else to do with Buddhism, the authentic approach is to put it to the test. *Try* smiling. Measure it against your own experience, both in meditation and in life. We may have noticed that the Buddha's smile is quite soft and gentle. It must feel very natural and light. [Serving Suggestion: For best results avoid the tight grin of the smug and the wild look of the insane. You might be left like that. Also people on the bus get scared.]

Contemplate how it feels *in the moment* and what the outcome is in the next moment. Test and observe the power of the smile.

Speaking personally, the introduction of a soft smile to my own posture turned my whole world upside down. Thich Nhat Hanh was teaching about it at his root temple in Hue, Viet Nam. It was like a light bulb had been switched on in my heart-mind. I felt more present and awake than ever. Aware and refreshed. I just couldn't believe that something so fundamental and so obvious had been missing before. Then, when I tried it in ordinary life, the smile seemed to colour the very fabric of whatever I was experiencing. I felt open and involved, quietly content and ready to benefit beings.

On a funnier note ... people tended to ask me less why I was so serious, or what was wrong. And, despite obsessing for many decades about my crooked, prominent teeth [and therefore never smiling] people started to comment I had a beautiful smile and that I was radiant. I didn't tell them about my super-whitening *Blanx* toothpaste or my new face-cream from *L'Oreal*.

I truly feel that consciously maintaining a natural, gentle smile bubbling away just under the surface *lifts* my entire perception. It also *opens* a heart and mind that otherwise might have tended towards the closed, inert side of the spectrum. It's almost like the face muscles are more natural and relaxed when you smile. And the subtle joy and freshness seems to emanate upwards from the Natural Mind itself and out through the eyes. Perhaps this is the radiance other people sometimes pick up on. It is not necessary to have a broad, beaming smile. In many ways that might actually be a bit creepy. But a small, natural smile is perhaps more genuine and easier to maintain.

Remember, at first, all we're doing with the smile is relaxing and opening things up. Then, when it becomes more natural for us, and we become more experienced as practitioners, we can actually use the smile in a more profound way.

A natural, subtle smile like that can become a kind of doorway. An opening through which we *engage* with the suffering of beings. The lips, the eyes, the whole face – even right down to the heart chakra – becomes a conduit through which we *send* beings our love and *remove* their suffering and ignorance. Once we establish this two-way flow of love and compassion, it is said the heart-mind of openness and bliss rises within us.

Smile, you are alive!

Staying In The Practice

The mind is always with us.

So, whatever pure awareness and spontaneous presence we awaken during formal practice can and must be carried into ordinary life.

More advanced meditators, therefore, aspire to *staying in the practice* at all times; fully present yet open to life.

We will find all the methods that help us focus during our meditation are also indispensible in post-meditation. Depending on our level of stability and realisation, we can use whatever technique currently works best for us.

The ideal situation is that we could continue to dwell in the Natural Mind itself. Or, if we have the view that unites the empty openness of Shunyata with the heart of compassion, that would come a very close second.

Alternatively, we could simply *remember* our Buddha Nature and touch it deeply from time to time, maintaining all the while an open, *non-conceptual* engagement with phenomena.

At the very least we should continue to develop our non-grasping, *non-stick* quality by continually *bringing the mind home* to the present moment. Using the objects of body-posture and the senses, the breath, or a mantra, continues to be extremely helpful even when we're not sitting on our meditation cushion.

The most important factor is not to be too uptight.

A relaxed, natural approach is key. When we integrate the qualities of the practice with ordinary life, everything begins to flow naturally and with great ease. As usual, whenever we become distracted we gently bring the mind back to base and continue with mindfulness, awareness and, above all, spaciousness.

Being in the world like this brings lasting happiness to all.

Teacher

Many people simply find an authentic, mainstream Dharma Centre just to learn how to meditate properly.

Of those people, some join that Sangha Community but most do not. They move on and take the meditation technique away with them – maybe developing a daily practice, maybe not.

But, for the ones who do stay, making a strong stable connection with the Buddha Nature through meditation is the priority. While some Buddhist lineages offer the teachings through qualified lay and monastic instructors, others emphasize the importance of receiving the Dharma directly from a living, highly realized Master [*Teacher*].

Either way, when making a choice of teacher, educate yourself. Bring your *Discriminating Awareness Wisdom* with you as you do your research. Making the wrong choice can lead to painful disillusionment further down the line.

The Buddhist lineages known as the *Mahayana* place great store by practitioners finding, and developing a direct heart connection with an appropriate master. For practitioners who are truly suited to this particular path, and who find a suitable Teacher, it can work out extremely well. The key issue is the crucial importance of finding the *right* Teacher for you in the first place, and establishing an *appropriate* connection with them.

We are strongly encouraged to check out the background, lineage, qualifications and personal history of any potential Teacher. The great saints and masters of the past, going all the way back to the Buddha himself, have instructed practitioners to thoroughly put the Teacher to the test before making any decision. And this is with very good reason! The world has always been plagued by spiritual charlatans, wannabe dominators and snake-oil merchants of every kind.

Even *within* the more mainstream Buddhist lineages themselves, regular reports emerge of Un-Awakened masters making all sorts of claims about themselves, the abusive or corrupt behavior of certain masters, and their close disciples who create personality cults and all the necessary media spin befitting of our Dark Age.

When searching for a suitable master we should be, as they say of old, like an expert in precious metals testing the purity of gold. Not only should we test the Teacher, but also take a good look at the content and clarity of their Dharma-teaching. Furthermore, we have to examine their Sangha members, especially the 'senior' students. We should examine how being with this particular master has shaped them; basic things like whether they are compassionate, caring people – whether their egos are flourishing or declining. When we check out the Sangha like this, we can discern for ourselves the hallmark qualities of the Teacher. A pure connection between Master and Sangha is crucial.

Personally, I would avoid like the plague *anything* that smells like a rat: abusive masters, guru-driven personality cults, local sangha groups led by manipulative strong egos. The list is endless but you get the general picture.

Searching for *your* master may take forever. You may not find one at all. Maybe there *isn't* one out there for you and you'll have to go it alone. Or maybe there's *three*! Whatever.

But remember... Life is too short for endlessly shopping around for the right Teacher. We might get caught in the loop of *spiritual materialism* and misguidedly approach the truth as a mere *consumer*. Sooner or later, we may just have to *pick* a teacher and get on the path. No need to waste too much time searching, going around the world like some *dharma-bum* looking for the perfect master.

The best advice I ever heard about *how* to make the most of the student-teacher connection is, having made a choice and embarked upon the path, to have no more doubts and develop unshakable, confident faith in the Master, Buddha, Dharma, and Sangha. When we perceive all four pillars *purely*, we benefit the most.

We must see beyond what appears. That *is* the Dharma, pure and simple.

It also holds true for viewing the Teacher – though very precious – as another type of phenomenon. We must see beyond the surface appearance of the Teacher; his personality, her manner, their image. Ever deeper, we must understand that the *teaching* they offer is the most important thing about them. We have to learn to connect with the deepest truth of those teachings and not just what they *appear* to be saying. To this end, *pure perception* is developed only by activating our non-judgemental *Wisdom Mind*. Our samsaric Surface Mind is what led to all our problems in the first place. So we obviously must abandon that now and receive the teachings with a different, more profound perspective.

This ancient Tibetan verse sums it up:

Rely on the message of the teacher, not on his personality;

Rely on the meaning, not just on the words;

Rely on the real meaning, not on the apparent ['provisional'] one;

Rely on your wisdom mind, not on your ordinary, judgemental mind.

At the deepest level, the channel that opens up between master and student is totally pure and brings *ultimate* benefit to the student as quickly and as directly as possible. It is a matter of Wisdom Mind speaking directly to Wisdom Mind. The heart opening to the heart. The primordially pure awakening the primordially pure; infinity gazing upon itself.

Perhaps the most *anarchic* of all the Buddha's teachings is that *we* create everything with our own mind: life, love, suffering, death...

This is also true for whatever charlatans or authentically enlightened spiritual masters we may encounter. *We* create them too. It's as though we manifest and summon before us the kind of teacher our karma attracts. But, as we know, we can *change* our karma by purifying it. We can get the *perfect teacher* if we become the perfect student.

Think about it: We have to become Shariputra to have the Buddha as our master; like Gampopa to have Milarepa.

If the teacher manifests in accordance with the state of my own mind, then I must resolve to awaken the vast openness and contentment of my own Buddha Mind in order to find my perfect teacher. I must become expert in accessing my Buddha Nature through pure awareness of the present moment. Then the perfect student-master connection can be forged in the furnace of the heart.

Dudjom Rinpoche, in his *Calling the Lama From Afar*, wrote:

> Pure awareness of nowness is the real Buddha,
> In openness and contentment,
> Find the Master in your heart.

Toxins

We are said to have a physical body and a subtle energy body. They're both very sensitive and, of course, interdependent.

It's quite easy not to notice how various toxins gradually make them obstructed, heavy and sluggish, when their natural state is to be clear and light.

This important point is easily proved in relation to the physical body. Certain foods make us feel heavy and sluggish. We often become so obstructed it's difficult to pass them through our digestive system. Unfortunately, they also might contain a lot of fat and sugar [which some people find very tasty and addictive]. That could also make us ill by triggering disease.

Similarly, toxins such as drugs and alcohol have very strong effects on the body. The five physical senses feel like they're almost *coated* by the toxins and become impaired. These particular toxins are highly addictive and may become extremely difficult to quit. But anyone who's been heavily addicted and yet somehow managed to withdraw from these substances can testify there's a veil that appears to slowly lift from the sense organs. It's like we can see, hear and taste anew with ever-increasing intensity and clarity. There is a freshness to our perception that can only be described as *clear* and *light*. At that time of re-awakening to reality it's crucial to understand that *this* is the natural state of the senses. It is the way they are meant to be.

Most people, however, do not perceive reality as it comes through the sense organs with that natural level of clarity. Even if we are not intoxicated, our minds become so used to this level of perception they simply stop experiencing it so clearly. We become lazy. For example, Science confirms that our nose nolonger smells odours that are present around us all the time [for example, household smells such as pets, foodstuffs, or even room air-fresheners]. We just get so used to them, they don't really register anymore.

Now, this leads us to the mind and all the particular toxins it has to deal with. Although the physical body really has an effect on the subtle energy body, it is the mind toxins that perhaps have the most negative effect.

Of course physical substances that intoxicate the brain organ also have a huge effect on the mind. The mind is smeared with an *extra* layer of murky disconnection. But the most dangerous toxins for the mind are not necessarily physical in origin at all. Contemplate the toxic nature of *Anger*, for example. It has the power to shape and destroy not only this current lifetime but many future lives too ... to say nothing of the destruction our anger brings to the lives of those around us.

Similarly with *Grasping*. The *I-want-I-need-What-about-me?!* tendancy knows no bounds and is always prone to ultimate disappointment.

These Mind Poisons are so dangerous yet they're all that stands between us and enlightenment if we could only start to work on them now. Poisons like grasping and anger [attachment and aversion] are fed and watered by the toxins we allow to enter our mindstream.

Contemplate all the negativity we feed the mind within our daily lives; the way we *are* with eachother, the way we think of ourselves in relation to others, the way we think of ourselves all the time; toxins pollute our mindstream by way of the people we hang out with, the way we *react* rather than *respond* to them; all the myriad ingenious and devious toxins that *invade* our mind-space by means of the kinds of TV programmes and other media we allow to penetrate us. We need more discernment or we'll never clarify our underlying confusion.

These are all factors that further obstruct our path to awakening. They just add to the thick layer of ignorance that already obscures our view of our Buddha Nature. It is the purpose of the practice to destroy the ego and all its poisonous, toxic suffering forever.

In order for full awakening to occur, both the physical and subtle body should be in harmony with eachother. Even if the physical body cannot be entirely clear of toxins, or is terminally ill, at least the subtle energy body should be as clear and light as possible.

Right from the day we start meditating up to the more advanced practices, they all work on opening up the natural flow of the subtle channels, energies, and essences. If this process of inner purification didn't occur, enlightenment could never happen. We'd just remain more or less as we are: good-hearted yet just as obstructed, heavy and sluggish as ever.

We don't realize it, but we're so caught up in our samsaric suffering mind and all the toxins that feed into it. It's not even good enough to *detox* from time to time only to *re-tox* again. We simply *have* to cut the problem at the root of the mind.

By cutting through the ego, we dissolve every obstacle, for once and for all.

Un-Distracted and Un-Altered

To perfect our meditation so we can rest naturally and with great ease in the Buddha Nature, we will need to have lots of personal experience and instruction in the profound meaning of these two vital words: *Undistracted* and *Unaltered*.

They are the very essence *and* method of realizing the Natural Mind.

The first of these crucial teachings comes under the scope of the fifth of the *Six Paramitas*: Meditative Concentration [the capacity to remain *undistracted*]. But we're not dealing here with the skill of coping with distractions like noise or thoughts while we are trying to meditate. *This* kind of non-distraction goes much much deeper than that; at this level we are learning how to remain *in the Buddha Mind* undistracted. That's an entirely different prospect and presupposes we have already glimpsed and connected with our Natural Mind, and are now ready to permanently stabilize that connection.

As beginners, we learn how to meditate using an *object* to help bring our mind home, such as 'watching the breath'. Then we take the crucial step of meditating *without* object;

we can sit for longer periods without needing a particular object to focus on – we become naturally mindful, aware, and spacious. Then we develop our practice through various stages, according to our lineage, hopefully awakening the heart of *bodhichitta* along the way.

When we enter the most profound phase of awakening through formal practice, we start to work on resting in the Buddha Mind all the time, undistracted and unaltered.

Even the most advanced practitioners [*yogis*] are working with the distractions of mind; expert meditators who have isolated themselves in caves, and so on, for the purpose of intensive practice may find they become distracted from the Buddha Nature too. Maybe because of ordinary distractions or because they are subtly attached to experiences like bliss, clarity and absence of thought. Another even more advanced pitfall is when a *yogi* becomes distracted from their true nature by *clinging to emptiness as an antidote*; they can get 'stuck' in their particular stage, the realisation of Shunyata, because they are using it as a coping mechanism *against* Samsara, as it were. Only when we completely *let go* of all attachment and aversion, even at the subtlest level, is full awakening possible. This concept-free mind that remains aware of, and engaged with, intrinsic reality is the essential nature of the Buddha Mind.

Once we have opened, and stabilized, this kind of non-stick yet compassionately engaged mind, we're said to have truly perfected the state of being *Undistracted* [Tibetan *ma yingpa*]. But, Yes you guessed it, that in itself is not enough. Now that we've reached the Essential Nature of Mind, we have to be able to *stay* there.

The quality of *remaining* in the Natural Mind, *Unaltered*, is the most subtle form of meditative realisation. Known as *ma chöpa* in Tibetan, the *Unaltered* state is the highest, most perfectly natural fruition of meditation. Resting in the Buddha Nature like this, one has realized the ultimate level *beyond meditation*, as it were. All we have to do then is maintain that *presence*. Do not alter it in any way. However, we mustn't become at all rigid or clinging. Until we have perfected the state of remaining **unaltered** in this '*Buddha Presence*', we must continue to practise it.

One profound method is to recognize the subtle difference in '*taste*' between *undistracted* and *unaltered*. Then allow the mind to shift, almost imperceptibly, from one state to the other as required... When we become distracted, bring the mind home [undistracted]. Then remain in that state [unaltered]. When we become distracted, bring the mind home again. Thus our subtle consciousness shifts gently back and forth from being undistracted to unaltered. This will keep the mind clear and the meditative experience fresh. At this penultimate level we are not so much *meditating on* anything; there is nothing to do really. We're simply *getting used to* the flavour of the Unaltered State.

If we are not yet ripe for realizing the natural state of the Buddha Mind, but are merely reading about it and contemplating its beautiful qualities, we should never imagine for one second that this experience is not open to *us*, right here right now. We must never permit wrong views to arise such as, *Oh poor me! Little old me! I could never experience that!*

The best and most highly realized masters teach meditation in such a way that their students are primed and prepared *from the very beginning* for precisely this realisation, *whenever* it may occur.

A *Wise* master views the student as a buddha, on the verge of awakening. And the same *Compassionate* master sets in motion the very path that will accomplish full awakening most directly. That is *their* job, and *our* destiny.

Who knows whether buddhahood will arise only after several more lifetimes, or with our next breath? But it *will* come. It's just a matter of *when*. Realizing the *unaltered* state is *how*.

The highest Tibetan teachings, known as *Mahamudra* or *Dzogchen*, include this tiny verse:

Chu ma nyok na dang,
Sem ma chö na de.

Water, if you don't stir it, becomes clear.
The mind, left unaltered, finds its own natural peace.

Vegan

The foundation stone upon which all the Buddha's teaching is built is an exhortation, from the heart to the heart: Do No Harm.

Now, either we're going to at least *aspire* to taking that appeal on board or we are not. If we don't take it seriously, we are not truly following a Buddhist path. If we do, we have to begin to shine the dharma light of mindful awareness on our own lives. We must reveal and face the areas of our daily lives we need to do some more work on. *Non-harming* is a general principle. But we have to try our best to decide exactly how to put it into action.

When it comes to what we eat, there are certain clear guidelines for Buddhists. One, of course, is *Do no harm.* Another is *Do not kill.* Many masters also take that to mean we shouldn't allow anyone else to kill on our behalf either. I *know* for sure I would never eat meat if I had to kill the animal myself first. Not to mention all those *Bodhichitta* and *Compassion* teachings about all creatures having been our mother in the past. Eating the bodies of other beings is therefore a *no-no*.

Even if we don't eat their bodies, by virtue of the non-harming principle, we shouldn't allow other beings to be used in any way for our benefit either. Let's face it, a whole variety of animals are bred, trapped, imprisoned and enslaved because of us. This covers a huge spectrum going from dairy products and eggs all the way to working animals, pets, zoos, hunting, fur and scientific experimentation.

The logical consequences of the Buddha's *non-harming* ethic are quite clear and very challenging in the extreme, especially if we don't agree with them.

So we know what we must aspire to at least. But the reality regarding this issue is a different matter altogether. *Very* few Buddhists are either vegan or vegetarian. This is so for many reasons. Some of us are very attached to eating meat or are just plain lazy. Others, although they're spiritually or culturally Buddhist, eat meat because that is what they do in those countries. For example, in Tibet most people live above the 'tree line' and have little or no access to vegetables. In Thailand, most people eat meat and even monastics are known to eat fish and seafood occasionally. Even when they settle in other countries, where vegetarianism is a viable option, many if not most highly realized spiritual masters continue to keep the habits of a lifetime and eat meat. Some *cannot* make the switch for health reasons; their digestive systems just couldn't handle the change. Others simply don't change, for whatever reason.

There are many interesting teachings to unlock here.

The Buddhist path is about working with attachment and other negative habitual tendencies. Veganism or vegetarianism raises a lot of difficult issues for us. '*I eat meat because I WANT TO*', just doesn't sit well with the teachings on ego. We must also work on our aversions too.

It's always possible an ordinary practitioner might become vegetarian because they don't like or even *hate* meat, in which case they may have developed an aversion to it. But generally speaking, most of us have no such baggage and aren't veggie simply because we just don't want to be.

Another interesting aspect is that becoming veggie could easily arise out of our general neurosis about *everything* these days. We tend to obsess about so much, that food and animal products might just become another head-trip for us and simply feed into our neurotic streak. One master famously even said, *I swear, my students appear to be so much up in their heads about what to eat that they're eating* **concepts** *not food!*

But, when we strip away all those 'red herrings' from the issue – sorry I just *couldn't* resist it – the plain truth remains. Meat *is* murder, and dairy is slavery. Furthermore, the Buddha seems to clearly say not to have any part in it.

Looking closely at the Buddha's own personal life, though, brings yet another *very* interesting perspective to the whole debate.

Are you sitting down? Well ... it appears the Buddha himself ate meat on occasion. In fact he's understood to have died as a direct result of eating some bad [possibly even poisoned] pork.

Just like the shocking discovery that many of today's enlightened beings continue to eat meat, the news that Buddha himself probably wasn't a strict vegan tells us a lot about how *we* should approach our own dietary dilemma. Buddha was a monk. He received daily food offerings on his morning alms round. Perhaps it was the tradition to eat *whatever* you were given, as a practice for dispelling attachment and aversion. Similarly most realized masters these days do not choose what they are going to eat. They remain open to eating whatever is offered.

In conclusion then, it has to be understood that the Buddha's exhortation for us to adopt a non-harming lifestyle is an *ideal*. A goal. An aspiration.

If we take that aspiration to our hearts, then we are on the right path. Many of us could so easily *reduce* the negative impact we are having on beings, by wholeheartedly *aspiring* towards total veganism while simply doing our best in the here and now. Avoiding meat just one day a year would be so easy to do and a huge step in the right direction.

One day a week is also not beyond the realms of possibility for most people. Or we could turn the whole thing on its head and only eat *meat* one day a week.

Whatever. As long as we're progressing towards the goal and doing our best. Who knows, *many of us* might find it no problem whatsoever to simply embrace full veganism for life starting today.

The most important thing is that we genuinely hold the aspiration in our heart, start where we are, seal it with a pledge, and progress mindfully towards that goal. We should rejoice when we succeed and share the merit for the benefit of all. And if we fall short, without judging ourselves we can just start anew.

> For the sake of awakening the heart of compassion,
> And for the benefit of all beings,
> who were once my loving mother,

I firmly resolve to stop killing, eating
and enslaving living creatures.
May I continue to do no harm and
cultivate a wealth of virtue!

Virtual Reality

Nowadays, many people – especially the young – are quite comfortable with the concept of 'virtual reality'. Computer games and movies like *The Matrix* bear witness to the fact. It has finally entered the common psyche that things are not necessarily as real as they appear. Indeed, some now theorize we may be living in an entirely fake and fabricated illusion.

From the *'holo-deck'* in *Star Trek,* to *The Matrix* movie, to the 'virtual' online realms which we can inhabit via proxies called avatars, we're becoming so comfortable with the concept of beings manifesting in 'unreal' dimensions that even children are now only a short step away from questioning just how 'real' *this* dimension we call 'reality' truly is.

Science tells us there are many parallel dimensions, and we may even be inhabiting several of them at once. Quantum Physics has discovered that the *consciousness* of the individual plays an enormous role in actually *creating* the matter that constitutes whatever form we are currently observing.

However, over 2500 years ago the Buddha realized and taught the same thing: *'With our minds we create the world'*.

He went on further still to warn that we create more and more mental suffering for ourselves the more 'real' we assume everything to be.

It is the natural radiance of the Buddha Nature within that manifests all that 'appears'. This is true for thoughts, emotions, places, people, situations, matter, energy. It all emanates from us. All appearances are therefore said to be *empty* of true existence. The 'reality' we cling to is *virtual*.

Like with the case of an online 'avatar', we mistakenly take the appearance of our own *Self* to be real too. All the drama, concerns, superficial joys and pains are just as unreal as cyber-games. We literally get caught up in a cosmic game and take it so seriously we simply *forget* that all the suffering we experience due to delusion, attachment and aversion, has been self-created.

Virtual Reality is a strong metaphor for the samsaric state of mind we have set in motion. We cling to the concept of *self-as-real* so desperately and so tightly the resultant *ego* that emerges appears to be the only 'self' for us to identify with. We are blind to the deeper truth. We know no better, so we simply go with the flow and get lost in the lie of what appears to be.

The most tragic part of it all is that we suffer so unnecessarily. Our very essence, the Buddha Nature, holds within it the truth that sheds light on the illusion and sets us free.

At the moment, our minds are turned outwards, lost in the illusion of our own projections. If we could only turn the mind inwards we'd access the power of that self-liberating truth, and find *rest* in our true nature.

Warrior

Be a warrior not a worrier, he said. It was like the earth stood still.

We were in the magnificent *Dzogchen Beara* retreat centre perched high on a spectacular Atlantic cliff-top situated on the South-Western tip of a remote peninsula in rural Ireland ... The edge of the world.

It was my first time to sit with Sogyal Rinpoche in person. Rinpoche's enigmatic words stuck in my mind ever since. So much of our suffering mind is preoccupied with worrying. We have an apparently deep-seated anxiety that stems from not realizing who or what we truly are, and which manifests as a flurry of painful attachment and aversion. The antidote is to go beyond Surface Mind and all the worry, right down to our core being and to rest there in the Buddha Nature. This protects and liberates the mind. But it's not so easy to achieve – and even harder to stabilize. To perfect this *awakened* state requires warrior-like training, determination and courage.

Enlightened courage is a very special quality. To awaken it we must develop unshakable confidence in our true nature. We must have all the cunning and skill of a *warrior*.

A *Dharma Warrior* goes into battle too, but our weapons are mindfulness, awareness and spaciousness. Our goal is to eliminate ego and its poisonous foot-soldiers: ignorance, attachment and aversion. Once we've defeated these inner enemies and liberated the Natural Mind from the tyranny of ego, we unleash and unblock the naturally limitless flow of peace, compassion and wisdom of the Buddha Nature within.

We *are* warriors not simply for the sake of our own liberation but for the sake of all beings enslaved by the suffering of their own minds. We must strive for *their* liberation too. In fact, releasing *them* first from suffering may even become our priority. In that case, we are following the courageous and compassionate path of the *Bodhisattva*. The last syllable of this Sanskrit word [-*va*] indicates the quality of being warrior-like.

So all together *Bodhi-sattva* has the nuance of 'Enlightened Warrior' or even 'Warrior who brings enlightenment'. There is no sense of aggression or force implied. The image of a warrior is used to evoke their determined courage, self-sacrifice, and expertise at using all the weapons at their disposal to *cut right through* the ego and all its selfishness. Such dharma practitioners possess all the self-less qualities of a warrior because it's their heart-felt wish to help all other beings find liberation before themselves. In reality, this self-*less* activity is the very embodiment of enlightenment. The action of a Bodhisattva is therefore, by definition, so *empty of self* they're hailed as already being fully enlightened.

The image of a dharma warrior is so potent because it takes a familiar concept and completely turns it around. We serve and protect others not ourselves. Our conviction springs from the power and the truth of the Buddha Nature and not from some misguided ideology. A Bodhisattva Warrior may even act alone in the world; there's no need to be part of an army with generals and politicians behind us. We don't even need armour or weapons to really help others become free. We might simply become invisible, just melt into the fabric of society and work undetected for the ultimate benefit of beings. What espionage! What subterfuge! Even if we wore a tee-shirt bearing the words *Dharma Ninja Spy*, nobody would suspect a thing!

'*Be a warrior not a worrier*' is perhaps the most liberating, outrageous, counter-cultural, revolutionary dharma teaching I've ever heard!

X Factor

There is an extremely popular TV 'talent' show in the UK called *X Factor*. Like other shows, and most 'reality' TV programmes for that matter, it's a competition that attempts to find one individual with exceptional characteristics. This person eventually wins the prize and all the horrendous celebrity that goes with it.

In today's crazy, mixed up world we *say* we recognize the 'special' quality of every individual yet we still perpetuate the lie that some people are somehow *more* special than others. We call this supposedly rare, elusive quality the *X Factor* and [even though it doesn't really exist] we embark on a monumental quest to find it.

As a society, we feed into the myth by creating all sorts of elitist competitions: talent, personality, beauty, sport, intelligence and so on. We invent an education system that relies on the success of a few while the vast majority is doomed to mediocrity or complete and utter failure. The inequity of the employment 'market' flows from that outcome. Entire lives are often decided on exam results. People are lauded or ruined on the basis of *IQ*, *DNA* or something as arbitrary as the quality of their local school and its teachers.

As individuals, we explore our own hidden talents to see if we ourselves might possess the X Factor in some field or other. If we *do*, we feel special. If we don't, we feel uninteresting and substandard. We console ourselves with empty reassurances like '*Everybody's beautiful, in their own way*'. But we don't believe it and our battered ego makes us feel bad and tries all the harder to assert itself.

We tell our children how *special* they are in the hope there's even an outside chance some part of them is. We suffer with our children when they seem to stick out from the crowd for all the 'wrong' reasons. Our anxiety forces us to pressure them into coming somewhere, *anywhere*, in the top half of their class at school. We lavish upon them expensive music, drama or dance lessons that we can ill-afford. And all this so they can rise above, or at least fit in with their peers - the 'competition'. What a rat-race we allow the suffering samsaric mind to make of life!

The power and the truth of the Buddha's teachings is that every one of us has the *X Factor*. Not just humans, but *all* beings. We all have the Buddha Nature.

It's not the showy spectacle we hope for and admire so much in today's so-called 'enlightened' world. How ignorant and deluded we are to have desired that shallow façade in the first place. Regardless of the quality of our body, our brain, or even the surface mind that produces thoughts and emotions, we have the Buddha Nature as our core being. Nothing, absolutely *nothing*, compares to the boundless peace, loving-compassion, and ultimate wisdom we already have. We are primordially perfect, unstainable and free.

The *Natural State* of our mind is clear, light, open and content. Our natural instinct is to act purely and compassionately for the benefit of others. The ego and all its fearsome, clingy nonsense is an illusion. See through it and we have glimpsed the truth. Cut through it and we're *already* completely liberated and awake.

We *are* Buddha.

There is *nothing* more precious for us to realize or embody.

Our children, their peers, and all living beings, are complete and *perfect* just as they are.

There is nothing more *urgent* to learn... *Nothing.*

X-Ray Vision

When I was a kid there was a comicbook super-hero who had x-ray vision. I remember wondering at the time what use that could possibly be.

To be able to see people naked is one thing. To an innocent child that would seem funny. But to see beneath the skin and look around the interior of the body with all its organs and their contents just struck me as a stupid power to have.

Later, when I got a bit older, I discovered that x-ray vision was extremely important in the medical field. It allowed doctors to detect and treat serious illness at an early stage. I was forced to reconsider my position. Then, in my late teens I observed cells and even atoms through a powerful microscope. I observed distant stars and galaxies through telescopes. I was *converted*! I understood that the human eye only sees a very superficial layer of what is really going on. Penetrate that apparently solid veneer and an entirely different level of truth is revealed. Fascinating, vibrant, ever-changing, impermanent. Seeing reality with a kind of x-ray vision had great value afterall. We have to penetrate the illusory exterior of things and see them for what they truly are.

Now I'm older, and have begun to contemplate the true nature of phenomena from a Buddhist perspective, I find it very useful indeed to apply my x-ray vision to reality and approach everything with the sense of wonder and openness I had when I was a child. I now realize, from personal experience, that nothing is the way it appears.

There is a vast difference between 'looking' and 'seeing'. The higher Buddhist teachings speak of 'outwardly looking' and 'inwardly seeing'. It's as different as 'wondering' and 'understanding'. And it can happen with training, in an instant: *The moment I look... I see.*

I look at a solid wall and *see* it's comprised almost entirely of the open space that exists between the buzzing atoms. I look at the ocean and *know* it to be hydrogen and oxygen combined in a dance. Looking at my own body, and even the mind itself, I *realize* they are not me.

Meditation helps us to attain this kind of profound panorama. Seeing things deeply *is* the path to awakening. Seeing *myself* deeply, I can penetrate the superficial outer layers of consciousness and experience the inner radiance and stability of the Buddha Nature. The Natural Mind that rests at the very core of our being is all there truly *is*. Manifesting all that appears, our true nature is pure mindfulness, awareness and spaciousness.

Like a blossoming lotus radiating clear light from the centre of our heart, the Buddha Mind shines like the sun.

There is the light of *Wisdom* that knows things as they really are and recognizes the Buddha Nature in all.

And there's the warmth of *Compassion* that works tirelessly to free all beings from the intense suffering of delusion and the terminally superficial.

Yes

We waste so much of this precious human life.

Vital life energies squandered amidst a haze of ignorance, attachment and aversion, our core vocabulary is reduced to three knee-jerk reactions:

I don't know! This expresses our almost total exasperation with not understanding the meaning of life. Most of all, we're driven to distraction because we have no clue whatsoever just who or what *we* are. Our ignorance blocks our inner view of the Buddha Nature. So we're forced to float adrift from the truth without a compass to navigate our way back. Although the darkness we experience appears all-pervasive, it is not. Yet we live in a constant state of high anxiety, always on the lookout for our own welfare.

I want! This second vital piece of vocab-for-the-bewildered builds on the first; because of ignorance, we are set adrift on the infinite ocean of Samsara – the Suffering Mind. We feel lost and anxious so our instinct is to *cling* to whatever passes by. This *attachment* is a reflex. It's almost involuntary at this point. We *hope* that grasping onto people, places, things, thoughts and emotions will comfort and stabilize us. Who knew it wouldn't?

No! Get away! This is the third and final phrase we have at our disposal. Granted, it's a rather basic toolbox but it covers everything. Imagine being adrift on the vast ocean of the unknown, the unpredictable waves, an abyss below, the dark night of the soul. This brings up perhaps the strongest human trait: *fear*. We dread monsters and demons to such an extent that our fear is activated whether they come or not. And when they do come, our instinct is to shout *No!* and chase them away.

'No' is such a basic instinct for us. I don't know how we ever manage to say 'Yes' at all.

Most of us find it very difficult to put ourselves in totally new or extremely challenging situations. There is a spectrum of *fear* that arises in this deluded Surface Mind of ours. It embraces everything from trying some new, exotic food for the first time, all the way to our reluctance to really open up to others and become friends or even life partners. The people who author their own big success stories are driven by *I want!* Meanwhile the rest of us – the silent, equally self-obsessed majority – are driven through the haze and the fog of the unknown quantity we call 'life' by the single-most toxic and fearful mantra possible: *No!*

The Buddha's words set out a perfect path before us that leads to total liberation from all this. All the heavy anxiety, desperate grasping, and fearful pushing away is a messed-up, self-induced nightmare. But it only consumes us as long as we dwell on the Surface of Mind. Once we go beyond, deep down towards our core being – the Buddha Nature – we avert and bypass all those problems.

The further we get from the superficial Suffering Mind, the closer we get to experiencing the perfect Buddha Mind. It has always existed within us and the possibility of living life from that perspective has always been available to us. The Buddha Mind has only pure, positive qualities. The three mind poisons [ignorance, attachment, aversion] and all their demonic vocabulary of chaos are dispelled into thin air just like the illusions both they and their creator, the ego, truly are.

The Buddha Nature radiates *Openness* and *Contentment*. If it had a favourite word, it would be *Yes*.

This single syllable encapsulates the essence of all the Buddha realized and taught. The openness and contentment that characterizes the Buddha Nature is so perfectly complete, in itself, that its primary function is to simply *be* as it is.

The Buddha Nature says *Yes* in all directions, both inward and outward. It's a primordially pure and spontaneously present mantra. The single syllable *Yes* both **accepts** and **lets go** at the same time. The essence of how to meditate well, it turns out, is also the meaning of life:

Breathing in: I accept.

*Breathing out: I **let go**.*

Since the Buddha Nature is both open and content we say *Yes* inwardly, fully accepting and letting go of the contentment. In the same way we say *Yes* outwardly, openly accepting then letting go of all phenomena. The twin aspects of this crucial point must be contemplated deeply and fully realized; we fully accept and rejoice in the nourishing qualities of the Buddha Nature, but without clinging; Then we *remain* content and open to life in the same way. By saying *Yes* to the Buddha Nature and to Life like this, we are both accepting and letting go of Nirvana and Samsara. By not clinging to either we completely go beyond both.

It seems *Yes* was the only word we ever needed.

Go on, baby buddha! Say a whole-hearted, fearless *Yes!* to life: the good and the bad.

Proclaim also a profound *Yes!* to the Buddha Nature awakening within.

Yogi

Particularly in the Tibetan Buddhist tradition, to be a *Yogi* [Skt. 'Yogin' for a male, 'Yogini' for a female] is to be a dedicated practitioner of advanced meditative and physical exercises that *unite* spiritual awakening with the energetic clearing of the *subtle body*.

The process of awakening the Natural Mind is united, through the various *yogas*, with the process of clearing the subtle body's *channels, energies,* and *essences*. In Tibetan, these are called *tsal, lung, tiglé*. In Sanskrit, *nadi, prana, bindu*.

These special yogas are not like ordinary, everyday yoga. However, they do find their origin in the same place. The higher Tibetan yogas came from the Buddha's teachings via two specific routes: directly from India, and from India by way of the Chan lineage of ancient China. These higher yogas only make sense if the practitioner is at the correct stage of development and is ready for them. Otherwise, they will have no effect or may even be harmful. Therefore, they are kept quite 'secret' and are only taught by qualified, realized masters to advanced students when the time is right and all the groundwork has been done. The so-called secret, hidden yogas of Tibet are not an end in themselves but a vitally important stage before embracing the highest *Tantric* practices – of which little or nothing is said in public, and rightly so.

But, for our purposes here, we must contemplate the advantages of becoming a *Yogi* ourselves. We can begin to see it as an aspiration, a calling. The path may not suit everyone, but maybe *we* are ripe for it. These particular yogic practices are mainly found within the older lineages of Tibetan Buddhism, known as the *Vajrayana*. They may be totally inappropriate for some practitioners, but they can also be entirely the right path for others. Just like a *thunderbolt* or a *diamond* ['Vajra'], these yogas can cut through anything and are seen as a 'direct fast track' to full awakening, provided the candidate is suitable. But what are they 'cutting through' exactly?

The whole Buddhist path is about cutting through *whatever* is blocking our internal and external *view* of the way things really *are*. The precious teachings on the Buddha Nature show us precisely what we must cut through. The *Ego* is the main problem. The self-clinging tendency is responsible for all our blockages and obstructions, both in terms of Mind *and* the Subtle Body. These obstructions and obscurations arise, via the ego-tendency, as ignorance, negative karma, and impure perception. *If* we want to break through these barriers at all, then at some stage we'll *have* to engage in spiritual yogas that *unite and clear* [almost 'realign'] the Natural Mind and the Subtle Body. Our goal must be to "[*re-*]unite with the Natural State". That's the Tibetan translation of the word 'Yoga'.

A *yogi*, therefore, is someone [maybe just like you or me] who is on the way to realizing that unification.

When we contemplate the nature of the yogi's path, we must be clear we're not simply talking about someone who does ordinary yoga stretches, and so on. The very heart of the yogi's practice is highly advanced *meditative absorption*.

Now this advanced, highly-skilled meditation work is ignited and made all the more 'real' when united with certain body postures that work with the subtle *energy body* and the rhythms of the breath and the heart. The body postures of ancient Tibetan yogis are depicted on the walls of HH Dalai Lama's secret summer temple, the *Lukhang*. It is situated on a small island in a lake just outside old Lhasa, the capital of Tibet. There are many books available with photographs of these fascinating and highly stylized ancient murals. They can even be seen nowadays, in great detail, by searching online. However, nothing much about the pictures tells us *how* to do these yogic practices. And that's as it should be. The teachings are given as part of a sacred oral tradition, and only when the conditions are right for success.

The whole concept of being a *yogi* also reveals a crucial point about the Buddhist path to awakening. If we're going to do Buddhist practices at all, then we must take them seriously and really *do* them. We must become devoted, *as yogis are*, to following the practices through to their ultimate conclusion. We must come to see the combination of this crazy mind and awkward body of ours as the very *vehicle* that will take us all the way to enlightenment. It's all we have. And it's all we need.

The more advanced we become as serious practitioners of whatever lineage we're following, the more we begin to live a quasi-secret life anyway.

We are not quite like ordinary people. We are not quite like monastics either. We are a third species altogether.

For the ultimate benefit of others, we simply get on with our practice of transforming our minds, opening our hearts, and awakening to reality as it is. Without creating too much fuss around us, and without leaving too much of a trace behind us, we quietly but *powerfully* get on with our practice.

The *formal* practice is done in private and in retreat.

The integrated *Engaged* Practice of bringing Peace, Compassion, and Awakening to beings is done ideally through our *every* action, both in practice *and* in the world, but with great humility, discretion, and natural ease.

Zeitgeist

Zeitgeist is a German word that's recently crept into common usage in the English language. It means the *Spirit of the Age*.

The times we live in are characterized by a globalisation of Western culture.

Concepts like consumerism, capitalism, the *I-can-make-it-on-my-own* brand of egocentrism, and the paramount importance of the individual are spreading everywhere. You can find a takeaway burger joint, internet porn, and ATMs on practically every corner, even in under-developed countries where most of the population have no food, water or medicine. It's not simply a case though of the West infecting the rest of the world with its misguided nonsense. It's more like the entire world is now primed and ready to embrace the 'false gods' of money and entertainment at the expense of almost everything else they cherish.

The authentic presence of a world view with selfless peace, loving-compassion, and spiritual awakening at its core is fast becoming extinct. For this reason, most mainstream world religions – especially Buddhism – consider the era in which now live a *Dark Age*.

Even the way we approach the spiritual path laid out by the Buddha himself is often shaped by the zeitgeist, the spirit of our times. We want to know what we will get out of it before we invest our time and energy even in something as harmless and simple as watching the breath. Our spiritual materialism turns us into consumers and the path into a product that comes without any health warnings or guarantees. Shouldn't the Buddhist label read: *Buyer Beware! Meditation could seriously damage your Ego!* Or *Enlightenment may not be guaranteed, at least not for this lifetime!* [*Terms and Conditions apply*].

As consumers of esoteric spirituality we grasp after possessing all the 'right' books and paraphernalia. We even cling to the 'right' master, once we think we've found one, for fear of losing our minds altogether. Our spiritual materialism, and its consumer complaints mentality, drives us to give up on the teacher or the whole path once our ego feels threatened or our feelings get a little hurt in some way.

The *zeitgeist* trains us to give up early if results don't show as quickly as we expected. Only the *very* dedicated, the obsessive, and possibly the psychotic in our society manage to stick with anything long enough for it to bear fruit. Even then our society can only lay claim to having created a *handful* of Olympic gymnasts, concert pianists, and serial killers.

If we approach the spiritual path [that leads to limitless happiness for all] in the same old 'quitter' fashion our impatience and lack of determination and self-confidence will always get the better of us. We're breeding a generation of hyper-active over-achievers at one extreme and disconnected, self-esteem impaired unfortunates with very low expectations at the other. Either way, most of our generation will quit the spiritual path when the going gets tough, provided of course we're capable of finding and recognizing genuine spirituality in the first place.

Yet it's also part of our Dark Age – often a very fashionable trend – to include a tolerably *safe* amount of the quasi-spiritual in our lives even though we may not be practising any path. Many people wear prayer beads for fashion and have Buddha statues, incense sticks from Tibet and exotic ritual *objets d'art* scattered noncommittally around their homes. Authentic, fully-realized masters must think it *bizarre*, to say the least, when they observe on the one hand our unbridled enthusiasm for things like tai-chi, feng shui, tarot cards and green tea, and on the other hand our almost total reluctance to reduce the ego tendency one iota or to prevent even a single negative emotional outburst.

These are dark days indeed when we *know* in our hearts the utter madness of allowing the rich to get richer while the vast majority of human beings have so little. The accumulation of wealth and possessions, wars about oil and other natural resources, and the basic inhumanity of our survival-of-the-fattest mentality have become the hallmark of our global civilization.

We as a *Culture* have so little awareness, and so little to recommend us for salvation.

We remain enslaved by a tiny number of wannabe dominator types. We are led by the least among us. And we are fast-losing our natural ability as a species to self-organize from the bottom up.

Consequently, Time itself appears to accelerate exponentially, untethered and headlong towards its rendezvous with apocalypse.

As the Eschaton screeches around us, we experience the resultant peaks *and* troughs of our chaotic culture simultaneously; commercial boom and financial collapse, United Nations' optimism and the misery of famine and war, not to mention the ultimate challenge of the environmental crisis that may be the end of us all anyway.

But even if the *zeitgeist* isn't looking too good in this bad light, there's still a glimmer of hope.

Beneath all the short-sighted selfishness, and regardless of the current trend for pseudo-spirituality and self-help books, there *is* a small but genuine movement towards true awakening that's happening both in and around us.

The fact you are reading this particular book at this particular time is no accident.

The authentic teachings of the Buddha are experiencing something of a mainstream revival. Especially in the West, but even in Asia, these precious teachings are beginning to flourish and blossom once again.

For now, it remains a sub-culture of sorts. But most successful revolutions – even *quiet revolutions of the heart* – start small.

Zenith

The *Zenith* of the Buddha's spiritual teaching is full awakening, enlightenment itself. It is the summit, the highest point, the final destination of the path.

The perfect blossoming of the Buddha Nature is to fully experience our ground, path and fruition as one. Openness and contentment flow boundlessly for the ultimate benefit of all.

But the absolute paradox of the Buddha's teachings is full awakening is not something that hopefully will occur at some point in the future. It happens in the *present* moment. It could *only* happen in the present moment. When we see it in this way we realize that enlightenment has *always* been available to us. Therefore we come to understand that the present moment is the *only* gateway to awakening. The most precious jewel of all.

The only way to go *through* that gateway is *Mindfulness* of the present moment. And the way to develop that mindful awareness is *Meditation*. The mind itself, properly trained, is the only vehicle we need to penetrate the outer murky layers of consciousness and so arrive at our true nature, the Buddha Mind of All.

Even a great master cannot awaken us. They can only be our guide. We must realize and awaken by ourselves. To think of all the countless lifetimes we have lived before, all leading up to this point! And to realize that awakening is a very real and present possibility! Given the right conditions, all we need do is apply the correct amount of mindfulness, awareness and spaciousness and we could awaken with this very breath, right here, right now. No wonder so many practitioners just burst out laughing when awakening dawns, saying things like: *I can't believe it! I should have known it was here all along!*

The absolute paradox of the path goes deeper still.

It's said the more profound and highly advanced teachings you receive, and the more profound and highly advanced your realisation becomes, the more you realize that all of the crucial points necessary for attaining full enlightenment were there right from the very beginning. Properly understood, and put into action, the *meditation teachings* we receive at the beginning of the path contain all the essential ingredients for awakening to unfold!

At every stage, the very essence of the Buddha's teaching is the same.

The true Nature of Mind is being pointed out to us over and over until we finally get it and go there and remain there.

We can look at the Dharma as a roadway with a beginning, middle and end. Or better still we can view it as a mountain having a broad stable foundation [*Ground*], a structured middle layer [*Path*], and a final *zenith* or summit [*Fruition*]. Understanding that the 'highest' teachings and the most 'basic' both have the same *essence*, we soon realize that the Ground of our being is simply *Resting in the Buddha Nature*, the Path is about practising *Resting in the Buddha Nature*, and the ultimate Fruition is nothing other than *Resting in the Buddha Nature*. They are one.

The zenith of the spiritual teachings, the highest and most sacred the Buddha could offer to you directly, in person ... the *crème de la crème*, Darlings ... is You Are A Buddha.

This *Heart Essence* is available to all, plain and simple, right here right now.

The Buddha's wisdom and compassion is freely available to all beings. It is especially potent for those who dwell in the here and now, for that's where *Awakening* unfolds.

The good news is radical, earth-shattering and profound, yet pure and simple:

> You are a buddha!
> Always remember that.
> You are already perfect and complete in every way.
> You must awaken from the dream that causes suffering.
> You must awaken to the limitless happiness
> that dwells within.
> You can guide all beings to the same realisation.
> Boundless peace, loving-compassion and awakening are
> the essential nature of everything.
> You can rest in your true nature, right here, right now,
> by mindfully entering the gate of the vast present moment.
> You are a buddha!
> The only question remaining is this:
> 'What are you going to do about it?'

Afterword

The essence of the Buddha's teachings is extremely profound yet very simple: *You are a buddha. Wake up!*
There is the *Wisdom* path that recognizes and emphasizes the innate buddha-potential of all beings. But it would not be complete without the path of *Compassion* whereby a buddha-to-be determines to bring *others* to total liberation from the suffering mind before themselves.

The *Mahayana* Buddhist lineages in particular emphasize both these aspects of the spiritual path. Although I'm quite familiar with the great richness of the *Theravada* Buddhist approach, it is from the Mahayana perspective that I have composed these contemplations.

In particular this volume is the direct result of contemplating the words of my own perfect teachers, Masters who embody all the wisdom and compassion of their own unique lineages. Their spiritual heritage stretches in a chain of awakened teachers and students all the way back to the Buddha.

The Mahayana spiritual tradition of my masters, including all *their* masters, joyfully finds its way onto these pages specifically with you the reader in mind. I pray that the inner environment of your own mind is inspired and uplifted, and that it unites with the spiritual landscapes of Tibet and Vietnam, with *Vajrayana* and *Zen*.

Therefore it is with a tremendous sense of rejoicing, and devotion, that *Buddha's Favourite Words* is offered here.

If anything has been helpful for you, it is because I have merely remembered and written down just what my teachers told me.

On the other hand, if anything has been unhelpful or confusing, I can only apologize and put it down to the useless chatter of my own deluded ego-mind.

DEDICATION

May all our precious Masters live long,
healthy and happy lives!

May any merit generated by contemplating
these teachings be joined with the vast ocean of merit
of all the buddhas.

And may all beings reach the far shore
of perfect, full Awakening!

www.ingramcontent.com/pod-product-compliance
Lightning Source LLC
Chambersburg PA
CBHW070042080526
44586CB00013B/878